MORE LOVE, SEX AND ASTROLOGY

More Love, Sex and Astrology

TERI KING

Allison & Busby
LONDON

First published in Great Britain by
Allison & Busby Ltd, 6a Noel Street,
London W1V 3RB

Copyright © 1986 Teri King

British Library Cataloguing in Publication Data
King, Teri
    More love, sex and astrology.
    1. Astrology   2. Interpersonal relationships
    I. Title
    133.5'8302   BF1729.I5/

ISBN 0–85031–610–3

Typeset in 10/12 Palatino by Falcon Graphic Art Ltd
Wallington, Surrey
Printed in Great Britain by
Billings & Sons Limited, Worcester

Contents

Introduction

Have you ever wondered how two people in a family can be so completely different in personality, even though their genes and environment are identical? Do you understand yourself, your talents and responsibilities well enough to make the most of your potential? Are you lucky with money or with love?

To these questions, and very many more, the planets hold the answers. Using your date, place and time of birth, astrology can, in fact, tell you more about yourself than a psychiatrist could after many expensive weeks of consultation. Astrology is the oldest science. It is, in fact, as old as civilization itself. Its roots are hidden in the mystery of our early beginnings. The earliest horoscope dates back to 2767 BC. No doubt our ancestors noted the effects of the phase of the Moon on the tides and crops, and indeed on all life on earth. Later, as such observations were extended, the influence of the Sun and other planetary movements on human affairs became the astrologer's concern. One of the most common remarks from the cynic is: "How can a forecast for any zodiac sign be accurate for everyone born under that sign?" The obvious answer, of course, is that all horoscopes must be general unless the astrologer is able to work from specific details about the hour, day, year and place of birth of a particular individual.

Now let me explain exactly what a birth-chart is. As an example let's take a person born on 3 September. Ordinarily speaking, he or she would be a subject of Virgo, a Virgoan, for the Sun occupies the section of sky known as Virgo between 24 August and 23 September, although even this can change from year to year. We must also, however, account for the position of the Moon, which enters a fresh sign approximately every forty-eight hours. It may have occupied Gemini on the day in question, and in this instance our subject would become a Virgoan/Geminian. (Here it must be explained that the Sun rules will-power and feelings and the Moon rules the subconscious, so our particular case will have the will-power of a Virgoan and the subconscious of a Gemini.)

We must further consider the sign rising at the exact time of birth. This is an ever-changing process as it takes approximately two hours for each sign to pass over the horizon. If Virgo was ascending on the hour in question, then the image presented to the world – the personality – would again be Virgoan, thus making our example a Virgoan/Geminian/Virgoan. This procedure is carried on through all nine planets, each of which depicts a feature of the subject's make-up; in addition, the signs they occupy and the aspects formed from one another all play an important part. Should an astrologer calculate and interpret these movements, then we would have what is known as a birth-chart. Because of the constant changing of the heavens, a person sharing a birth-chart with another is very rare, though it would happen if two babies were born in the same place at exactly the same time. In this event, as both children are endowed with identical gifts, environment will be their deciding factor, dictating which characteristics are used constructively and which are used destructively. If we return to our example, we will notice that two of the three important characteristics are in Virgo, and so our subject will be a typical Virgoan. If, on the other hand, the Sun were to be in Virgo with the Moon and ascendant both in Scorpio, then he or she would display all of the traits associated with a true Scorpion, despite probable belief to the contrary.

Astrology can be used to assess many aspects of human life. Birth complexity cannot be tackled during the following pages, therefore the subject has of necessity been treated in a general way. What is the purpose of this book? Well, no matter how beautiful, rich or successful we may be, life is a pretty miserable affair unless we can find ourselves that special relationship. And in order to achieve this we must first understand ourselves as well as other people. I hope this book will help you to understand that special someone in your life. There is a general character analysis for members of each sign of the zodiac, with sections for those types in whom the typical characteristics are exaggerated or perverted – the difference between Dr Jekyll and Mr Hyde, hence my title for these sub-divisions: The Hyde side. The book offers advice on how to catch and keep your mate, understand his or her sexuality, discover what sort of person will be your ideal partner and, when things go wrong, how to end the affair. Almost all types of relationship are tackled, everything from love and sexual affairs to friendship and business.

Astrology should be used as a guide to character – its original and true purpose – and no better form of character analysis exists. With luck you will learn about yourself, your friends and also find this book amusing as well as informative. Once the information has been understood and digested it becomes easier to accept our limitations and our weaknesses, and this is sure to lead to greater inner peace. I hope you will be amused by the contents but will none the less come to realize that there is much truth within these pages.

TERI KING

Aries (the Ram)
Sign of the Crusader and Leader

March 21 – April 20

The first Fire sign: Vital, enthusiastic, impulsive, quick-thinking, quick-witted
Ruler: Mars
Colour: Red
Career: Soldier, surgeon, engineer, mechanic, professional sportsman or woman, explorer
Famous Arietians: Bismarck, Marlon Brando, Casanova, Julie Christie, Doris Day, Billie Holiday, Houdini, Thomas Jefferson, Omar Sharif, Vincent Van Gogh

---

ARIES MAN

The planet Mars gives the typical Arietian man fire and brilliance. He has enough vitality to drive four steam engines at the same time. He possesses a great sense of adventure and an aggressive, pioneering spirit. He is original, in sympathy with new thought; he forever chases progress. One of his problems is that he may hit on fifteen great new schemes in the course of one morning but may have absolutely no desire to fill in the details or carry them out. If he isn't able to find a sympathetic ear or hit upon the chance to develop projects immediately, other ideas that he finds equally interesting will take their

11

place. For this reason it is very hard for him, once he encounters obstacles, to persist in one course. He needs to find someone who will help him to stick to a single goal until he has achieved success. As a rule, the Arietian male prefers work which offers some opportunity for personal leadership, for he enjoys overcoming difficulties and may go out of his way to challenge opposition.

He is always hopeful, no matter where life takes him, and his happy knack of forgetting failure can aid his endurance in times of stress. Unfortunately Aries also confers upon its subjects a strong impulsive streak which frequently land them in situations which could have been avoided with a little more thought. Even when successful, this type needs someone to follow on after him. He is a trail-blazer, a leader; but he leaves it to someone else to build the settlement and maintain order, since it is rare for those with the Sun in Aries to finish what they start. Love and friendship fill a large part in his life, though he projects excitement rather than soothing domesticity. He tends to attract others because of his spirit and dash, but while he pleases and stimulates loved ones, he never satisfies. Often he loves by sight: his woman's looks are very important to him. Yet in the final analysis, he usually chooses more with the head than with the heart and intellectual qualities greatly influence his choice.

He goes after the object of his affection with single-minded drive, though he tends to be more interested in conquest than in settling down. If he appears fickle, it is because he is searching for an ideal that can never be found. He dreams of love, but won't be content with the imperfect reality. In a perfect world Mr Aries would stay away from marriage until aged at least 30: before then he is likely to be too busy attempting to discover his professional path in life; however this is not a perfect world, and his boyish charm and impulsiveness often lead him to commit himself to the wrong woman simply because it seems a good idea at the time.

The young Arietian male is likely to take more trouble choosing a car than he does a wife. However, once fully matured his warmth, affection and energy are hard to resist.

ARIES WOMAN

The typical Aries characteristics are slightly softened in the female, although she will still display all of the warmth and vitality associated with this sign. However, she does not suffer fools gladly, always saying what she thinks. She is given to organizing herself and others. Righteous indignation will spur her to remedy injustice with a sharply honed ironic tongue. She should beware of her quick temper and curb critical outbursts aimed at loyal friends or workmates. Like her male counterpart, she is filled with enterprise and enthusiasm. She is always ready to offer friends excellent advice, and is unselfish with help to those who are less wise or less fortunate than herself. Unless you know her well, she may give the impression of distinct bossiness, even insensitivity; but don't be fooled, for underneath she is kind, romantic and sympathetic. She has a delightful sense of humour, is attracted to the opposite sex and makes friends easily. Scope is needed for her energies, and she seeks opportunities which will enable her to lead her fellow creatures. She is rarely fulfilled in the ordinary round of domestic duties; she makes a fine mother and wife, but is quickly bored with the routine of housekeeping and longs to get back to an outside job and life of her own. The Aries woman can frequently be found on committees or running both a career and marriage quite successfully. In love, she really needs a super strong-willed and masterful man who can bring out the feminine side of her character. All too often, though, the weaker types sense her hidden strengths and latch on; and as she is not the best judge of character she only discovers her mistake when it is too late. But when she does, don't expect to see her heels for dust. There's only one thing that beats the rapidity of her falling in love and that's a quick exit.

THE HYDE SIDE

The faults associated with this sign are selfishness, impatience, argumentativeness, quick temper, foolhardiness, aggression, insensitivity to the feelings of others, bossiness, over-impulsiveness and restlessness. This character suffers from an excess of the qualities typical of Aries. Hope and enthusiasm are replaced by recklessness and fickleness. Where the well balanced Arietian rushes in with an amount of co-ordination, this one lowers the horns, charges and beats his or her head against a brick wall until someone comes to the rescue. This type chases novelty and is always engaged in some new project or idea, which is never seen through to any conclusion. Tact is a word that does not exist in his or her dictionary.

Such a person runs headlong into relationships and activities doomed to failure. Few Arietians ever learn from past mistakes, but this individual makes more of them. The opposite sex and enterprises are abandoned whenever the going gets rough. This Ram stares in total disbelief when a problem that has been ignored for some time, in the hope that it will disappear, suddenly reaches up and taps him or her on the brain. This type only lives in the present, therefore loyalty is an undeveloped part of the character. Little or no thought is ever spared for the partner. On occasions, somewhat pathetic efforts are made to form lasting relationships. But the inability to consider anyone else usually leads to separation, and, being insensitive, these characters hardly notice the weeping wreck they have left behind. It is "onward, forever onward". Somewhere perhaps, a dream or two away, must be the real thing. But then they wouldn't even recognize it. When badly perverted or unbalanced, the sadistic streak comes to the fore in the sex life. Any unsuspecting person with a negative Arietian in tow should check out his or her closet. The explanation given for the ball and chain may be that it is for beating carpets, but it's probably time to get out of there quickly before the dust begins to collect on your back.

HOW TO CATCH AND KEEP YOUR ARIES MAN

An Arietian falling in love can be compared to a ten-ton juggernaut careering down a very steep hill. But whereas the vehicle may have a driver capable of slamming on the brakes or reversing, in the case of the typical Arietian, this is not so until the damage has been done, and then his retreat can be equally as dramatic. So any woman involved with such a man should be wary of any early declarations of love, and while it is important that she outwardly appear to be giving herself totally, in fact she should only partially commit herself.

This man is not attracted to the clinging-vine kind of female. He prefers his women to display a certain amount of independence; this he can respect, although he is likely to show alarm if it is taken too far, for he will still want to feel that he is the most important part of her life. The Arietian man loves to argue; mental combat stimulates him, so his woman need not feel she will lose him if she stands up for herself. In fact, these heated moments will possibly be an important part of the relationship. Any highly complex or emotional lady would be wise to run in the opposite direction from this type. For although warm-hearted and affectionate, female moods leave him completely baffled, and any woman who expects understanding from him is in for disappointment.

It is extremely easy to recognize an Arietian in pursuit or retreat. If his partner wishes to hang on to him once he begins to back away, she will have to be quick before he completely disappears over the horizon. As soon as she detects the first symptoms, she is advised to suggest immediately they see less of each other. The Arietian loves a challenge and his interest may be rekindled. With any luck, by being denied so much of her company he may very well realize how much she has come to mean to him. There are several things to bear in mind. Never bring the Arietian face to face with past mistakes, for he rarely looks over his shoulder and is unconcerned by the years gone by. He flatly refuses to learn from them. He is also an enthusiast and will look to his woman for support: no matter how crazy his ideas may appear, she must at first agree with him, although it is permissible at a later date to point out tactfully one or two weak areas in his scheme. Open criticism will only result in a blow to his ego and could possibly stimulate one of his rapid exits.

HOW TO CATCH AND KEEP YOUR ARIES WOMAN

The Arietian woman is a strong personality and any suitor who still believes in the old adage that only men should wear the trousers could be in for a bit of a shock. This is the kind of female who will find herself an unsuspecting male, rearrange and organize him and his life and then wonder what happened to his spirit and manhood. Because of this, she doesn't find forming a serious relationship easy. Time and time again she will become involved with a weak and indecisive individual. Impulsiveness in her character does not improve the situation. She crashes headfirst into relationships, prepared to give all, then suddenly discovers that the man in question does not come up to certain standards, so she rushes out again equally dramatically.

A man determined to catch the Arietian lady's heart will certainly need his wits about him. He is advised to give full vent to his masculinity, and flatly refuse to have his life taken over. In fact, he could try to dominate her instead, for the caveman approach might well pay off in this particular instance. The Arietian woman will be so surprised when she realizes that for once the roles have been reversed that she could be relatively manageable. After a while, however, she is bound to make a bid for leadership again and while it is natural for her mate to give in on small points which make her happy, he should firmly stand his ground.

The Martian in this female inclines her to make war as much as she makes love; for arguments are part of her personality. She finds them stimulating and will assume that a male who refuses to argue with her does not care. Flare-ups will be short, fiery and inevitable but the Aries woman has a large, warm heart and making-up will be tremendous fun. One last word of warning: the Arietian is not a purely domestic animal. She cannot be expected to live her life purely in the home and any man with designs on her will need to accept this. The type of man who wishes to lock his woman away would be wise to look around for a very different lady.

HIS IDEAL PARTNER

The Arietian man's ideal partner may well be born under the signs of Leo, Sagittarius or Pisces. Physically speaking, whether blonde or brunette, she will be all female from her cleavage to her ankles – at least on the surface. For while this man loathes any kind of sexual confusion and likes to recognize the opposite sex instantly, he does admire a certain amount of independence. This isn't to say he'll be glad to pat his woman on the head and send her out to the office every morning, but it does mean that he is repelled by clinging, possessive women.

The Aries man has been called, and not unfairly, insensitive. He is pretty uncomplicated and simply does not understand feminine moods. In some instances he cannot even recognize female needs. Aries men tend to "wear" women. By that I mean that the male of this species likes his woman to be admired by all and sundry. He enjoys watching the effect she has on other men. But just let her flirt with one of those admirers, and she will be dropped so quickly she won't notice she is escortless until it comes to calling a cab to take her home. But jealousy on her part needs to be kept under control. All those animated conversations, the heads together and the laughter, all innocent. Forget it ever happened. In a close relationship, honesty is definitely the best policy, at least from his standpoint. Another thing important to this man is the attraction of a challenge. Once he has scored, above all else he loves a playmate, although his games are likely to be a "me Tarzan, you Jane" variety; nothing too elaborate. You don't have to worry about swinging from tree to tree, in order to satisfy a whim.

Any Arietian chasers will be well advised to remember that he prefers to do the pursuing. Keep in mind that old song that goes, "A man chases a girl until she catches him", and you won't go far wrong. When this character sets his sights on a girl and she ignores him, totally, he will go to any lengths to attract her attention, to the point of being rude and thoroughly objectionable. This, to him, is preferable to total indifference. She may only realize after a long period of time that the man who sticks his tongue out at her at every opportunity is, in fact, madly attracted to her. It may also then dawn on her that her own irritation and annoyance is stimulated by a similar attraction. If she can prove to him that she is the ultimate female, then she could just last the course – if she's lucky.

HER IDEAL PARTNER

Believe it or not, the Aries woman does have an ideal. This is another thing she won't readily admit, but there, in the back of her head, her Sir Lancelot exists. Her ideal mate will be born under the signs of Leo, Sagittarius or Pisces, for these types find her relatively easy to understand. But they had better be quick. All too often, and despite her independent nature, she allows her sexual desires, plus temporary emotions, to lead her into rash commitments which are later retracted. It is not unusual to find women of this sign multimarried or on their own because of the constant pressure applied by the opposite sex. It's important that in early life her mother teaches her the difference between love and sex and the fact that both can be enjoyed quite separately. When she has learned the difference, she will probably find herself much more sought after. Mind you, she may be the one to go down on one knee and ask for his hand in marriage. It's so much quicker that way.

Although the Aries girl loves to play at love, too much emotional ping-pong will lead to tension and hangups. Any man not immediately taken by her feminine wiles will intrigue her greatly. Who is this character who can resist *her*? When the answer is not forthcoming, she will go to almost any lengths to prove her desirability to this blind male. Somewhere along the way she may lose real interest, but that will not stop her. She has got to make him realize that SHE IS DESIRABLE! When she has eventually given him proof, she will walk away satisfied.

Above all else, she needs to feel free. She will not use her freedom to bed-hop, but she must feel trusted. Don't expect blind faith in return, for you won't get it. But if she loves her man, she loves him. Her passions are deep, her emotions honest, and she expects total honesty in return. She will have a stock of flirtatious ways but the ideal man won't notice. When his little green jealousy lamps begin to flicker, she'll feel that his weakness is showing.

She is a contradictory and complex character; regrettably, she is also selfish, possibly without realizing it. For all Arietians demand plenty from their mate, but in certain areas are unable to give in return. Romantic, over-sensitive or highly strung types had better stay out of a lengthy relationship with this woman. She is full of Martian fire that will burn sensitive fingers every time they try to touch her.

SEXUALLY (MALE)

Although the Arietian likes complexity in his personality, this

18

is not necessarily true where sex is concerned. Because he lives a lot in his mind he probably won't experiment as much as he should do on the physical levels. However, if his lady love is wise enough to give him the lead occasionally, she will discover that his variations on a theme can be quite enlightening. He tends to dominate and organize his business life and will, no doubt, bring these tendencies home and apply them to his mate. When he's had a rough time during the day at work, there's no way that life is going to be a bed of roses in the evening. The Arietian male's sexual appetite is influenced by his success in life.

SEXUALLY (FEMALE)

Miss Aries is like her male counterpart in that she enjoys sex but is not dominated by it and is certainly equally interested in other facets of life. But when in love, she is warm and passionate, although perhaps the teeniest bit selfish. She is attracted to the strong and positive type of male, but no man will be left in doubt as to whether she wants him or whether he may as well forget it. On occasions her unabashed approach can take the opposite sex aback. The male needs to be quick, collect his thoughts, untie his tongue and bear in mind that he is probably on the verge of a highly charged sexual affair. He should have plenty of stamina; she has boundless energy and will expect the same from him.

There's no doubt about it, you may love her you may hate her, but one thing is for sure: she is quite irresistible.

HOW TO END THE AFFAIR

One of the quickest ways to dispose of Arietians is to let them think that they've got you. Then they usually make a very rapid exit. Apart from this, all Arietians have sensitive egos, so you could try letting your Ram think that you have found someone more attractive. Once they believe this, you can wave your white handkerchief at them as they walk down the road. Yet another ploy is to be possessive and jealous. The Arietian cannot bear the thought of being owned and will be soon gone.

19

But hold back those tears as you say goodbye. It takes more than this to break the heart of an Arietian. This type's nature is to forget as soon as possible and that means in about the time it takes for your Ram to reach the front gate. Furthermore, the break in romance is never their fault. How could it possibly be? Arietians are never, never wrong – or so they think.

Once you have lost your Arietian, you will look back over the affair and wonder what hit you, at least if you were involved with the strong type. You will miss the warmth and generosity, the verve and excitement, the idealism and egotism. But if you were involved with the weaker type, you'll clap your hands and celebrate the departure, for never was there a bigger fool, nor a more self-deceived person.

ATTRACTING THE SUN SIGNS

ARIES WOMAN WITH ARIES MAN

These two should have no trouble at all attracting each other; it's a very fiery match, with great sparks of passion and surges of vitality. If the relationship is to work, they'll need to take turns at leadership, but with two such sensitive egos this could be somewhat difficult, unless other influences are at work on her chart, when there may be a chance. She does basically understand him, since he is just as ambitious, aggressive and adventurous as she is. Initially he will be attracted to the mutually shared characteristics but it is necessary for her to realize that, on occasion, she is simply going to have to allow him to play boss. Without this concession they will both be constantly juggling for position, which can be purely creative or just plain frustrating. If she can learn sometimes to bow to his ego, she'll discover she has got an extravagant lover. He will wine, dine, gift and court her in a most irresistible fashion. But they should probably keep to a purely sexual or business relationship.

ARIES WOMAN WITH TAURUS MAN

There are a myriad differences between these two. If they are to succeed, she will have to learn to be more practical and less impulsive and he must try to climb out of his rut and be prepared for anything. He loves listening to music; she prefers to dance. He adores his food and drink, is a pretty hot chef, and is capable of consuming a seven-course feast; she prefers something simple like a steak and salad. He is faithful, affectionate and fearful every time she goes off on one of her madcap schemes. More than likely he will have to make some concessions, as he is an obstinate lover. But in the end he is sure to find her pace a little too hectic, though at least he will try to keep up. A frustrating match.

ARIES WOMAN WITH GEMINI MAN

She'll have no difficulty in attracting him with her warmth, dynamic energy and optimism. She'll be attracted to his ready wit, intelligent mind and also initially to the fact that he is constantly surrounded by milling admirers, since anything that appears to be a challenge is always irresistible to her. One of her greatest difficulties is ensuring that she does not give in too readily to him. Once the Gemini man feels that he knows her and what she has to offer, he will be off. This relationship may be something of an emotional treadmill. He makes love with his mind, while she loves with emotional burners at full blast. For him, sexual variety is essential; there's no point in expecting him to be faithful, unless there are other influences at work on his chart. He is an outrageous flirt and will tease her unmercifully. Her sense of ego will not be amused. Ideally a hot, passionate affair, but little else.

ARIES WOMAN WITH CANCER MAN

If she is typically Aries, then she is a go-getting lady who lives life to the fullest extent on a professional as well as on a social level. Therefore ideally she should look elsewhere. The Cancer man is domesticated and needs a woman who is feminine to the point of being tenderly maternal. Her idea of taking it easy is to cut down from three parties a night to two. His version of enjoyment is a quiet evening at home and a romantic dinner for two. She is temperamental and changeable, yet tenacious. The things that he asks from life are security and homely smells emitting from the kitchen. She may be able to seduce him with a lobster thermidor but not with a quick sandwich, grabbed on the way to a fancy-dress party. Bearing in mind that Cancer is water and Aries is fire, the result is bound to be one hell of a lot of steam! Unless she genuinely possesses a domesticated side to her character, it will be dishonest of her to do anything but admit they are just not compatible. An intimate relationship or even friendship will be difficult.

ARIES WOMAN WITH LEO MAN

These two fire signs can create a positive blaze between them. Both are egoists and both recognize the need to pander to this. The Lion is perhaps one of the few men that she is prepared to give in to without feeling that she has lost something of herself. He is the king of the jungle, remember, and requires a lot of understanding; and he expects to be treated as royalty. But he has all the equipment for winning at any game, including love. His pride and confidence rival only her own. He is an insatiable lover and has the kind of warm charm that constantly feeds her electric sexiness. To appeal to this character, all she has to do is be herself. A relationship that can succeed at all levels: friendship, business and love.

ARIES WOMAN WITH VIRGO MAN

There's precious little mutual ground between these two. She will want to teach him to sky-dive, he'll want to show her how to do tax returns. If she allows him to teach her economics, maybe at least he'll form part of the audience while she performs her dare-devil interests. But at least his "take-over" attitude shouldn't cramp her ambitions. She ought not to be too surprised if he expects her to take the sexual initiative – frequently. What is most likely to happen, however, is that the first time he criticizes her she will decide it's time she took off – but quick! A tricky relationship.

ARIES WOMAN WITH LIBRA MAN

These signs are totally opposite – which doesn't mean that they won't attract. When she rings him at 4 o'clock in the morning to suggest they drive down to the coast, he'll be delighted. He loves spontaneous women. But if when he arrives to pick her up she is dressed in scruffy denims with her hair unkempt, he will be immediately disillusioned. Furthermore, he will be quick to notice that her home is something short of spotless and glamorous. This is a gentle, sensitive and totally romantic man, something that the Aries lady must bear in mind at all times. Denims are permissible, of course, at the right time provided they are clean and that her hair is gleaming and she has topped the whole lot off with a French perfume. Being something of a tomboy she may object to all this. In which case, something has got to give and it's bound to be their relationship. A good sexual relationship.

ARIES WOMAN WITH SCORPIO MAN

With a Scorpio man who can be even more outrageously aggressive and sexy than she is, Miss Aries will find it is rarely pure lust. His desires come from deep within him and are strictly of an emotional variety. However, be warned that he is capable of finishing anything sexual that she starts. One must always be careful with a Scorpio man. A love affair with this character is an unforgettable experience but after a while she will find his constant jealousy claustrophobic. This is likely to be a relationship that burns white-hot – for a while . . . until she asks herself whether it's really worth all the aggravation.

ARIES WOMAN WITH SAGITTARIUS MAN

Provided both partners are typical to their signs, then this is one of those relationships which is literally made in the heavens. He'll adore her spontaneity and impulse and respond to it at a moment's notice. These are two fire signs and two egoists. She may find him a little tactless and maybe clumsy verbally, but she must never put him down. Initially he may

23

resent the fact that she seems capable of sorting out his professional life, until he realizes she is right. These two are likely to be friends as well as lovers. She will try hard to share his interest in football or motor racing and he in turn will be happy to leave the great outdoors in order to occasionally socialize with her friends. There's much natural give-and-take in this relationship. It's an excellent one for love, sex, business and pleasure.

ARIES WOMAN WITH CAPRICORN MAN

He is probably attracted to her warmth and energy and she may initially see him as a steadying influence in her rather erratic life. It's difficult for him to stay near her flames for too long. He will appreciate and love her tendency to lead him into new exciting adventures, both social and sexual, but she must never lose sight of the fact that he will always question everything when it looks as if it might interfere with his work or ambitions. There will be many occasions when she will need to accept playing second fiddle to his job – the question is, will her ego allow this? This can be an excellent business partnership. Anything more could be decidedly touchy.

ARIES WOMAN WITH AQUARIUS MAN

This is best described as a fun relationship. Anything else could get very sticky. He will promise to call her on Friday but won't get around to it until the following Tuesday. She will make a date with him for dinner one night and then break it to work late an hour before he is supposed to pick her up. The question is, will these two ever have enough time to get together? He's erratic, somewhat eccentric and unpredictable; she is flighty and likes to live in the present. This relationship is likely to finish up as some sort of complicated game rather than anything more serious.

ARIES WOMAN WITH PISCES MAN

She has it within her power to put the unworldly Piscean male through emotional turmoil. One minute she is feminine and warm, allowing him to think he's the only man who's ever entered her life – the next she is aggressive, fiercely independent and a workaholic. He simply won't know where he stands. He loves flowers, animals, soft music and romantic breakfasts for two; she prefers loud music, the company of friends, a cup of black coffee and a cigarette for breakfast. The delicate approach is what is needed here, although it's doubtful that the Aries woman will be able to maintain it long enough to catch this particular man.

HOW WELL DO YOU KNOW YOUR ARIES WOMAN?

Answer honestly the questions below, scoring 3 for every Yes, 2 for Sometimes and 1 for No, then add up your total.

1. Would she rather have one expensive outfit than three cheap ones?
2. Does she ever get angry with you when you refuse to argue?
3. Do weak people seem to cling to her?
4. Is she impressed by extravagant gifts?
5. Would it be difficult for her to be a full-time housewife?
6. Is she an organizer?
7. Could you take a couple of friends around to her place for dinner without an invitation?
8. Is she impulsive?
9. Would she be an asset to your career?
10. Is she happy to take the lead in sex?
11. If you went away on a business trip, would she go out with friends rather than sit at home?
12. Does she tell you when she is physically frustrated?
13. Does she have difficulty in remembering special dates or anniversaries?
14. Does she prefer to open doors for herself and light her own cigarettes?
15. Does she belong to any committees?
16. Is she extravagant?
17. Is she happier in the company of men than women?
18. Has she been known to throw the odd tantrum?
19. Is it difficult for her to take criticism?
20. Does she strive for the dominant role in your relationship?

(Answers)

1–30
Either you don't know your woman at all or she is not a typical Arietian. It may be that some of the planets were in an air sign, say Gemini, Aquarius and Libra, and perhaps you could find her underneath these. If not, I suggest you talk to her more and get to know her.

31–50

This is an excellent score, from her point of view anyway. You know her about as well as she wants you to and no more. You have an extremely promising relationship which could develop along serious lines. If you've only just met, either you are psychic or, if you don't want to be caught, I suggest you run rather quickly.

51–60

She is typically Arietian all right and you seem to be able to accept that fact, though heaven knows it can't be easy for you. However, take care; this is a pretty tough lady and one who likes to remain something of a mystery. If she scores well answering the quiz on you, it's likely that you've been together for quite some time and are in danger of taking each other for granted.

HOW WELL DO YOU KNOW YOUR ARIES MAN?

Answer honestly the questions below, scoring 3 for every Yes, 2 for Sometimes and 1 for No, then add up your total.

1. Does he resent being reminded of past mistakes?
2. Is he fussy about his appearance?
3. Does he always forget your birthday?
4. Does he find it difficult to read you?
5. Are you the financial wizard in your relationship?
6. Does he get upset if he thinks you are ordering him around?
7. Does he find it difficult to switch off from work when he comes home?
8. Does he consider himself a good driver?
9. Does he get a little rough on occasions when making love?
10. Does he find it hard to express deep emotion?
11. Does he enjoy luxury?
12. If you say no to sex, is he offended?
13. Is he insensitive to touch?
14. Does he leave chores unfinished?
15. Does he need constant ego-boosting?
16. Does he enjoy some kind of sport?

17. Does he invariably flirt with your friends?
18. Does he think you flirt with his workmates?
19. Is he a member of any kind of committee?
20. Does he possess a jealous streak?

(Answers)

1–30

You seem not to know your man at all or else he is not typically Aries. It is possible there is some water on his actual birth chart; if so, you'll find the chapters on Cancer, Scorpio or Pisces more applicable. Maybe this quiz had helped you to learn more about him.

31–50

This is a good score. You know as much about your Arietian man as he wants you to know. I shouldn't probe any deeper. You seem to have the basis of a good relationship. He is a strong person, knows what he wants out of life and is able to get it. Fortunately, you should make a good support for him.

51–60

Does he know you know him as well as this? Most Arietian men like to think of themselves as challenges, otherwise they get a little bored. However, you have my sympathy, for he is a true Arietian for good or bad, and that will take some coping with.

Taurus (the Bull)
Sign of the Constructor or Producer

April 21 – May 21

The first Earth sign: Practical, patient, persevering, productive
Ruler: Venus
Colours: Pink, blue
Career: Builder, farmer, banker, civil servant, industrialist, architect, surveyor, accountant, auctioneer, jeweller, artiste – especially singer
Famous Taureans: Charlotte Bronte, Salvador Dali, Queen Elizabeth II, Ella Fitzgerald, Sigmund Freud, Adolf Hitler, Liberace, Karl Marx, Stevie Wonder

---

TAURUS MAN

This individual is practical, reliable and steadfast. He must have security for his peace of mind. He has excellent powers of endurance and patience. He instinctively conserves, witholds and needs to possess; he has a sound sense of material values. However, all this dependability doesn't necessarily make him dull, because he can be warmly emotional. While finance does play a big part in his plans, it's not that he is mercenary, but in order to be happy or successful in any way a secure foundation is essential. This is a kind and generous man. He has an excellent sense of humour which makes him good company.

His interest in others leads him to offer warmth and hospitality wherever he goes. He enjoys the good things in life and, being sensible with money, can usually afford to indulge himself. He has tremendous reserves of patience and energy and is capable of waiting a considerable time for plans to mature. Whenever an appeal has been made to his feelings, he sticks to a losing cause long after others know that it is hopeless. He'll be obstinate, and even violently enraged, when others try to drive him into doing something, though perfectly friendly and calm if appealed to in the correct way. But try to cajole or bully him into making changes he does not agree with and he will dig in his heels and lower his horns – and you'd better watch out. A Bull in full charge is something to avoid. His stubbornness is frequently reflected in his opinions and emotions. He should learn to compromise and not expect life always to adapt itself to him. He must remember that although other people's views may be wrong, they have a right to air them and he should at least be willing to listen.

In love the Bull has a strongly romantic streak, and when happily mated it doesn't take long for him to become placid, domesticated and affectionate. No matter how passionate an affair may be in the beginning, it usually develops into a warm, friendly relationship which augers well for being happily settled in the married state. The Bull makes a faithful and contented husband.

TAURUS WOMAN

The Taurus lady is extremely feminine and is in fact a softer version of her male counterpart. She too is something of a financial wizard; although she's never mean, she can, over a long period of time, build up quite a formidable bank balance, mainly because this makes her feel secure. Apart from this she has a keen love of the comforts and luxuries that money can bring her. But she can be somewhat contradictory. Having saved for months on end, stinting herself even on necessities at times, she will suddenly splurge out on a binge when she will indulge on all the good things in life – good company, good entertainment and above all else good food and wine. This leads to one of her main problems, for the love of eating and imbibing often results in an unwelcome bulge of fat. The typical Taurus woman spends much of her life trying to diet off such binges.

She is neither an idealist nor a dreamer, but constructive and for the most part stable. She never relies on luck, but insists on the just rewards for good steady work at her vocation. She slowly builds towards ultimate but solid success. She loves system in all that she is involved with and is a great organizer; once she has made up her mind about what needs to be done and the best way to proceed, she is unstoppable. The notorious Taurean stubbornness means that, having made up her mind or reached an opinion, she can be immovable. No wise man will attempt to nag or manipulate her, for she is capable of great anger, although fortunately these outbursts are rare. However, when those eyes narrow and her pretty heels are dug in, it's wise to clear a path and get out of sight as quickly as possible.

For all her practicality, don't be fooled into believing she is not all woman. Physical attraction is important to her. Platonic love simply doesn't exist. She is very direct in her relationships. One thing she cannot stand is to feel that she is being kept on a string, that the object of her affections perhaps does not return her warm feelings, and she may ruin many a relationship by insisting on being told exactly where she stands. She would rather be rejected than kept in doubt. She may have been a late developer physically but she is bound always to have attracted male admirers. She doesn't fall in love easily, but when she does it's usually for life. Once she feels that she can trust her mate, she is tremendously affectionate, demonstrative and madly romantic. She will fall every time for those unexpected presents, flowers and dinners for two which to her are an essential part of love-making.

Lastly, there's an artistic streak to this lady; if she is not actually an artist, she has an appreciation of art which is great providing she can afford it. If so she's bound to have a collection of some kind. The opposite sex should also bear in mind that she regards love-making as an art and is therefore generally averse to casual relationships.

31

THE HYDE SIDE

Although this type has the splendid patience associated with their Jekyll counterparts, they are also extremely obstinate and pig-headed, they despise contradiction and believe themselves to be always right. They are overly possessive and averse to all change and therefore frequently become stuck in a rut. They are stodgy, self-centred, grasping and will slavishly adhere to routine. They therefore totally lack spontaneity. These Bulls are lazy, luxury-loving and self-indulgent. All Taureans need to watch a tendency to overeat and over imbibe, and these types find it hard to deny themselves any kind of pleasure.

They never give unless they are sure of receiving. Where money is concerned, they believe the only person it's worth spending on is themselves. It's almost impossible for them to find true happiness, for love is a giving emotion. When some poor unsuspecting member of the opposite sex does eventually come along with an open heart, this Bull is suspicious, believing that basically you don't get anything for nothing, including love. If it isn't forthcoming during the third hour of the first date, they demand to know why. Not surprisingly, most of their relationships are doomed before they begin.

Should they ever actually make it in the marriage stakes, almost overnight they become complacent, slothful and begin to take their mate for granted. For some reason, they seem to relish the idea of jumping into the deepest rut as quickly as possible, perhaps because they believe that they have already put themselves out to catch their mate, so now why bother? Not surprisingly, these Taureans more often than not finish up alone.

HOW TO CATCH AND KEEP YOUR TAURUS MAN

The true Taurean male likes his woman to be dependent on him, for it makes him feel important; any female wishing to attract his attention will be wise to take note of this.

He loves his home and spends much time in it, and his artistic streak will lead him to spend quite extravagantly on decorations and furnishings. He loves to entertain, so when thinking of settling down into a serious relationship he will be immediately attracted to the well dressed female who appears to be quite capable of acting as hostess while remaining cool, calm and beautiful. All Taurean men are fond of their food and many excel in the culinary arts. Nevertheless, he does prefer to believe that his woman is able to rustle up a Chateaubriand or a soufflé at a moment's notice. All this may make him sound rather dull and domesticated – but not a bit of it.

Somewhere beneath his usually heavy exterior lurks a romantic. Therefore while it's true that he may extract the maximum enjoyment out of his home, he will not expect his wife to become a drudge in front of his eyes. Any lady who hopes to be important to him must be well groomed and poised even while changing a nappy or doing the washing. Invite him round to a sumptuous meal, put on your sexiest dress and within moments he should be putty in your hands. His most glaring fault is his unbelievable stubbornness. When a clash of opinion arises, open battle would be most unwise, for he'll refuse to budge – that is until he walks out the door. Any pursuing woman should resort to feminine wiles, women's liberation notwithstanding. Helpless looks and gestures work miracles with this type.

One further word of warning: the Taurean man is very money-conscious and lives with a constant horror of debt. Naturally, then, he is unlikely to be attracted to those females who have a talent for spending money quicker than it's earned. Rather he will be fascinated by the one who displays common sense in this direction. Not that the Taurean man could be accused of being mean; with loved ones he is very generous, but he'll never spend more than he earns, no matter how much he is nagged or how many tears are wept. Therefore if in hot pursuit of a Taurean, you are advised to get out your cookery book and take an overnight course in how to turn pennies into pounds. Don't forget to look ladylike while you are doing it.

HOW TO CATCH AND KEEP YOUR TAURUS WOMAN

Like male members of this sign, this woman is stubborn and determined, two attributes which in certain circumstances can be most useful, helping her to achieve her objectives in life and to withstand harsh conditions. Conversely, they can also be most unattractive, and anyone close to a Taurean female will know there are times when she can appear unbearably self-opinionated.

She is also prone to over-indulgence and someone who can keep up with her will appeal to her. Men who have been involved with a Taurean for any length of time may begin to wonder whether she has a bottomless pit for a stomach, but don't be misled into believing quantity triumphs over quality. No, it's a case of both! Any admirer taking this lady out for dinner will need to rob his piggy-bank first, for it's likely to be an expensive occasion. Despite this, it's important that he does not show any sign of meanness. The Taurean lady likes a generous man. Neither will the macho approach pay dividends; more subtlety is called for. Initially she should be allowed to have her own way, but very gradually the man concerned can begin to assert himself. And it is important that he does so; to let himself become a doormat will be the beginning of the end. She will soon lose interest and respect and begin to look around for a stronger individual.

Work-wise, no matter how dull her job or occupation may be, she is sure to have some artistic hobby and any man with his eye on her should attempt to interest himself in this, for she will naturally value his opinion. Disagreements are handled in one of two ways: either she loses her temper and can be likened to an out-of-control bulldozer – in which case the man concerned may be tempted to take cover, though the best couse of action will be to remain undaunted and give as good as he gets – or else she becomes impossibly stubborn, digs her heels in and refuses even to discuss. When this occurs, there's no point in even the most intelligent and diplomatic of men attempting to either argue or reason with her. This will be a pure waste of time. The best course of action is to wait until she is in a more favourable frame of mind, and then, after a few loving words, a kiss and a cuddle, confront her once more with the subject in dispute. In these circumstances, her unyielding disposition is likely to melt away.

HIS IDEAL PARTNER

When choosing a mate, the Bull is no impulsive bargain-hunter. He can never be accused of picking the first girl who happens along. Even if her astrological label is Capricorn, Virgo or Cancer, it doesn't follow that she'll automatically find her way into his heart. She may be listed as his most compatible mate, but that doesn't mean she won't have to try. Besides, he'll be in the throes of enjoying the other nine sun signs and may not be ready to be disturbed. Much depends too on whether he has been recently hurt. Once his fingers have been burned, they smart for many a month and he'll think twice before becoming involved again. But if some girl thinks she is right for him, and he has given some sign that he thinks so too, then she is clearly a very special lady. For she will be capable of rustling up a cordon-bleu meal for his boss or friends at the drop of a hat while remaining calm, chic and feminine, and she will have earned his admiration. She is also capable of making love on the spur of the moment. At the end of both proceedings, she'll hardly have a hair out of place!

The extravagant female will have trouble with this individual; she will have to cure the hole in her purse, but quick. The Taurean is nobody's fool and isn't soon parted from his cash; not that he has moths in his wallet, you understand – far from it, but he certainly does have a sense of value where money is concerned. His ideal partner, then, will have to learn to be sensible and he will reward her with fine clothes and expensive perfume. All she need be in return is feminine and superhuman. Once he has made up his mind that he has found the ideal lady, one of whom his mother would approve, he will chase her until he is finally accepted or rejected. He doesn't take kindly to being left dangling like a spare piece of string. He definitely wants to know where he stands.

If she fools around with his emotions or teases him, I'm afraid there's going to be an unpleasant scene. To have his chosen woman totally dependent on him both boosts his ego and enhances his masculinity. But he won't expect his mate to become his slave or want her to stick to him like jam on a blanket. He won't mind if she is occasionally disorganized and even panicky, this for him is typically female. Just so long as, underneath, they both know who is boss, she'll be fine.

35

Lastly, the right mate for him will never lose sight of the fact that he is Stubborn with a capital S. She would be well advised to find out just exactly what it is that gets him into this mood. But she'll only exhaust herself in efforts to change him. She must accept him for what he is, be content to be his woman, keep the children's toys out of his way when he comes home from work and wants to rest, substitute a gentle Brahms lullaby for rock 'n' roll, feed him regularly and lie lovingly in his arms every night – it's not too much to ask, is it? Well, perhaps it is, but not for his ideal partner.

HER IDEAL PARTNER

The female Bull will probably find her ideal partner under the same signs as her brothers: maybe Cancer, Virgo or Capricorn, for these three are all acutely aware of financial responsibility and can be relied upon to supply the security she so badly needs for her peace of mind. A Taurean lady with creditors all over town isn't the happiest person in the world, and when she is unsure of where the next penny is coming from, she becomes irritable and bad-tempered. Clearly she needs a responsible influence in her life. And that's where her ideal mate comes into the picture.

Apart from being able to keep her in the manner to which she will undoubtedly have become accustomed, he should have a romantic streak in his manner. Love and devotion mean a lot to her and if he supplies it she will return the compliment with unswerving loyalty.

She requires a man who can also enjoy himself. She won't mind if he occasionally eyes another pair of legs, or even helps a pretty neighbour across the street, but if he takes things to extremes and puts one toe across her line of fair play, then he'll be in trouble. She likes a man whose appetites in every way match her own. If she has decided to eat a ten-course meal, then he had better shape up. If she wants to make love morning, afternoon and evening, not only will he be a lucky man, he'll also have to have the stamina to stand the pace. Furthermore, her ideal partner must enjoy the comfort of a domestic scene. He's not called ideal for nothing. And there's more to come!

She may not often show it – not to him, at any rate – but she can be quite jealous and possessive. Therefore, on no account should he make a bid to become the local Casanova. Once she has made a commitment, even if not in document form, it's good for all time, and she expects similar behaviour from her mate. Would-be Romeos who only require her as an interesting sexual interlude should be warned not to let her in on the secret. If a man explains to her that he thinks they are basically wrong for each other although he still finds her fascinating, she may be a little disappointed but will lap up this wonderful flattery. The worst thing he can do is lie to her or intimate that he means more than he actually does. Not only will this give her a severe case of depression, but the after-effects are likely to be a traumatic and dramatic row. She may not mind being taken, but does resent being taken for a fool.

Her ideal man must be practical and have a reasonable grasp of the fundamentals of life. He doesn't have to have a university degree to gain her admiration and on the other hand she isn't depressed or worried if he only has the IQ of a retarded ant. How to strike a happy balance? If his feet are firmly planted on the ground, and he doesn't give in to too many flights of fancy, then this could be the chap for her.

She will remain loyal to him from the penthouse to the gutter, as long as he treats her right. And he should bear in mind that having a Taurean lady to rely upon in any emergency – from a bruised thumb to the collapse of his company – is more than anyone can expect from another human being. When treated correctly she is party to all her man's expectations.

SEXUALLY (MALE)

When it comes to sex, the Taurean man is fairly basic, earthy and usually an early developer. Any woman who has baby-sat for the neighbour only to discover a 9-year-old attempting to make a pass at her can be quite sure he is born under the sign of Taurus. From the time he learns to run, the opposite sex is on his mind. He could be classified as "over-active" but one could more accurately call him lustful. As a young man he can't wait to get to grips with this mystery of life and, once that has been achieved, there's no stopping him. Mind you, there'll be ladies who complain that his approach is sometimes primitive; he may not hit you on the top of the head with a club, but his approach is neither complicated nor original. If his mate is looking for any kind of variation, then it's up to her to take the initiative.

Because of his inherent stubbornness, patience will be needed if she hopes to introduce him to anything new. Never expect him to be too outrageous, or you'll be disappointed for sure. Because of his highly sexual character, Mr Taurus will never let his mate forget that she is a woman, and no matter how long they've been married or involved, he will always be good for physical contact. Clearly, then, this character's sexuality lies largely in the hands of his woman. She should never complain about his performance, without first checking on her own.

Lastly, some excellent wine, a superb meal (but a light one), soft music and exotic perfume are really about all it takes to interest the Taurean man.

SEXUALLY (FEMALE)

There's absolutely nothing prudish about the Taurean woman when it comes to sex – and eventually it will. She is one of the first to stand up and be counted when it's a matter of acknowledging sexual needs, but deviations from the norm won't occur to her unless introduced carefully by a clever partner. There's little point coming home laden with goodies from the sex shop and expecting an ecstatic response. Many men tend to make a quick assessment of her on first meeting, which turns out totally wrong. Because she is happy and emancipated enough to admit that she would like to share your bed on occasions, don't get the impression that you are in for an orgy of experimentation. "I man, you woman," is all she wants when it comes to a night of love.

Romance and the right atmosphere play a great part in her love life. If a man is to get anywhere with her, he needs to set the scene carefully. Soft lights, pleasant smells, good food, soft music are all good props and she is the first to admit she falls for them every time. But let's get back to her versatility. Probably her biggest problem is her age. If she is under 23 and above 17 she is still open-minded and ready to learn all things regarding the physical side of life, from the right man. Once past this age, she tends to say to herself, "You can't teach an old dog new tricks" though with luck she may find out that she is wrong. If she is over 30, then I'm afraid she will be well stuck in her sexual rut, probably believing that her standards are the only ones. The way out of this situation is for her to fall madly in love, for then her mind will automatically become more flexible. Over 50, the years of over-indulgence tell on her physical appearance which may have been allowed to disintegrate. The old girl may look just a little over-ripe but she will believe she is totally undesirable. She may even become slovenly. When she has reached this stage of degeneration, it's up to her man or any man to put her back together again. You'll have to build her confidence starting from scratch. It isn't often that the Taurean woman's legs lose their shape; they are frequently the show-piece of her anatomy, so flattery can be laid on in this direction. Admiring advances can do a lot for her morale too.

Just because she is strong and practical, no man should ever fool himself into believing she doesn't need those compliments or the same protection as her smaller sisters do. If she believes a man admires her, and she can always rely upon him in a crisis, then she will be his.

HOW TO END THE AFFAIR

Disposing of a Taurean isn't easy, the reason being that notorious stubborn streak again. But it isn't only that: if you've been together for any length of time, then you'll be looking on a good and steadfast friend, and breaking off with a friend is never the easiest thing. Anyway it's difficult to get the Bull to do something it doesn't want to do.

At the beginning of the relationship, the matter is simple. A string of "dont's" will soon put the lid on any budding romance. Don't be too keen to give in to him sexually, don't stand up for him, don't save money, don't be modest, don't tell the truth, don't keep your mouth shut, etc. etc. And don't forget that he likes to know exactly where he stands. If you tell him the best place is about ten miles from you, he'll soon get the idea. He may even be thankful for this advice if you haven't been stringing him along. He's unlikely to make a scene; he hasn't got the energy. The quickest way to send him on his way is to step out of character, but do it gracefully. For example, if you are used to spending pleasant nights out drinking together, let him get drunk on his own. Be a blabbermouth, poke fun at him in front of his friends. Go to a swish social function dressed like a tramp. This type of treatment followed by a clean break will be the easiest way out. But are you really certain you want to be rid of him? If so, then you must have found someone who is worth his weight in gold.

If you are a man and you are attempting to get rid of your Taurean lady, this can be a little more difficult. She too will appreciate a clean break, but maybe a few hints should be thrown her way before the final bombshell is aimed and dropped. Try your hardest not to satisfy her sexually, refuse to allow her to cook for you. If she does cook, lose your appetite. A week of this behaviour and she will probably be off. With the Bull you have to be firm, unwavering and as kind as possible. If, after the affair, you find you miss your Taurean, don't come crying to me; you may be able to catch him or her as they leave, they don't move quickly.

HOW TO ATTRACT THE SUN SIGNS

TAURUS WOMAN WITH TAURUS MAN

Physical, material, emotional creature-comforts are important for both parties here. If she can afford Christian Dior wardrobes, cook gourmet meals, keep a mansion neat and manage to look fragile in the face of all this, then the Taurean man will worship her, but it's rather a lot to ask. Sexually, there's little trouble; his love-making is forthright and direct – not terribly imaginative, but affectionate and fulfilling, and that's the way she likes it. One of the biggest problems is a double helping of Taurean stubbornness lurking within them both, although she may learn to back down graciously, especially if there's some other influence on her birth-chart. But if not, in a matter of weeks this passionate relationship will have reduced itself to a stony silence and, unless someone is prepared to give, this could go on for years. Taureans make excellent business partners, and possibly even friends, but this is not a wise coupling for a love affair.

TAURUS WOMAN WITH GEMINI MAN

The Taurean sensuality and deep-seated need to own and to hold on to things and people can easily overpower the freedom-loving Gemini. He'll have her chewing her nails down to the elbows when he is not home at 3 o'clock in the morning, or doesn't answer his phone when she needs solace. He is also absolutely hopeless on the financial front and may have them both in debt within a couple of months. Not that he is always prone to this sort of behaviour, but it may come out in open rebellion against what he sees as her miserly tendencies. Worse than this, while she is a faithful sort who expects a loyal mate, this man is a flirt, and there's nothing to be done about it. Try to shut him in and he'll become more and more promiscuous. Quite obviously, then, it's a relationship to be entered into at one's peril.

TAURUS WOMAN WITH CANCER MAN

This promises to be a very good relationship. Cancer is a water sign, Taurus is an earth sign; mix earth and water you get mud, which these two are unlikely to use to throw at each other, but rather for sitting and wallowing in. He loves to pamper; he'll invite her to a meal and thoroughly spoil her. Apart from being a super chef, he is affectionate, warm and likes physical contact. His many moods may confuse her at first, but she will soon adjust to them, anticipate them and even head them off. Attracting this man presents no difficulty at all for her. A mutual love of home comforts and the culinary arts is enough to stimulate interest for both partners.

TAURUS WOMAN WITH LEO MAN

Initially, at least, there are certain things these two have in common. Both like good food, luxury and the best things in life. However, she will need to hide that common sense until she gets to know him a little better, though he may still be too much in love with her to care about it. He will be impressed by her elegance and poise. She will let herself be charmed by this

41

expert lady-killer. But when guards are dropped at a later date, vast differences between them will be uncovered. He constantly lives above his means, something she would never dream of doing. He adores the company of attractive women; she won't approve. But both are equally fixed about preferring to get their own way. This is a rather difficult relationship, then, and is best confined to business.

TAURUS WOMAN WITH VIRGO MAN

The Virgo man will be attracted to Miss Taurus's elegance and he will be doubly impressed if she displays financial common sense. But it will take her a while to get used to him. She won't understand his tendency to transform her panoramic vision of life into little details – she'll find it unnerving. When she knows him better she will swear he is the only man who can come home falling drunk, sleep in his suit and get up looking fresh and uncreased. He needs to control his sharp tongue, though. The Taurus woman doesn't mind some gentle criticism, but if he turns into a nag it will only bring out her notorious obstinacy. Mutual outlooks on life make this an exemplary partnership, whether it be for love, sex, business or companionship.

TAURUS WOMAN WITH LIBRA MAN

Both signs are ruled by Venus, so this partnership contains most of the ingredients for a successful love affair, although not necessarily marriage. Both have an interest in the arts, in good food, in fashion, a shared love of culture and good conversation. Socially, emotionally and intellectually it's a fairly winning combination – so long as she never takes him for granted. The Libran man is in love with love; the problem is that the object of his affections tends to change monthly. She won't appreciate his tendency to attract all the prettiest girls wherever they go, but should she display any jealous tantrums, this lover of peace and harmony will be off, leaving her ranting and raving on her own. These two may well attract each other effortlessly, but the staying power of the relationship remains in question.

TAURUS WOMAN WITH SCORPIO MAN

This is sure to be an attraction of opposites. Of the two she is the more stable, for the most part being ruled by common sense, whereas he uses his intuitions and deep emotions. It's also debatable whether she can handle the passion that's likely to come her way, for anything longer than a short period. In the end she may decide it's all a bit heavy-going. However, there are certain things these signs have in common. Both can be fiercely jealous and stubborn in their own ways. Because of this, the mildest flirtation may well break them up. Hardly a basis, then, for a long-term relationship.

TAURUS WOMAN WITH SAGITTARIUS MAN

Miss Taurus will have little trouble appealing to this gentleman with her feminine wiles. However he is strictly a man's man. He's forever plotting schemes with workmates, out buying drinks for the boys, or deeply wrapped up in personal projects – infuriating her because she isn't involved. Furthermore, he likes the great outdoors, which to the Taurean lady is alien, with the possible exception of a little bit of gardening. His characteristic generosity with everybody else is likely, too, to stir up her jealousy. But if she shows it, he'll get his running shoes out of hock and be gone from her life before she has a chance to stop him. This is a combination which may work if one or either of the parties is not typical to their sign. Otherwise it's sheer hard work and frustration.

TAURUS WOMAN WITH CAPRICORN MAN

This is one of those propitious astrological unions. She'll have little trouble attracting him: all she has to do is assure him that he really will be rich and famous one day, show him she believes in him totally. Once she does this, that icy saturnine exterior will melt away. When she gets to know him better, she will understand his depressions, while he will understand her need for stability. Sexually speaking, where she is timid, he is as persistent in bed as he is at work – in fact he's an overachiever! Nevertheless there are times when this ambitious man needs to relax and the Taurus woman can assist him to do so. As both characters are probably striving towards common objectives, this is an admirable relationship, be it for love, friendship or business.

TAURUS WOMAN WITH AQUARIUS MAN

A Taurean woman going through a lonely phase in life may be drawn to this rather special man, for he is the most imaginative and least conventional lover in the Zodiac. Life with him can be impossibly chaotic for the calm-craving Taurean, so it's probable that the novelty will very soon wear off. He may well be attracted by the way her brain works, far more so than by her body, and his myriad outside interests are likely to take him away from her when she needs him the most. This is probably a rather short-lived affair.

TAURUS WOMAN WITH PISCES MAN

Although this is not generally thought to be a particularly successful alliance, in many instances it does work. For the enigmatic, sentimental, artistic and magical man that this Piscean lover is brings the Taurean woman the wonderful feeling of being needed and wanted. He will adore her and express his love in the most delightful fashion, sending her flowers on every weekly anniversary, maybe even daily if she is lucky. She in turn will help him find his briefcase and keys so that he can get to work at some point. She may end up regarding him as rather a scatty child, but some women find this attractive. But initially she shouldn't allow him to see her overly practical side, rather she should give in to the romantic being within. Common sense can always be applied a dose at a time. An excellent friendship and a possible romance.

TAURUS WOMAN WITH ARIES MAN

Although basically the Taurus woman is totally incompatible

with the Arietian, she may succeed in tempting him into her cosy lair, where he will revel in her flair for colours, tastes and textures. However, it can only be a matter of time before her obstinacy surfaces each time he tries to direct her life – and try he will. She must allow him to be boss if she wants the relationship to last. She may well consider the fires he awakens in her are worth submissiveness. After all, it isn't often one comes across a man who understands so well one's need for independence and, at the same time, gives encouragement and approval. This all sounds perfect, but what is likely to happen is that passion will be short-lived and eventually these two will become very close friends.

HOW WELL DO YOU KNOW YOUR TAURUS WOMAN?

Answer honestly the questions below, scoring 3 for every Yes, 2 for Sometimes and 1 for No, then add up your total.

1. Does she have a well developed sense of smell?
2. Is it impossible to change her mind once she has made it up?
3. Are there times when she gladly spends the day's food money on expensive bottles of perfume?
4. Does she become ravenous after love-making?
5. No matter how clever or practical she is, does she sometimes feel like an unprotected little girl?
6. Does she overeat when she is unhappy?
7. If you lost your job, would she gladly take over the role of breadwinner?
8. Does she find it hard to forget an injury or a slight?
9. Is she totally thrown when faced with a change of plan?
10. Is she lacking in spontaneity?
11. Would she be reluctant to try anything new sexually?
12. Does she have a physically lazy side?
13. Would it worry her if you got into debt?
14. Does she have a weight problem?
15. Does she prefer the company of women to men?
16. Does she have a creative hobby?
17. Do you think she would secretly like to be more frivolous?
18. Does she like it when you wait on her?
19. Is she sexually fairly predictable?
20. Is she loyal?

(Answers)

1–30
Your lady may have a Sun in Taurus, but she's anything but typical; or perhaps you haven't known her long or haven't bothered to get to know the real woman. However, it's more likely that there's a Piscean, Sagittarian or Arietian influence there and the relevant chapters may help you get to know how she ticks. Of course it could be that she is deliberately playing

an evasive game, in which case you haven't a hope with her.

31–50
You are involved with a typical Taurean lady all right, and you know her as well as she wants you to know her. Allow her to keep one or two little secrets and mysteries; it will add piquancy to your relationship. If you've just met, then you are in with a fair chance of making a success out of your relationship, but it's more than likely you've been together for some considerable time.

51–60
How can you know her so well and still be together? It's probable that the two of you need a break in order to rediscover some of that old romance. Otherwise your relationship could deteriorate into one of complacency, and that won't do.

HOW WELL DO YOU KNOW YOUR TAURUS MAN?

Answer honestly the questions below, scoring 3 for every Yes, 2 for Sometimes and 1 for No, then add up your total.

1. Is he a real home body?
2. Is he unbelievably stubborn?
3. Does he have an eye for colour?
4. Is he stimulated by the countryside?
5. Does he sometimes secretly wish to shake off his responsibilities?
6. Does he resent being the rock of Gibraltar in the family?
7. Does he often fall asleep when you want to make love?
8. Does he have a gargantuan appetite?
9. Although you know he never hurts you, does he look quite fierce when angry?
10. Is he turned on by silks and satin?
11. No matter how good or bad you may be at it, does he prefer home cooking?
12. Is he bad-tempered when woken up?
13. Is he averse to physical exercise?
14. Is he oblivious to your more sensitive needs?
15. Is he sexually an early developer?

16. Does he have tremendous powers of recuperation?
17. Does he like to cook?
18. Would he like to spend more time in his garden?
19. Is it difficult for him to be spontaneous about love-making?
20. Do you wish he would be more experimental when it comes to sex?

(Answers)

1–30
Either you don't know this character at all – perhaps you may have just met – or he is not typical of his sign and perhaps there's a strong fire influence, such as Leo, Aries or Sagittarius. If you have known him for any length of time, it may be wise for you to devote more of your energies to finding out exactly what makes him tick.

31–50
Your man is typically Taurean. And you know him pretty well. Not too well, you understand, not enough to become bored with him, and that's the way it should be. If you've only just met, then the stars look promising for you. If you've been together for some time, then look after your relationship; it really is very special.

51-60
Do you know your Taurean man? Yes, you do! Perhaps sometimes you wish you didn't quite so thoroughly. But there is time for you to do something in an attempt to recover some of that old sparkle. It's difficult to know someone this well and retain any excitement.

Gemini (the Twins)
Sign of the Agent or Writer

May 22 – June 21

The first Air sign: Adaptable, communicative, versatile, incessantly on the go, restless, acquisitive
Ruler: Mercury
Colour: Yellow
Careers: Commercial traveller, news reporter, clerk, shorthand-typist, secretary, lecturer, teacher, broker, solicitor, printer, publisher
Famous Geminians: Bob Dylan, Ian Fleming, Errol Flynn, Judy Garland, John F. Kennedy, Paul McCartney, Marilyn Monroe, Laurence Olivier, Prince Philip, Cole Porter

---

GEMINI MAN

The Gemini man is intellectual and many-sided. His energies come from the brain and nerves but not the heart. He possesses a very sensitive, highly-strung disposition, and needs plenty of fresh air, rest and exercise. The Gemini symbol resembles the Roman numeral II and symbolizes the duality and a "never two, three or four minds alike" nature. The only certain thing about the true Geminian man is that he is never the same for any length of time. Even he rarely knows who he is at any given time. If typical of his sign, then he is vivacious, with a surplus of intellectual energy which seeks expression in many ways. He is longing for new interests and knowledge, plus his impatience

49

with routine, can lead to a brilliant career in literature or some other artistic field. Whatever his chosen job, it is essential that he is able to express his character in some way through it.

Settled contentment is not for this type, no matter how successful he is in personal or professional life. Even when at the top of his particular tree, he is not one to rest on his laurels; rather he will go out to find yet another tree to climb.

It is an impossible task to try to pigeon-hole the Gemini, for it would be necessary to put a little bit of him here and a little bit of him there. In his work he must have variety and change. That's why you'll often find him either as a journalist or a travelling salesman. Put the Geminian man in an office where he is chair-bound and you sentence him to mental death. Not only that, but as soon as he is outside of such an uncongenial atmosphere he will compensate by seeking diversification in his personal life. That nervous energy just has to have an outlet.

This individual has a strong sense of justice and is able to see both sides of any argument – and sometimes a third – so he is apt to contradict himself continually. That's why you'll never get anything from him in writing. At the beginning of a letter he may have decided on one course of action, by the time he gets to "Yours sincerely" he will have changed his mind. His verbal ability is quite amazing. He has such a way with words that even a politician can be struck dumb when confronted with this man. A Geminian real-estate agent trying to sell you a house in need of complete renovation will soon persuade you and himself that all it needs is a lick of paint. Never mind the leaking roof and the rotting floorboards. And if the ceiling caves in on your tour of inspection, he will convince you that it was supposed to do that.

This positive type is a reminder that Gemini is a masculine sign. He displays much force and initiative. He is very definite in his views, is multi-talented and makes an excellent manager or executive. But he is not particuarly domesticated and does not participate wholeheartedly in family life. There's a somewhat superficial attitude towards relationships with relatives or his wife. He is ruled by the mind, and, unless other influences in his chart contradict this, his emotions are somewhat shallow. He tends to be a flirt but this part of his nature should not be taken seriously. His experience of love is rarely deep.

Lastly, Gemini rules the hands and the arms as well as the

upper respiratory system, the nerves and the part of the brain controlling higher thought processes. Therefore this character tends to be clever with his hands and likes to use them constantly. An uncommunicative and relaxed Gemini would indeed be a rarity.

GEMINI WOMAN

Gemini female shares many characteristics with her male counterpart. Playing it cool is her forte. She studies, reasons and observes. She is dispassionately rational. Fear of being fenced in keeps her moving constantly. And she is so calculating and adaptable that she can adjust to anything, with an eccentric air which leaves other people breathless. When she can't get a taxi, she's not above hailing a milk float.

In relationships, her quicksilver humour and knack of communication fascinates and confuses. Older men are impressed with her witty repartee as well as her talent for listening. Younger men see her as a mimic and are astounded that she can make them believe anything. Beneath that svelte exterior lurk myriad personalities, each waiting to burst forth to surprise and delight. She can frustrate, infuriate, anger, titillate, tempt, hate and love, all within the space of a morning.

With such an abundance of attributes, it is difficult to imagine her ever being alone. She needs plenty of activity around her, and she usually manages to find it, or create it. Nine times out of ten, her tantrum-throwing is her way of keeping everyone on their mental toes. Men are attracted to her stimulating company.She is always on the look-out for something to discuss or criticize. Her concentration is not a strong point, neither is short-term memory. In the middle of a world-shattering debate she may suddenly decide that your hair is parted on the wrong side, or that your new sweater doesn't match her carpet. Emotionally speaking, she is similar to the male Gemini, appearing to be flirtatious and a sore trial to her lover. Men may find her fickle and unpredictable, but nevertheless something of a challenge.

The true Gemini woman is usually above average height and rarely suffers from weight problems. She looks good in expensive clothes and generally has an elegant appearance, but this is only one of the many images she likes to project. Do you want a femme fatale, mysterious and sexy? A girl-next-door in pigtails and denims? A mother? A slut? You've got them all and many, many more besides. If this aspect of her character is smothered, she becomes introspective and introverted. She simply cannot pick out one of her personalities and stick to it; you might as well ask a chameleon to stop changing colour. It's important that she is allowed to grow freely, develop naturally and be how she wants to be. She is unlikely to be fulfilled by a purely domesticated existence. The worst thing anyone can do is try to chain her to the cooker, day after day. And although she yearns for motherhood eventually, rigid domestic routine will bore her stiff. Pressure of any description will only drive her within herself or, worse still, out of the family home. Nevertheless, the silly side of being a mother appeals to her tremendously. Crawling over the floor pretending to be Champion the Wonder Horse or the Midnight Special Engine is right up her street, but let the child become demanding and impatience will take over. Nevertheless her offspring will be surrounded by love. And she will care desperately about their intellectual and mental development, even if their socks are a little grubby. Maybe she has got her priorities right.

Anyone becoming involved with this lady had better be warned that they are taking on a harem: she is a different woman for every day of the year. Whether you like this female or not very much depends on your ability to keep up with her pace.

THE HYDE SIDE

Those with more of the faults than virtues associated with this sign are liable to be superficial, lacking in continuity, two-faced, inconsistent, cunning, with a tendency to dissipate nervous energy. The Gemini curiosity here degenerates into a tendency to spread themselves too thinly, to do everything haphazardly and nothing particularly well. They fritter their time away frivolously instead of concentrating their energies in order to achieve excellence or success. They are easily distracted and restless, unable to stick to any regular or repetitious occupation for long. And how exhausting they are! They drain everybody they come into contact with, demanding sympathy, attention, consideration and time. Invariably they believe themselves to be right, and consider anything that does not affect them directly to be of no consequence.

All Geminians talk. Incessantly. And not only with their voices: all parts of the anatomy are used in communication. That's the easiest way to recognize them. They gabble and wave their arms around like demented windmills. But they've rarely got anything to say – anything worthwhile, that is.

Whereas the strong Gemini leads an eventful professional life, the weak types tend to be "jacks of all trades" and just can't be bothered to settle to one career. They go from one job to another, resigning as soon as they run into any form of opposition. Not to put too fine a point on it, they are irresponsible. Because they are takers, they will often turn to stealing as a hobby. They see something they want, cannot afford it, but have decided that they SHOULD have it. If they get caught they don't possess the facility to lie, unlike the stronger type. They believe that no one is as smart as them.

Novelty-seeking and insincerity make life very difficult on the personal level. These types are continually attracted to what they can't have; and should they manage to get over to that greener grass, they will soon be off to the next valley. They are quite at ease running a number of affairs all at the same time.

Loved ones shouldn't fool themselves that this Gemini will become more practical with age. These types never mature. They take a long time to grow up. Many of them just never make it. Because of this they get along with people many years their junior, especially children.

Most Geminians are a mixture of both the good and the bad, so do not despair. There's hope for them. Basically the Gemini is capable, loyal and faithful; it just takes the right partner to bring out the best in the personality, but in this weak type you may have to dig pretty deep.

HOW TO CATCH AND KEEP YOUR GEMINI MAN

If you are looking for a man as strong as the Rock of Gibraltar or perhaps a protector, then you had better leave this character well alone. A many-sided Gemini man finds these two roles anything but his favourite. There will be days when he needs a lover; others when he is searching for a mother-figure and still others when he will become all male and want to shield his loved one from the cruel harsh world.

He can be quite tiring. He needs constant novelty, for he dreads boredom. A female determined to snare this individual must keep him constantly on his toes, for as soon as he has figured her out he will be off. In order to captivate him, she should be prepared for a lot of hard work: attempting to keep up with this man can be exhausting. She will need to project a variety of images, and even when she has managed to catch the Gemini male, she will still have to maintain this constant flow of differing roles to keep him really happy.

Those closely associated with this type have several crosses to bear. For the Gemini man is a flirt. He simply needs endlessly to pit his wits against members of the opposite sex, though once his charm has won through, he loses interest. This should always be borne in mind; tantrums, tears and jealous outbursts only make him feel claustrophobic and then all will be lost. Finances may also be a bone of contention, since his man cannot withstand pressure from any direction. Any pursuer of Gemini must be prepared to shoulder financial responsibility.

Most Geminians mature very late, if at all. Life is guaranteed to be tremendous fun, but any attempt to organize him will be disastrous. Simply accept him as he is, or forget about him.

HOW TO CATCH AND KEEP YOUR GEMINI WOMAN

Any possessive, jealous or domineering male should dismiss this woman from his life, for otherwise he can only be in for heartache and aggravation. Unless he is equally mentally devious, it can be extremely difficult to put one over this lady, as it were. Her active mind rules her completely and at times she will deliberately make a relationship complicated, in order to exercise her mental faculties in solving a problem. Once she has fully understood her man, she immediately loses interest. Boredom is the greatest threat to her relationships. She is a flirt, but fits of jealousy only encourage her to become more outrageous. When the man concerned really feels he can take no more, he is advised to give her a taste of her own medicine: he should look around for the most attractive female and advance. Any designing male would be most unwise to allow himself to be won over one hundred per cent by the Geminian woman. He should always keep something back and try to remain an enigma for as long as possible. This lady cannot resist a challenge, but when that has been won, she is off.

Once a Geminian's heart has been captured, however, she will be a devoted lover, though she must always be allowed a certain amount of freedom. She won't wander far if she feels free to be herself. But if she believes her individuality is threatened, she will rebel and feel justified in seeking a more easygoing mate. Declarations of love come very quickly to this female, but by the following week she may have changed her mind. If one finds an uncertain and eventful life stimulating, then this is the ideal woman to provide it.

HIS IDEAL PARTNER

The Gemini man is attracted to the naturally sophisticated and chic female, just as a moth is to a candle. He appraises and correctly assesses the opposite sex very quickly. Glamour to him means more than a set of false eyelashes and fingernails to match.

His ideal partner will need to adapt to his changes of mood and be more practical than he is. Someone has got to keep an eye on the more mundane things of life, such as paying bills and doing weekend shopping – things which tend to make him yawn. He needs an exciting, mentally stimulating mate; he won't shy away like a frightened deer if she has a good brain and he won't even mind if she finishes a crossword before he does. His ego is not that sensitive. He thrives on mental challenge. Whatever else his lady is, she must never be an intellectual doormat.

Another essential is that she is not over-sensitive to his flirtations. True, he may be surrounded by women so that all she can see is the top of his head above the crowd, but when the party is over she will be the one he takes home. Regrettably for his admirers, though, he does seem to attract the opposite sex rather effortlessly. Women are part of his scene. Take them away from him and you have Mona Lisa without her smile. But his ideal mate will ignore the rumours or suspicions: it's a rare Gemini man who betrays any trust given to him.

In a general sense, those born under Libra or Aquarius have the best chance of hooking this man. Attitudes to life are very similar. These Sun signs are not tied to their home and willingly change their environment at a moment's notice. Certain characteristics frowned upon by other more practical characters are admired by Mr Gemini. He'll grin from ear to ear when he finds out that his latest love travels light and that her best friend is her toothbrush. Although he needs a certain amount of guidance, this must be given without nagging. While home ties can be nurtured within him, he will be off at a startling pace if his mate becomes overbearing. He needs room to breathe, otherwise a hopeful mate may just as well try to catch the wind.

Affections are clearly ruled by the mind and he is capable of calculated action. He can be quite an opportunist, for example if he thinks that by forming a relationship he will further his ambitions. Bosses' daughters with a Gemini in tow had better make sure they are not being used.

All of this isn't to say he doesn't like the idea of marriage. Far from it. But he does need to be perfectly in tune with his prospective spouse, both mentally and sexually. He may run across the sexiest lady on two legs, but however glamorous she is, if her mental cupboard is bare, then she doesn't stand a chance.

HER IDEAL PARTNER

This lady can usually take her pick of the multitude, but it is to be hoped that in the front line there will be some Librans or Aquarians. Other Sun signs are generally speaking short-term prospects, whereas Libra and Aquarius, the other Air signs, possess similar attitudes to life, sex and love, though not necessarily in that order.

Like her brother, the Gemini woman is not the most practical of people so needs someone to take care of her – but unobtrusively. It's difficult enough to get her to settle down or to take love seriously. She needs someone to worry about her physical welfare and she needs plenty of fresh air, exercise and the right food. Her health breaks down very quickly under any kind of pressure. Protection of her must be done without her know-ledge, for she becomes easily claustrophobic.

Apart from a protector, she also needs a lover and a playmate. Her ideal partner will recognize that her mind must be kept active and developing, will keep romance alive and kicking and always come up with the unexpected sexually. And when she can't find one man to measure up to all these requirements then she is quite happy to keep half a dozen knocking at her door. Variety is the spice of life. Mind you, she does understand that he is hard to please, and if she cares enough for the man in her life, she may adapt to his limitations fairly easily. But she should never be forced to do so, or she will become resentful and dissatisfied and will be on her way.

If she decides the new man in her life doesn't shape up and has a head full of sawdust, she is likely to use him as a doormat. To sum up, her ideal man should be highly sexed, but also able to provide mental stimulation. There's no point in having a fire in the heart if all you've got upstairs is an empty room.

SEXUALLY (MALE)

This is a mental man who derives more pleasure from the chase than from the actual spoils. Don't make the mistake of thinking he is undersexed. He just needs the right kind of stimulation. He also likes his sex to be unexpected. And the more out-rageous you are, the more delighted he will be. He fully appreciates the funny side of a physical relationship and when it comes to approaching ladies on a sexual level, he knows quite a few tricks and some that haven't been invented yet!

This man loves to tease, but don't worry; he will eventually rescue you. And while you are playing his game no one else is going to walk away with his playmate. It may be difficult for an admirer of his to sort out whether she is the only female in his life. The chances are, she isn't. He prefers to be all things to all women. Because of his basic irresponsibility, the thought of contraception may never enter his head; and if nine months later some playmate presents him with an unexpected gift in the form of a little bundle of humanity, he will be amazed at how such a thing could have occurred and will show no paternal feelings.

GEMINI   May 22 – June 21

Any Gemini admirer is warned to take heed of the Boy Scouts' motto: "be prepared." Try to develop a knack of anticipating any of his moods as they approach. This way when he wants to play a sexual version of the *Jungle Book*, she will already have her gorilla suit laid out. There's something of the sexual fantasizer in him. The thing to remember where this character is concerned is that an active head will lead to an active body.

SEXUALLY (FEMALE)

The Gemini woman's approach to sex is easily discussed: she doesn't. Like her brother she is a teaser, deriving more pleasure from the warm-up than the actual game. When being wooed, she likes to be taken by surprise. A reputedly successful stud trotting out all the old lines will be greeted by a far-away look in her eyes. Her mind is probably on the nice little dress she saw round the corner, or she may be thinking about having the room decorated. If her lover doesn't keep her mind busy she will do it for herself, and this could take her a million miles away from what is supposed to be happening. Ideally she should never know exactly when sex is going to take place. The man who is programmed to have sex on Mondays, Thursdays and Saturdays, after dinner and invariably in the same position, isn't going to be around for very long. Once sex becomes a chore she loses total interest and desire.

If asked, the Gemini woman would find it very difficult to tell you exactly what attracts her sexually to any one man. She may like the fact that she can talk to him or she may be turned on by the way he walks. But no man should ever make the mistake of thinking that just because he can converse with her he can also have his evil way. Also remember that while she may flirt, she isn't necessarily offering an invitation to join her in the boudoir. Sex could be the farthest thing from her mind. Unless she is obviously trying to drag an admirer into her bedroom, it will be wise of him to remember that this lady believes a gentleman takes his time.

HOW TO END THE AFFAIR

Not the most difficult of operations, whether you are handling the male or the female of the species. This type becomes claustrophobic rather quickly, therefore possessive or over-protective behaviour can be guaranteed to drive your Geminian into someone else's arms.

The ideal time for showing your jealousy is at a party when the Geminian is surrounded by panting admirers. Cling to or embarrass this type and he or she will have collected someone else's phone number before you go home. But if you dare to ring soon after this, then act the outraged party. You'll probably be deafened by the sound of the receiver being crashed down on your ear. Honesty is not necessarily the best policy here, for Geminians usually like to do the dropping, and are, indeed, used to doing so. It never occurs to them that someone doesn't want them. Good heavens what an assumption! So if you are too open about wishing to end the relationship, you are quite likely to increase your attraction.

You may need a couple of weeks to get rid of this particular limpet but that is preferable to a couple of months of unwelcome phone calls and pestering. Those two weeks should be spent zealously displaying over-demanding behaviour. If, for good measure, you can throw in an attractive member of the opposite sex, then your manoeuvre cannot possibly fail. But don't dampen your handkerchief or worry once the relationship is over; Gemini will be fixed up elsewhere within an hour. There's always someone ready to take on this type.

ATTRACTING THE SUN SIGNS

GEMINI WOMAN WITH GEMINI MAN

There may only be two physical bodies in this combination but there'll be anything from four to forty personalities to contend with. Nevertheless, it can be a compatible partnership, if somewhat exhausting. Both are able to understand and tolerate mutually changing moods. He will be as impressed with her ability to complete a crossword in five minutes as with her ability to make him feel all male. However, if this relationship is to end in marriage, then someone will have to develop some financial muscle. Otherwise love is definitely going to fly out of the window as soon as the debts start piling up. Of one thing you can be sure, no one will be bored. The combination can work matrimonially, but it is more likely to be suited to a white-hot love affair.

GEMINI WOMAN WITH CANCER MAN

This man needs to feel and express love, and to be with a female who can soothe his insecurity; and it usually isn't the Gemini woman. He will be totally lost attempting to keep up with her mercurial changes of mood and appetite. He'll appreciate her sense of humour, unless it is aimed at him, when he'll be terribly hurt. She may be initially attracted to his nest-building instincts, but when he wants to spend too much time in it, she will quickly bore. In turn he will find her independence not only a turn-off but extremely worrying. A difficult relationship.

GEMINI WOMAN WITH LEO MAN

She can shatter his dreams with a perfectly timed comment, yet somehow manage to make him not only accept this but laugh about it. On a social level, life will be glamorous and interesting, which will help to cement their relationship, initially anyway. He will be attracted to her because she is brilliant and capable. She will be attracted by his regal bearing and the way he stands out in a crowd. After a while, however, she will be exhausted and bored by his constant need for flattery and his demands for affection and shows of loyalty. And when he gets to know her well, he will realize that she isn't one hundred per cent glamour but a tomboy, housewife, shrew, critic and friend all rolled into one. It's rather doubtful that he can cope, I'm afraid. Affairwise or for friendship, can be a good combination.

GEMINI WOMAN WITH VIRGO MAN

A rather unpredictable relationship, for Mercury rules both

signs. On the negative side, this makes her logical and calculating while it enhances his flair for nagging. He may approve of her clothes and her friends, but will question new projects in which he becomes involved. He is likely to ask her to make herself look more natural, forget about so much make-up. Any kind of theatricality unnerves him. Such criticism won't go down well with her. Nevertheless, these are both intellectual signs and this couple can spend hours dissecting themselves and other people. Romance has been known to work here, but one would expect to find business partners and friends under this combination.

GEMINI WOMAN WITH LIBRA MAN

One of those partnerships blessed by astrology. He loves to romance and court her; this excites her and she lets him know it. He'll love her combination of intelligence and glamour and will even remain resilient and adaptable to her many changing moods. She'll love his interest in everything female and will be able to discuss everything with him, including fashion. Neither have a jealous bone in their body and they will be amused by each other's mild flirtations, understanding only too well that they mean nothing. An excellent relationship, be it for love, marriage, friendship or business.

GEMINI WOMAN WITH SCORPIO MAN

Initially she may enjoy his passionate sexual demands, but his jealousy and possessive nature leave her rather tight-lipped. He will regard her as something of a puzzle he would like to put together, according to *his* plan, though it's unlikely that he'll ever be able to do so. When he fails, his sarcasm will surface, as will his sharp tongue; and that's when she'll begin to hurt. If she is considering a liaison with a Scorpio then the best way to attract him is to make him believe that she can shore up his economic position. This is hardly a satisfactory basis for any relationship. On the whole, these two are likely to tear each other to pieces and both will finish up nervous wrecks. An unwise relationship.

GEMINI WOMAN WITH SAGITTARIUS MAN

These two are bound to fight, but when they do it's because making up is so much fun. Her wise-cracking sense of humour will never cease to delight him; and he will be impressed by her accomplishments at work. He will love her spontaneity and madcap ideas. These all help to enhance his lifestyle of freedom. Sexually they may also have fun. But on the whole it's a rather superficial relationship. Furthermore, both parties tend to be involved with multiple relationships, so it can only be a matter of time before one or the other meets someone else. A fun relationship, but hardly one to be taken seriously.

GEMINI WOMAN WITH CAPRICORN MAN

The typical Gemini lady likes her night life, her career and possibly wading in the park fountain when the mood takes her; this will make a Capricornian man lose his wits. The only way she will appeal to him is by offering the prospect of tranquillity. She may be tempted to give this a try, for he is the most caring man of all – supportive, gentle and reliable. If she really does mean business and is sufficiently attracted to his rather stiff exterior, then she'll need to submerge her whimsical ways. Putting the boot on the other foot, he will need to loosen up quite considerably and realize how important she intends to be in his life. But is it fair to ask people to change so drastically? I doubt it. Therefore this isn't an ideal match.

GEMINI WOMAN WITH AQUARIUS MAN

Another astrological textbook goodie, if both are typical. He dislikes clinging females but will appreciate this lady's changing moods and probing mind. He will be greatly attracted to her independence and will desperately want her to be as successful professionally as he is, provided that's what she too wants. For it is what she wants that is important to him. He will also respect her need for privacy. If she can respect his occasional need to be alone, then all will go well. It's her intelligent, quick mind which will really hold him, her ability to become interested in all of his hobbies and causes. His effortless way of adapting to her moods will be the big attraction for her. An excellent union.

GEMINI WOMAN WITH PISCES MAN

Pisces man is always intuitive, mysterious – adaptable, impressionable and romantic. But he may smoke, drink or cling too much for her to tolerate. In one of her many moods, she may send him some poetry she has written. He will be greatly impressed, not realizing the mood may not descend again for another year. If all is to go well in this relationship, she will need to be dramatically desirable and prepared to devote her time and attention to his many and varied whims. Rather a lot to ask from a Gemini lady, I'm afraid. He on the other hand should not take anything she does or says too seriously, for she is changeable and likely to contradict herself the following day. A great friendship may develop between these two, but a marriage could be heavy-going.

GEMINI WOMAN WITH ARIES MAN

Typical Aries man is short on patience, caution and subtlety – a bit too rough at the edges for her refined and intellectual approach to life. But platonic companionship could certainly be fun. She will need to be careful before she uses her razor-sharp wit on anything he takes seriously – he can counteract quite savagely, and is even capable of turning her friends against her. However, he can be a loyal protector and a true-blue friend in need. You are super lucky if he is the boss or a pal; but husband – that's something else.

GEMINI WOMAN WITH TAURUS MAN

Her parents will probably be more pleased about this match than she will. They will believe that their scatty daughter desperately needs this solid and reliable individual. She is able to charm him with words and confuse him too. But she will drive him to distraction with what he sees as her flightiness. He is definitely a plodder, but dependable and courtly towards her. She had better be prepared for the fact that his love-making is just as proper as he is. If determined to attract him, she will need to be more serious, take up an interest in food and drink and prove her loyalty. He will need to open his mind to the many interests she indulges herself in and not take her flirting too seriously. All a bit much, wouldn't you say?

HOW WELL DO YOU KNOW YOUR GEMINI WOMAN?

Answer honestly the questions below, scoring 3 for every Yes, 2 for Sometimes and 1 for No, then add up your total.

1. Does she enjoy letter-writing?
2. Is she averse to quick sex?
3. Is she moody?
4. Does she enjoy a good gossip?
5. Does she wave her arms and hands around when she talks?
6. Can you influence her sexually through the mind?
7. Did you have to beat off a bevy of admirers before you began your relationship?
8. Was she more considerate when you were chasing her than she is now?
9. Is she naturally a late riser?
10. Does she like to be romanced?
11. Does she like to talk about herself?
12. Is it difficult for her to relax?
13. Is she a great reader?
14. Does she dress to please herself rather than the opposite sex?
15. Does she find domesticity boring?
16. More often than not, does she ask you what you think rather than what you feel?
17. Does she contradict herself in an argument?
18. Would you be unhappy about leaving her with your best friend for the evening?
19. Does she like to travel?
20. Has she ever taken a pill in order to help her to sleep?

(Answers)

1–30

Either you've an awful lot to learn about your Gemini woman or she is not typical of her sign. If the latter applies, there's probably a considerable amount of earth lurking on her birth chart, and it may be a good idea for you to read the chapters devoted to Taurus, Capricorn or Virgo. If this is a new relationship, perhaps there's hope for you, but you'll need to brush up that grey matter if you are to make any impression on her.

31–50

This lady of yours doesn't appear to have many of the Hyde qualities in her personality, luckily for you. Also you seem to know her fairly well, well enough anyway to carry on a successful relationship. Don't worry that you didn't score more; this is the way she likes you to be – uncertain. Delve any deeper and you could be in trouble.

51–60

It's unlikely that your Gemini mate will be happy with this score, for you know her too well and no Geminian likes to be read like the daily newspaper. In future you'd be wise to keep your knowledge to yourself, for you are in danger of being a little bit too complacent or, perhaps worse, taking her for granted.

HOW WELL DO YOU KNOW YOUR GEMINI MAN?

Answer honestly the questions below, scoring 3 for every Yes, 2 for Sometimes and 1 for No, then add up your total.

1. Was he a real Casanova before you met him?
2. Did he have a penchant for married ladies?
3. Is he boastful of his sexual conquests?
4. Does he know a little about most subjects?
5. Does he hate it when you are jealous?
6. Is he hopeless with money?
7. Is he critical?
8. Would he rather have stimulating conversation than inferior sex?
9. Is he many-sided?
10. Is he a flirt?
11. Is his professional life somewhat chequered?
12. Does he enjoy talking about himself?
13. Does he have a bad memory?
14. Is he a playful lover?

15. Does he think of himself as a woman's man?
16. Does he move quickly?
17. Does he find it hard to turn off his head at night?
18. Does he like to find new forms of entertainment?
19. Does he need a lot of rest?
20. Does he like change?

(Answers)

1–30

Let's hope you haven't been with this man very long, for you don't seem to know him at all. Either that or he is not typical of his sign. It's possible that there's a strong earth element on his birth chart. If you are desperate for understanding, I suggest you read under Virgo, Taurus or Capricorn to see if you can find your elusive Geminian there.

31–50

Not only is this the ideal score, it is quite likely that you could turn out to be the ideal mate for your Geminian man, so long as you don't probe any deeper. You have enough understanding of him to stand you in good stead over the years.

51–60

This high score is what one would expect of someone involved with a Geminian man with a considerable chunk of Mr Hyde in him. He probably doesn't stop talking about himself, so how could you fail to understand him? But will such knowledge lead to boredom and complacency? Very likely; if you want this relationship to work, some changes will have to be made.

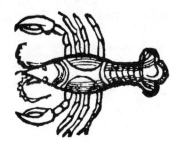

Cancer (the Crab)
Sign of the Parent and the Patriot

June 22 – July 22

The first Water sign: Shrewd, intuitive, receptive, retentive, good memory, impressionable, apt to let emotions colour thoughts
Ruler: The Moon
Colour: Purple
Career: Archaeologist, gardener, caterer, brewer, publican, any career connected with the sea
Famous Cancerians: Louis Armstrong, Arthur Ashe, Yul Brynner, John Glenn, Ernest Hemingway, Lena Horne, Helen Keller, George Orwell, Rembrandt, Ginger Rogers, Ringo Starr

---

CANCER MAN

The Cancerian male is highly sensitive and easily hurt but outwardly gives the impression of impenetrable self-assurance and toughness. He is protective and loyal to his family, possessing an instinctive clannishness and patriotism. He is very attached to his home and needs security and a womb-like shelter to withdraw into while restoring self-confidence. He is sympathetic, sentimental, moody and reserved.

Many born under this sign are great collectors. Sometimes at a serious or professional level, at other times because of an abhorrence of throwing anything away.

If you've ever stood at the sea's edge and watched the tides, you will have noticed the way they bounce in over the rocks and swirl up the beach. Then there's the ebb, drifting out and seemingly hanging on to every stone, never wanting to let go. Now if you observe the Moon, you'll see how it waxes and wanes. One evening it is a beautiful orb hanging there, but over the days it slowly changes until it is a thin curve of silver light in the night sky. Now look at your Cancer man. In him you will find the lunar influences. His moods are in tune with the Moon's changing face, just like the ocean's tides. And yet this man never really changes. Underneath the moods, he remains the same character. Even his inconsistency is constant.

But even the strongest Cancerian man is not as strong as the members of other Sun signs. For all Crabs possess an extremely soft centre; and what has a soft centre usually has a hard shell. The human Crab is no exception. His strongest characteristic is tenacity. Remember how the crab at the seaside hung on to your big toe and just would not be shaken off? Once the Cancerian has something, be it a person or object, he clings to it. The Crab would rather lose a claw than let go. This attitude applies to both his professional and his personal life. The Cancerian male is stimulated by his emotions, which go far deeper than most. He feels anger, love or hate just as keenly and passionately. His imagination is equally well developed. Because of this he makes a sensitive lover and a sympathetic friend. Success to him is meaningless without someone to share it with. Therefore, he makes an excellent family man and husband. He finds frivolous people an absolute mystery. He takes his love life seriously and cannot understand those who don't. Self-pity is another characteristic associated with this sign. Add to this a strong imagination, and this man can make a mountain out of any simple molehill. When he is depressed and retreats, whether through despair or uncertainty, he is very hard to contact. No point attempting to phone him; don't expect him to answer your letters, or your knocking at the door. As far as the outside world is concerned, he has gone away.

Resilience is the last characteristic owned by most Cancerians. When they make mistakes, they tend to brood. They don't find it easy to shrug off disappointment and it's a long time before they try again. They absorb ideas and sense impressions, and after digesting them convert them to new use.

They are resourceful and active in this way, even though they may not be physically active.

The Cancerian usually has an easy-going disposition and is faithful in love, a combination which makes for happiness in marriage. He is very sensitive, however, and is deeply hurt by unkind criticism. He can feel very sorry for himself, especially when he doesn't get his own way. If this happens often, he may take a perverse pleasure in a martyr complex. He is very emotional and responds to love, approval and sympathy. He likes the adulation of a crowd and to feel popular. For this reason, he loves to act, even if only as an amateur. He enjoys publicity, and the limelight, tries to capture it in any way he can.

His anger is aroused most when he feels a threat to his self-preservation. He is a resolute and defensive opponent who wins by dint of persistent attrition and gradual encroachment, rather than open declaration of all-out war. Quite obviously, then, a complex man is the Cancerian. It is of the utmost importance that, when it comes to settling down, he finds the correct mate.

THE INDIVIDUAL (FEMALE)

The pyschic Moon-child can charm a stone Buddha. She can be gregarious, imaginative and talkative, at which time people gravitate to her, especially with projects that need publicizing or problems best solved by her subtle, emotional approach. Despite a belief to the contrary, she need not be alone unless she wants to be. This frequently occurs when those oh-so-sensitive feelings have been hurt.

It's very hard for the Cancerian lady to separate what she feels from what she thinks; she is a sponge for the emotional ups and downs of other people. Like the male Crab, when the romantic and practical within her are at odds, she takes refuge under a self-protective shell. But if you are looking for a woman who can take life by the scruff of the neck and give it a good shake, or to stand behind you like a prop and shove you in the right direction where your career is concerned, you needn't start wiping your feet on this girl's doormat, it's just not her scene. Like her male counterpart, she isn't as strong as other Sun signs, but where her strength is, it's paramount. In terms of the ability to love and cherish, she is a winner. Should her man decide to go off chasing moonbeams and fairytale dreams, he can be sure that when he returns empty-handed she will be waiting for him, his slippers warming by the fire and his favourite meal ready to be served. Cancer is the maternal sign.

Unfortunately the Cancerian woman isn't always able to find her true soulmate. But when she doesn't, it affects her far more deeply than those born under the more resilient signs. She can then become a burden on friends and family alike, leaning heavily on their time and sympathies. Her man won't have to worry about her taking off with his cheque book. She'll only spend, spend, spend if she is seeking an embrocation for strained emotions. Normally her balance of payments is in a far superior position to most governments.

The Crab draws her confidence from her man, so he will need plenty to spare. She is very easy to undermine, but very difficult to build up again. It won't hurt to tell her a hundred times a day that she is young, lovely and desirable.

Like her brother Cancerian, she will have a store of treasures that only she can appreciate. To anyone else a bus ticket is, well, just a bus ticket; not to her. It can recall whatever happened on that particular trip – the first meeting with her man, or her decision to stop smoking, or it may simply be a reminder of when the car broke down and she had to seek out other means of transport.

Her greatest asset is her devotion, her deep sincerity and loving tenacity through thick and thin. She will sacrifice anything for the one she loves. She can be a rock for him to cling to in the crashing waters of despair, or the delicate moonbeam that softens his heart and makes him giggle. For someone looking for a superb mistress in the form of a wife, or vice versa, this is the right lady.

THE HYDE SIDE

These types of Cancerians are discontented, lackadaisical and idle. They have no desire to bestir themselves or make the effort necessary for accomplishment, taking the line of least resistance whenever possible. However, they cling tenaciously to what they already have, as do their stronger brothers. Other faults, and there are many, include being very touchy, moody, inclined to self-pity, timid, untidy, unstable, easily flattered, too clannish. They harbour slights, and invariably suffer from an inferiority complex, as perhaps they should.

They try constantly to attract attention and go to extremes in order to do so. Being also notorious hypochondriacs, they may use ill health in order to capture the limelight. I met a weak Cancerian once who could make himself physically sick, anywhere, anytime, whenever he felt he was being ignored. Very nauseating!

Fierce pride and independence alternate with helplessness and hopelessness. For long periods of time they deliberately hide while indulging in bouts of self-pity, morbid thoughts and depressions – anything to draw attention to themselves. Obviously, then, these types are totally at the mercy of their moods. They fairly throw themselves into sensationalism, sentimentality and all forms of exaggerated emotion. When sad, although there may be no tears, a more forlorn and self-pitying character will be difficult to find. And when these types cry, umbrellas are the order of the day. It's also fairly common to discover in the male of this species a gigantic Oedipus complex.

When they are single, these Cancerians flit from one partner to another, draining them and leaving them feeling like half-chewed sponges. Emotional vampire, I suppose, is a fitting description. It takes a lot of loving to keep these types happy. And even then it's never enough. Members of the opposite sex involved with these types will not find it easy to decide which of their moods are genuine and which are feigned; but then they really don't know themselves. One of the strange things about these types of Cancerians is that while they take, take, take and go on taking, they will tell you how sympathetic and sensitive they are, but continue to give nothing back whatsoever.

Fortunately, most Cancerians are a mixture of the two types. If they lean too far in the negative direction, they could be nothing short of monstrous.

HOW TO CATCH AND KEEP YOUR CANCER MAN

There are certain signs which the rest of us either love or hate, and this is one of them. This is Mr Homebody. Scatty or career-minded females will be well advised to leave him alone, for he will only cause a tremendous amount of frustration in their lives. This character would be attracted to the gentle and feminine kind of woman. She should not, however, appear to be too organized, for he loves to protect and cherish his loved ones and should be given the opportunity to do so. When confronted with the type of woman who has her life laid out like a well oiled machine, he becomes uncertain of himself and will eventually be repelled by her. He is interested in everything connected with the home, the garden, children and food. He is generally only attracted to the kind of woman whom he believes can supply all of these.

The Cancerian male's faults can appear to others most amusing at times, though it would be extremely unadvisable to laugh at him, for he may sink into one of his infuriating self-pitying moods. Many hypochondriacs are born under this sign, so any woman prepared to take him on will need to exercise the patience of a saint at times. In return for such devotion he can offer a strong shoulder to cry on, financial security and he is extremely sensitive to love. One of the things that incenses the more dynamic characters is the Cancerian's slowness. He works and moves at a leisurely pace; nobody can hurry a Crab if he does not wish to be hurried. Any aspiring mate of his would be wise to accept this trait. Impatient females who cannot bring themselves to live with it will save themselves a great deal of frustration and unhappiness if they recognize that fact. A gentle and homely image is the one to be adopted in this particular instance.

HOW TO CATCH AND KEEP YOUR CANCER WOMAN

The female Cancerian's attitude to men largely depends on her age. When very young, she is sensitive, vulnerable and ready to love at the drop of a hat. As she grows older, however, she learns to protect herself and throw up an almost impenetrable barrier between her sensitivity and any designing male. With the Cancerian who falls into the first category, the man concerned should remember that he is in a position to inflict great pain on her and he should only commit himself if his feelings are serious. With the latter variety, life is going to be difficult, for in order to melt the hard shell around this woman's heart one must win her trust and this operation can take a considerable amount of time.

Impatient and impulsive types should beware of the Cancerian female for she will only regard them with disdain and adopt a patronizing attitude towards them. Through tenderness and love he may eventually triumph, though this sign does have certain faults that can be rather irritating to others. The female Crab's vivid imagination needs to be channelled out or she may become a hypochondriac and tend to wallow in self-pitying moods. The only thing to do when she allows herself to be bogged down in one of her martyr complexes is to be sympathetic at all times. A pillar of strength, then, is the image to go for.

HIS IDEAL PARTNER

This man's ideal mate will want a partnership for life, since that is how long he expects the nuptials to last. Once she wears his wedding ring, it will be impossible to shake him off. The equally emotional signs of Scorpio or Pisces are best fitted to understand our complex friend.

He is not attracted to women who emit organizing vibrations. He enjoys protecting and cherishing and must be given the opportunity to do so. When he runs into a highly independent female, he will become uncertain of himself and eventually she will repel him. But if he is convinced she is his woman, then catching him is fairly easy, and his ideal woman needs to be someone who can provide him with children, good food and a comfortable home. In return he will take care of the materialistic side of life and never take her for granted. Any liberated woman who wishes to hang on to her freedom, sanity and equality should stop reading right now and give this man a miss.

However, this man is prepared to devote himself entirely to the right lady. He will work his fingers to the bone and make her life as happy as possible. She must be able to contend with his moods. She will have to be able to smile every time he pours cold water over her ego, and to keep smiling when he brings out the family photograph album. His family tree is very important to him, and the more interest she shows in that, the more interest he will show in her. Remember that when this man has you marked down as his woman, he will stop at nothing to offer his proposal. He works overtime to woo his chosen mate like she has never been wooed before. And if she accepts his proposal she must be prepared for a life that is ruled by the lunar changes. It's quite likely then that her best friend will be an almanack.

HER IDEAL PARTNER

This "moonlight maiden" has the best chance of happiness with those born under the signs of Scorpio and Pisces, who are equally emotional and have a good understanding of her hypersensitivity. Scorpio is just as possessive and Pisces shares the same need for affection and ego-boosting. They also tend to be more patient with the Crab than, for example, the Geminian or Sagittarian, who cannot be bothered with sentimentality or gush.

The Cancerian woman needs someone who is looking for a home and, later on, children. She will be attracted to a man who can handle financial affairs, doesn't have a permanent hole in his pocket and is ready to settle down.

The Crab is generally considered one of the shrewd members of the Zodiac. When it comes to business, those born under this sign cling to money as to everything else. Her mate must be able to handle this side of life in a similar manner, otherwise he will be up against a barrage of criticism and nagging. Apart from this, she needs a sympathetic and sensitive man, one with imagination to match her own, so that both can whirl away on flights of fantasy and romanticism. Born liars or those who are unable to face up to the bare facts of life will send shivers of horror down her spine.

To be honest, this isn't the easiest of women to live with, despite the face that she craves the home atmosphere; taking her on for a lifetime needs careful thought. Any man who rushes on a trip down the aisle without first weighing up the pros and cons will either destroy her or be destroyed by her. Her retentive mind can rake up troubles which he thought were long forgotten. Even years later she may gather them up by the handful and deposit them squarely in his face. There's no point in disputing the facts. Her elephantine memory will have everything in its right place.

So members of the opposite sex are warned to tread very cautiously. The Cancerian will either make you exquisitely happy or bloody miserable.

SEXUALLY (MALE)

The Cancerian man is not as promiscuous as the more gregarious signs. But this doesn't mean that he is sexless. He could be of indeterminate sex but never sexless. Mind you, he is often timid in his approach to women. Rebuff and defeat are the greatest deterrents to his advances, and he is often beaten before he begins. Many a female has found herself unwittingly placed on a pedestal before she has even spoken to him. And when she doesn't measure up to his idea of what he thought she was, he is totally disillusioned.

Don't ever forget that he is a sentimentalist and a romantic. He is tender, kind and considerate as a lover. It is no good any female attempting to drag him off to bed, he will probably run and hide underneath it. A crowded vivid imagination can aid him greatly in his sexual life. But he is quite content to live out his fantasies without letting you in on the subject at all. And when you do find out what is going on under that shell of his, you could be quite shocked. But if you are past that stage in your growth, encourage him to tell you, although he is unlikely to reveal all until he knows you well. The Cancerian man remains a gentleman just as long as she remains a lady. But when the barriers are down, it's a different set of rules.

In many respects this individual is infuriatingly old-fashioned. He is still inclined to the belief that there are only two types of women: those you marry and those you don't. No matter how experienced a lover may be, she should show interest in everything he attempts to teach her and not be offended if he also tells her what her reactions are supposed to be. What she must never do is tell him she has tried it all before.

He likes to believe he is opening up a wide and wonderful new world to her; if he thinks for a moment that he isn't educating her, he will retreat into his shell and his fantasies.

SEXUALLY (FEMALE)

The Cancerian female finds it extremely difficult to separate love from sex. She does at least have to pretend to be in love before closing the bedroom door behind her. Any man in her life will need to understand this. But despite her big watery eyes, which appear to be full of love, as soon as his side of the bed has gone cold, so will her pretence. There's no point in trying to make her see the bare facts, as it were; they'll be totally unacceptable. This is the way she is made; no point in attempting to change her. If she wants to live her life swathed in cotton wool, then I suppose it's one way of cushioning her vulnerability. Like her male counterpart, she is not noted for any outrageous sexual deviations. Attempting to pressure her sexually at the drive-in will only leave her attacker watching the movie alone. She prefers somewhere safe, and she doesn't feel secure, at least on the first few encounters, until she is in her own bed.

This female has an extremely vivid imagination, which also means that she can be quite adaptable. If handled correctly over a period of time, she can be made to accept most things, provided she believes that love is the motivation. For the Cancerian lady, kissing constantly is half the fun. Love is all to this woman and constant reassurance in this direction when you tangle up in the blankets will make all the difference. Cuddle and caress her and make her feel totally secure within your big strong arms and you'll have a happy Cancerian lady.

HOW TO END THE AFFAIR

Those who wish to dump a Cancerian have something of an almighty task on their hands. It's difficult at the best of times. Whether you are attempting to lose a male or female of this species, you really have your work cut out. Prising loose from these claws is no easy matter. If the situation is handled wrongly, you could be in for months of aggravation.

The safest way to dispose of these individuals is to disillusion them, but totally. By now you should know what your Cancerian's image is of you. If you've projected the homely comfortable type, then proceed immediately to be quite the opposite. Be outrageous. With any luck, it won't take long before you are toppled from your pedestal; although the Cancerian male will be too gentlemanly to end the relationship himself, he will certainly be relieved if you do it for him. Of course it's possible that your Crab will temporarily enjoy the change in your character; but despair not, it won't last.

For a woman attempting to get rid of the male Crab, I suggest you take over the double role, especially in bed. A few minor criticisms about his sexual technique won't do any harm either. He's a bit rickety in this direction anyway, so a slight push may work. The male attempting to rid himself of the female Crab should, I suggest, become totally insensitive to her needs and desires. Criticize her cooking and perhaps her love-making, shout at her a few times. She may dig in her toes and fight back for a while, but not for long.

HOW TO ATTRACT THE SUN SIGNS

CANCER WOMAN WITH CANCER MAN

Both partners here can make each other's romantic and sexual dreams come true. Romeo and Juliet, eat your heart out. They'll also share the deepest understanding, even when at the opposite ends of a turbulent argument – and there are bound to be quite a few. The biggest problem in this union is the double dose of sensitivity. The slightest criticism, a wrong word or look will be enough to send them crying and screaming into a full-blown drama. If looking for a turbulent life, filled with constant trauma, then maybe they'll settle for each other – though even those born under this sign do on occasions like a bit of peace. In general, this relationship works best confined to friendship, business or maybe a sexual affair.

CANCER WOMAN WITH LEO MAN

The Leonine man likes to be where the spotlight burns brightest, so the Cancerian woman in this union will need to stifle her own love of the limelight and be prepared to join the sycophants that he surrounds himself with. But how long before she finds the whole procedure sickening? Cancerian feelings run deep – far more deeply than he can ever understand. Remember that this is a fire-and-water relationship. If determined to hang on to him, she'll need to revamp her wardrobe and make it more dramatic in order to keep him intrigued and amused. If he wishes to stay in her life for longer than a few weeks, he will quickly have to develop some domestic instincts and perhaps a little more sincerity. An unwise relationship.

CANCER WOMAN WITH VIRGO MAN

Although the Cancerian lady could hardly be described as sloppy or dirty, neither is she one hundred per cent sterile; and if involved with this fussy character, she will need to make sure that not only is she super clean, but also her home. When he comes to visit, he will expect crisp ironed sheets, fluffy towels and a tangy, clean odour of eucalyptus or some other natural herb. But be warned, he is unlikely to satisfy fully her amorous nature, and his direct approach on occasion could prove to be something of a turn-off. To attract her, he will have to try to relax more, be more spontaneous and homely. Yes, I know your flat is clean and tidy, but does it look as if you actually live there? It's hearts and flowers all the way with this lady, and the Virgo man may not be able to cope with this for more than a few days. A good business relationship, but hardly a love-match likened to Antony and Cleopatra.

CANCER WOMAN WITH LIBRA MAN

The way she looks and acts will appeal to his sense of correctness. He will have confidence in her always being properly outfitted, whether on the tennis court, at the theatre or when his boss invites them to dinner. But one wrong word can send both of them into a sullen silence that will seem to last for ever. Social life is so important to him that she may eventually decide he is superficial, but if he wishes to hang on to this lady – and it's going to be difficult – he'll need to show her that he can enjoy quiet evenings at home without getting restless; and above all else he must praise her cooking, even if it's not up to the standard he is used to. He plays at romance whilst she is sincere, so the poor old Crab could be in for something of a battering in this relationship. Not a wise union.

CANCER WOMAN WITH SCORPIO MAN

A successful astrological combination, however you look at it: friendship, sex, love or marriage. This man is able and willing to love as deeply as she needs. And it won't be long before she becomes his number-one fan. He's a walking sex manual and she's only too ready to learn; and the more enthusiasm she shows, the more enchanted he will be. It's important that she bear in mind, though, that this man demands one hundred per cent loyalty; nothing short of this will do. The Cancerian woman will be quite happy to oblige, if she really cares about him. He doesn't need telling how to attract or keep her. He instinctively knows the things to do and say to please and turn her on. A very auspicious relationship.

CANCER WOMAN WITH SAGITTARIUS MAN

Another of those fire-and-water relationships, and everyone knows that when you mix these two elements you get a hell of a lot of steam; as a result of their constant quarrelling, they are both likely to finish up covered in condensation and a lot of regret. For this partnership to stand a chance, the Cancerian woman would have to give him all the emotional, intellectual and physical elbow-room he needs. There's no point in her expecting him to be faithful; he simply can't be. And if she starts making demands in this direction, then she is heading for trouble. Can she take it? Does she want to? She should think about it carefully. She is liable to end up believing him to be an unscrupulous cad, and this will only serve to make him more outrageous and quite convinced that she's a wet blanket. A relationship fit only for the bravest.

CANCER WOMAN WITH CAPRICORN MAN

Although these two are opposites, they have a lot in common and such a match could work. He has the persistence that makes her dreamy fantasies come true. Conventional women attract him – therefore she can put away her trendy outfits in favour of simple but expensive little numbers. He likes the good but unflashy things of life. Wine and caviare on the bedside table, if you can afford it, will be greatly appreciated. He likes a lot of attention too, so she needn't feel that he will think her pushy if she telephones him often. We are dealing with two financial wizards here, so there'll be no trouble in that direction. Their biggest hang-up will be of the emotional variety. Mr Capricorn keeps his deep feelings to himself. He is a cool and reserved individual. She, on the other hand, wears her heart on her sleeve and needs loud protestations of love. If they can overcome this emotional incompatibility, then the relationship has some hope.

CANCER WOMAN WITH AQUARIUS MAN

Love to the Aquarian man is only a diversion; it is certainly not one of life's biggest delights, as it is to her. But he is basically faithful. However, his various involvements will seem to drag him away from her almost constantly. She will need to control her possessiveness and her anxiety about losing him. Once she gives in to these, this will be an interesting though short-lived match. These two are so diametrically opposed, it is difficult to imagine that they will be able to compromise. He must try hard to interest her in his many outside pursuits; she must be prepared to get enthusiastic about the dying of the Blue Whale or any other cause he happens to feel like chasing. He will have to make allowances for her emotional needs, while she should attempt to be less demanding. It's an awful lot to ask, isn't it?

CANCER WOMAN WITH PISCES MAN

She will quickly discover that on the sexual front this man can be as correct as a Capricornian, as delicate as a Libran, as persistent as a Taurean, as adventurous as a Sagittarian or as casual as an Arietian – it varies with his many, many moods. And she'll be able to appreciate them, being a moody person herself. She will be able to cry with him at sentimental movies, laugh with him at the absurdity of sex and try to make yearly pilgrimages to the hotel where they spent their first weekend together. She is probably the best lady under the Zodiac for him, and if they are both typical of their signs, they should have no difficulty in getting on with each other. Attraction should be almost instantaneous. An excellent union.

CANCER WOMAN WITH ARIES MAN

Being intuitive and perceptive, the Cancerian woman will see all his faults the first time she meets this character, and with any luck will spend the rest of their relationship discovering his virtues. He is the dominant one, but she'll happily follow his lead, although she'll be miserable at times over slights that are more in her emotional imagination than of his doing. Eventually, though, his bursts of anger (he does throw tantrums) may prove too much for her Cancerian calm to withstand. She may come to the conclusion that he is really not worth all the grief she has to put up with – he's just too childish for her. It won't be long before he decides that she is too complacent and boring. Water-and-fire relationships like these always have the toughest time.

CANCER WOMAN WITH TAURUS MAN

He will find it easy to respect her totally and he will be charmed by her ability to whip up a magnificent dinner for six on a limited budget. Both are domesticated creatures, relishing the joys of their own hearth and home, preferably with an enormous dog snoozing before the fire and acres of plants at the windows. This couple will find it quite delicious to wallow in the mud resulting from this water (Cancer) and earth (Taurus) relationship.

CANCER WOMAN WITH GEMINI MAN

Life is an ever-changing MGM musical to the Geminian man. He cannot be trained into being a domesticated animal; he cannnot understand the depth of the Cancerian's moods or the sensitivity of her soul. She had better bear in mind, if she wants to attract him, that he dedicates himself to women who provide more puzzlement than protection. She will need to be more of an intriguing moonchild and less of a mother figure to win his interest. As for him, well, he's an adaptable kind of individual and he'll happily accommodate himself to her – for a while. But in general this is not a partnership made in heaven.

HOW WELL DO YOU KNOW YOUR CANCER WOMAN?

Answer honestly the questions below, scoring 3 for every Yes, 2 for Sometimes and 1 for No, then add up your total.

1. Does she have a sweet tooth?
2. Does she have a feeling for the past?
3. Does she need to save some money each week, no matter how small the amount?
4. Is it difficult for her to separate love from sex?
5. Does she weep at the movies?
6. Does she develop a headache when she senses your motives are pure lust?
7. Is she a hypochondriac?
8. Does she have a retentive memory?
9. Does she like to eat immediately after sex?
10. Would you leave town if you forgot a special anniversary?
11. Does she always get sentimental when she sees a young child or baby?
12. Is she attracted to the sea?
13. Is she emotionally very dependent on you?
14. Would she have a nervous breakdown if you lost your job?
15. Does she constantly diet?
16. When you flirt does she get very upset?
17. Does she hold grudges?
18. Would she find it difficult to carry on more than one sexual affair at the same time?
19. Despite her ability does she love to cook?
20. Does she suffer from deep depression?
21. Are her moods influenced by her surroundings?

(Answers)

1–30
There are three possible alternatives here: (1) you've only just met, (2) you never really have taken the trouble to get to know your woman or (3) she is not typically Cancer. If you both think that this is the case, then it's quite likely that there is an "Air" influence on her chart. Try reading under Aquarius, Gemini or Libra; you may find your lady here.

31–50

You are lucky enough to be involved with one of the nicer Cancerians, and you know her pretty well. Either you have been involved with each other for a very long time, or you are a very perceptive man. Either way, your relationship has a great chance of working.

51–60

It's a wonder you have the energy to fill out this quiz, for you appear to be involved with a Cancerian lady with a considerable amount of Hyde in her. You must be exhausted. At least you seem to know her very well and presumably have accepted her with all her faults. If this is the case you are a very brave man. There must be an awful lot of give in your relationship and my guess is that it all comes from you.

HOW WELL DO YOU KNOW YOUR CANCERIAN MAN?

Answer honestly the questions below, scoring 3 for every Yes, 2 for Sometimes and 1 for No then add up your total.

1. Does he like to protect you?
2. Does he drink when depressed?
3. Does he have an over-active imagination?
4. Is he a hypochondriac?
5. Does he consider himself a genius in the kitchen?
6. Is he possessive?
7. Is he close to his mother?
8. Does he like to draw attention to himself?
9. Has he always taken his relationships, even the briefest ones, too seriously?
10. Is he anti-feminist?
11. Is he easy to shock?
12. Financially is he a bit of a meany?
13. Does he ever wallow in self-pity?
14. Does he insist that you make attempts at getting on with his family?
15. Does he have a sweet tooth?
16. Does he rather obviously flirt with your friends?
17. Does he sulk when you don't feel like making love?

18. Do you suspect "Mummy spoiled him"?
19. Does he buy girlie magazines?
20. Is he paternal?

(Answers)

1–30
It's quite possible that this Cancerian man of yours has several other planets in one of the Air signs, such as Gemini, Aquarius and Sagittarius. If you both agree that he is untypical of his sign, perhaps you can learn more about him by reading these chapters. If he believes he is a true-blue member of this sign, then you obviously haven't known him very long, or are totally lacking in intuition. You know as much about him as you would a total stranger.

31–50
You know and accept your man well enough to make a good go of a lengthy relationship. If you are not committed to him, be warned that he is probably on the verge of committing himself to you. And your chances of success are great.

51-60
There's obviously something of the masochist in your personality; you clearly enjoy being a doormat. This man is born on the darker side of Cancer, and unless you are prepared to submerge your own personality and devote yourself to him I suggest you get out quick – assuming that he'll let go.

Leo (the Lion)
Sign of the Director or Chairman

July 23 – August 23

The second Fire sign: Self-expressive, energetic, assertive, intense, steadfast, spontaneous
Ruler: The Sun
Colour: Orange
Career: Manager, social organizer, overseer, artist, actor
Famous Leonines: James Baldwin, Napoleon Bonaparte, Fidel Castro, Alfred Hitchcock, Mick Jagger, Mussolini, Jacqueline Onassis, Princess Anne, Princess Margaret, Robert Redford, Shelley, Ted Hughes.

LEO MAN

The Leo man is generous, warm-hearted, a born leader, enthusiastic, dignified, broad-minded, outspoken and a good organizer. He loves to do things in a big way and can't be bothered with details. He has a strong sense for the dramatic and is usually very self-assured. He has a keen love of luxury and of pleasure. He is demanding, exciting, dramatic in everything he does – he can't help but be sheer dynamite. His dynamism attracts and dazzles the opposite sex and makes them think that he is in charge of the situation. But the rest of us should always remember what Leo wants, Leo gets.

Whether he resembles a shaggy-maned lion or a homely purring pussycat matters not at all; regardless of his stature, he will be difficult to overlook. He emanates confidence and has a way of drawing attention. His appearance and his choice of clothes can cause quite a stir, being usually expensive and ostentatious.

Professionally speaking, the Leo man makes an excellent leader. He never has any trouble delegating responsibility and has a nack of sifting out the right man for the right job. The right side of life is always the bright side where Leo is concerned. He has heard of pessimism, but there is no reason to believe in its existence. Mind you, he is rather impulsive on occasion and this can lead him to gamble away the family fortune. But nothing is too good for those he loves and respects.

Regrettably he is not as organized in his personal life. Because of a tendency to cloud his judgement with emotion, he frequently gives his affections to the wrong people. Pride is a Leo trait and his ego is all. With the right girl, he is an excellent husband and good provider. He really likes to see those he loves looked after and cherished.

Most Lions know what the word "work" is all about. Don't be surprised if he doesn't visit your lair for days on end. He is probably out hunting up a few extra pound notes or chasing a business deal. But his routine is rather erratic. In work he can achieve a great deal, in fact will probably get more done in a day than most of us would accomplish in a week. Then quite suddenly he will lapse into a thoroughly lazy phase during which he will be immovable. Like a lion in the jungle, he will rest until ready to spring into action once more. There is nothing anybody can do about it except wait.

It doesn't matter whether you pour flattery upon his head as many as ten times during one day, of one thing you can be sure, not one drop of it will run on to the ground. For Leo soaks up compliments of all descriptions, so much so that it is quite possible for him to choose business partners and lovers for the beautiful things they say about him. Stop building up his ego and see how long it is before he begins to roar. The Lion is undisputedly king of the jungle. His courtiers will be "Yes, sir, no, sir" kind of people. This is a side of his personality which he needs to keep under control, for it can lead to all sorts of problems. Furthermore, this man never apologizes. His intense pride would make him feel this to be an admission of being at a lower level. He might recognize that he is totally wrong, but he will not admit it; and don't try to push him too hard in this direction. Lions have claws and it might take some unsuspecting victim a few weeks to get over the scars.

For a Leonine who appears to be masterful and strong to the outside world and yet has a wonderful sunny and generous interior, life can be tough. Especially once people discover his big warm heart. He is often taken advantage of, not surprisingly. It is important that the Leo man comes to grips with his situation early in life in order to avoid serious heartbreak.

LEO WOMAN

Like her male counterpart, the Leo woman makes a wonderful, loyal and warm friend, possesses fierce pride and a love of luxury. She cares about her appearance and would not dream of wearing anything but the best. She will probably be a collector of jewellery – and it is no good expecting her to make do with glass beads or plastic bracelets.

Unfortunately, she invariably places her boundless faith in the wrong people. Her judgement is far too easily deceived by appearances, and her desire for comfort can lead to marriage for material reasons. Any man who is living in a log cabin by a railway track and driving a 1948 Ford and still wearing his father's hand-me-downs had better look elsewhere for a mate. The Leo lady is not about to become a common-or-garden alley cat, so don't expect her to dirty her paws on your front gate. When she does make the mistake of falling into the money trap and getting herself involved with a walking cheque book, she is guaranteed failure. For this girl needs to feel deeply and loved constantly if she is to remain well balanced. Remember that fierce pride. No one in their right mind would attempt to dent it.

Professionally speaking – and most Leo ladies are career-minded – she is quite a different animal. The sweet purring pussycat curled up at her man's feet can turn out to be a snarling, spitting, hackles-raised fireball when out to achieve her professional ambitions. Many a businessman has had his contracts scratched to shreds by her. When married with financial security she can make an ideal housewife; but if she can't get what she wants in a personal relationship, she will be out and about, involved in the world around her. She has to feel she is an interesting person to be with, and the domestic role may not offer her the scope needed for her energies and ambitions.

THE HYDE SIDE

Even this type of Leonine is never quite as bad as other weak members of other signs. For all Leonines possess that basic warm heart.

However, these Lions are plagued with delusions of grandeur. Even if their den is of the eight-foot-by-eight-foot variety they will attempt to make it look like the interior of Buckingham Palace. They believe that the very best in life is their birthright, and they have an unquenchable thirst for personal glory. But don't expect them to work for it; toil is for mere mortals. The gods never ever work. And if laziness was a measure of godliness, these characters would reside on Mount Olympus. They expect and demand a high position in life, even if they cannot hope to fill the footprint left by a predecessor. These individuals always choose to be a big fish in a little pond rather than the reverse. In practically every instance they try to get too far too soon, losing out through lack of experience, laziness or restlessness.

Here again the biggest weakness is the love of flattery. They select workmates and friends for their pandering ability. When it comes to marriage, they will invariably choose someone in a socially inferior position to themselves, for in this way at least they are assured of one person to dominate and before whom they can strut. They don't realize the image they project is one of pomposity and arrogance. Although they like to show off their status symbols to friends and acquaintances, they rarely put themselves out to do so. Rather they prefer to surround themselves with an audience and proceed to play a game of one-up-manship, inflating minor successes and deliberately hiding failure. When in a mood to entertain extravagantly they do not hesitate not even to obtain a loan from somewhere for the purpose. Clearly not the most practical of people.

It must be pointed out, though, that your particular Leonine mate may not slot conveniently into either one of these categories; he/she maybe a mixture of both. But Leo is never an evil sign – just downright hopeless on occasions.

HOW TO CATCH AND KEEP YOUR LEO MAN

Few can be totally indifferent to the Lion: we either find him irresistible or are totally opposed to him. Many women really cannot be bothered to take the trouble to look any further than the arrogant and lazy façade and will dismiss this type immediately. But in general it is not too difficult to uncover his warm and generous heart.

When the Lion loves, he does so with his heart, body and mind and he is nearly always attracted to the sophisticated type of women. He has a keenly developed sense of luxury and comfort. He is also extremely extravagant, especially where loved ones are concerned.

Any woman determined to achieve success in a career of her own is in for a pretty trying time if she's attracted to this man. He must be king of all he surveys and this means that his mate must be dependent on him. He has a hypersensitive ego and a strong sense of pride, so it is very rare for a Leonine's wife to be allowed to work. She must simply sit around looking beautiful and be expert in covering him in compliments. Being particularly susceptible to flattery, the Leo is often misguided enough to choose partners who can boost his ego, however unsuitable they may be. To keep a Leonine man happy, never make him feel threatened in any way. He must be the most important thing in his woman's life and she must be happy to have it this way. He is totally unable to accept anything else. A Leonine is always attracted to the big and beautiful and this is always carried over into his finances and career. He generally tries to associate himself with over-ambitious and sometimes totally impractical ideas. His woman will be courting disaster, however, if she should ever shoot his ideas down. Rather, she should try to persuade one of his friends to talk some common sense to him; even if he is not more receptive to a third party, at least she will not have run the risk of causing a large rift in their relationship.

Any woman chasing a Leonine man should try to treat him as she would a big pampered cat. Give him lots of love, affection, warmth and comfort and she will have her Lion for life.

HOW TO CATCH AND KEEP YOUR LEO WOMAN

The Leonine woman can have an adverse effect on men, who are inclined to take one look at her arrogance and run in the opposite direction. If, however, they allow themselves to stick around for any length of time, they will soon discover a generous warm and loving nature.

This type of female has notoriously bad judgement. She is inclined to rely on outward appearances, which are often misleading. She has a well developed sense of luxury, comfort and beauty. It is nothing but the best for this young lady, and because she is prepared to give her maximum she expects to be loved as intensely in return. It is an easy matter to impress this woman but it can be rather costly. Men who loathe parting with money should watch out, for this lady needs to be wined and dined at the best and most expensive restaurants. She is also extremely susceptible to flattery and is quite able to sit all day while some adoring male applies liberal praise. The Leonine lady constantly needs her ego boosted. Pride is paramount in this type and any man who dares to attack her hyper-sensitive ego is sure to be dismissed in no uncertain fashion.

A man in pursuit of her must be affectionate, generous to the point of extreme and the possessor of a silver tongue. Those who grow close to her will soon realize that the arrogant front displayed so convincingly is a cover-up for her soft centre, and is part of her personality that must be accepted. The Leonine woman could rightly be accused of being the last of the big-time spenders but bullying or threatening behaviour will only worsen the situation. The way to this woman's heart is through lavish affection; only then will she be ready to listen to reason.

HIS IDEAL PARTNER

Subjects of Aries, Sagittarius and possibly Gemini, have a good chance of making it with the Lion. These signs' basic needs coincide to a degree and because of this understanding can be reached. But if you are a female Scorpion, don't waste your time following his tracks; when you finally snare him you will be able to see through him in an instant, and he won't like that one little bit. No, his ideal mate needs to have as much enthusiasm and optimism as himself, someone to offer him continuous praise and support in all he does.

Above all else he needs a mate who will not point out his failures. According to him, you see, he does not have any. He is not kindly disposed to dream-shatterers. The Lion is a highly sexed creature, so cold-hearted Hannahs had better stay out of his lair. His ideal mate will also need to be a status symbol, for Leo the Lion, like Aries the Ram, tends to wear women. He won't like the idea of being seen around his territory with a mouse on his arm. She will need to have something about her which makes her flash like a neon sign. He likes other men to notice her, but he won't expect her to flirt. Any innocent male who smiles at her will probably find his teeth clamped firmly around his rear collar stud. But despite this, he needs the encouragement and reassurance of his male friends that he has indeed scored highly.

His ideal mate won't have a career, or if she does she will need to drop it. Refusal to do so will mean that she will be regarded as a rival and he has no wish to compete against a woman he has chosen. His ego just could not handle any glory she may attain. There is only room for one monarch in his domain and it is not a female of the species. Oh, yes – he is pompous, over-demanding and sometimes quite impossible. But he is also irresistible and extremely lovable. And his lady will have to worship him, unless she wishes to observe him pining away before her very eyes. In return, she can expect to eat at the finest restaurants, wear the most expensive clothes and be seen in the smartest places. She will need a lot of stamina too, for the Lion likes to play hard. Faithfulness does not come easily to this man for he likes to be loved, by as many people as possible. His mate will need to spread her love very thickly unless she wishes him to go on the prowl night after night. Nevertheless a big cat in the bed is worth twenty on the roof top. Mind you, she will never stop him eyeing up the opposition, even if the relationship has progressed to the diamond on the third finger of the left hand stage.

Once he has found his ideal and has whisked her up the aisle, all things change. You have seen pictures of lions sitting contentedly surrounded by their families. That is just how he will behave. If she looks after his domain, he will look after her. Not many Leonine men raise large families, but what children there are will respect their dear Leo dad. He will allow them the odd misdemeanour and they will be able to pull at his whiskers on occasions; but when he roars, the whole jungle knows about it and everybody else snaps to attention, including his brood.

HER IDEAL PARTNER

Like her male counterpart this lady's ideal partner will possibly be found under the sign of Sagittarius, Aries or maybe Gemini, for these three Sun signs, generally speaking, are the ones which can offer her most in the way of true happiness. Most of the other signs would only prove to be wet blankets to her. Ideally, though, even if she can find a man who owns a Rolls Royce and is prepared to shower her with presents and compliments, she should not rush straight into marriage. Because there is a real danger of this, she is often a much married lady; she cannot be totally impartial to a man with a good position. This is one side of her character that she should try to get straightened out and face up to the cold fact that even millionaires do tend to have just one or two faults, which should be analysed carefully. After all, if he is going to share the throne with her, he had better be worthy of the crown.

Her ideal mate will be prepared to let her follow her own career. No use arguing about it; that is the way it is. No man is going to tame her into a life of dishcloths and tea towels. Neither is it her style to bow down to all his wishes.

Her substantial sexual appetite will also need satisfying. Think twice before volunteering; she is really not going to be happy with the twice-a-week man and her appetite is likely to grow with maturity. Neither will she wish to become involved with someone who wants a large pride of cubs. You can put this down to vanity, for she is concerned about losing her figure. However, this does not mean she does not want children at all, but where they are concerned, she can't count further than two.

As you will have gathered, she appreciates a man with whom she can share the luxuries of life. It's not too important if he isn't a millionaire, just so long as he can occasionally take her to the best places and spend some money on her, particularly on special occasions. Types that carry pocket calculators around with them for checking bills may as well forget this young lady. Any man showing penny-pinching tendencies just once will be eating alone. She feels a good standard of living is her birthright. How good, depends on her depth of feeling for her mate, though if a man intends to trap her into a dreary apartment on the wrong side of town, he can be sure that she will be very unhappy in a short space of time.

Her ideal partner will know that while money will get him some of the way and gifts will get him a little further, it is flattery that will complete the journey. Despite the impression I may have given, she is not a gold-digger. Nevertheless, with her there is only one thing that money can't buy – poverty.

SEXUALLY (MALE)

The Lion has a very developed sexual appetite; all things carnal are of paramount importance to him. He abandons himself heart and soul to his affairs. Women are naturally drawn to this man. They sense his masculinity and everything that is Leonine is irresistible. Because his ruling planet is the Sun, warmth and life positively radiate from him. If invited back to his den, don't expect to find it filled with the bare essentials. And when he gets round to making love, it will either be on a velvet quilt or a fur rug. He is susceptible to the texture of materials and sometimes this can lead to a degree of fetishism. Furthermore, the greater amount of success he has had in the day, the greater his sexuality at night.

His run up to love-making will usually take the form of an expensive dinner with champagne, for when he tries to impress he does it properly. The egg-and-chips or hamburger establishments are definitely out. And if, after all the bother he has put himself to, the lady he is pursuing is not ready to consummate the relationship just yet, he will be a good loser. His pride may find it difficult to accept a poke in the eye and it will definitely sting a bit, but disappointment is well hidden. He'll philosophically reason that he can't win them all and will be so gallant about the whole thing, she may even change her mind.

When strongly attracted to a member of the opposite sex he is happy to spend vast sums wooing her – that is, of course, in relation to his resources. Obviously you can't expect a pink Rolls Royce to arrive gift-wrapped if your Leonine lover is only a grocery boy. (But in time he will probably own the shop and in the meantime his lady will have to make do with the occasional free pound of butter.) Expensive presents and flowers will be utilized if this will help him to achieve his ambition.

The Lion possesses an ability to make every girl he meets feel like a lady. But don't be surprised if he conveniently forgets this, once he has got her on the goatskin rug. For that is when the Lion really begins to roar. He may be considerate and loving at the beginning of the relationship, but it won't be long before she begins to think she has a wild animal in the bed – and realizes that she is quite enjoying the experience. A Leonine lover is difficult to forget.

One problem does exist, however, and that is laziness. And in a lengthy relationship he may reach the stage where he can't be bothered to put himself out. A bit of stimulation and imagination on his woman's part is called for then, and if they get through this sticky phase all will be well with their relationship probably lasing for ever.

SEXUALLY (FEMALE)

Any man looking for a quick conquest one evening can forget it with a Leo woman. Getting anywhere with her needs to be planned like a wartime campaign. Furthermore, she will burn a hole in his pocket. If a suitor does succeed with her, it will only be in comfortable surroundings. A brave fellow attempting to pounce on her in the back seat of a car, or the front seat, for that matter, is asking for trouble.

Once she has chosen a mate, inhibitions are not for her. She is very open-minded. She will try anything once and can probably improve it anyway. The worst thing any man can do is

96

to criticize her bedroom technique. No matter how inexperienced she may be, her man must be tactful when acting as her teacher. She is a willing pupil and learns quickly. Like her male counterpart she enjoys a romp on the goatskin rug and relishes the feel of soft materials against her flesh. Try to remember she is akin to a great big pussy cat. Keep her warm, well fed and loved and she will purr contentedly in your ear. Otherwise she is liable to bite it off.

A word of warning: sexually, she prefers to remain faithful to one man, but I did say prefers. If that man is not working out too well when it comes to night play she may look for another playmate down the block. There is nothing in her book that says she must not drop you if you don't come up to standard, whether in or out of bed. Clearly, then, not a lady for the faint-hearted.

HOW TO END THE AFFAIR

Not an easy procedure. For even when your interest in your Leonine lover has totally waned, it is unlikely that you will be filled with any ill feeling or resentment. You are sure at least to like this type and not harbour any desire to hurt them. The first thing to remember is that it is unthinkable to allow your fiercely proud Lion to believe that you are tired of him or her. Ideally a mutual split should be agreed upon.

Try something like: "It has been working up to this for some time now, don't you agree? . . . Of course, I'm not saying it's anybody's fault – certainly not yours. It must be that we are just incompatible. What do you think?" Your Lion will, more often than not, agree with you. And your ways will part smoothly without any animosity, and with any luck the day will have been saved.

For heaven's sake don't tell the Lion: "You're a beast – you've never understood me. I can't go on – I really can't. . . ." That ego will have been deflated quicker than a fairground balloon and the pride will have taken one hell of a knock. Leos think they understand EVERYBODY. What's more this approach will arouse that Leonine arrogance. "What do you mean, you can't go on – what about me?" Now you feel bad and on the defensive, and here comes an argument, so I'll leave you to pick up the black eyes.

A jilted Lion is a very sorry sight, and don't imagine that simply because your Leo is female that the hurt will be any less, although the affair can always be ended simply by the use of the wrong words. If you must take yourself off, then at least leave your Leo with pride and confidence in tact.

Whatever you do, don't list their faults and proceed to analyse them one by one and it wouldn't be kind to explain how much you fancy his or her friend. Far better to get your Leo to agree that you are just not good for each other. That way you'll be able to leave without claw marks all over your image, or, worse still, your body.

HOW TO ATTRACT THE SUN SIGNS

LEO WOMAN WITH LEO MAN

This is a pretty exotic coupling. Although it has all the exciting possibilities of the battle of the sexes, these two will try to outdo each other at work, socially and in bed. Competition for the limelight will be fierce and intriguing but it will be exhausting for both parties. She is bright, independent, attractive – and not always available. And the same is true of him. Both will expect the other to flatter, cajole and generally make a fuss of them . . . but neither will. Once this fact has sunk in, I'm afraid there's bound to be trouble. Ideally, two Leos should settle for a business partnership, or perhaps they will make it as good friends. Anything else could make life somewhat difficult.

LEO WOMAN WITH VIRGO MAN

She is the type who only uses cleaning fluid to wash her diamonds, while the Virgo man will want her to wash his shirts in it. He'll be a most incisive critic when she basically doesn't want one. Nevertheless, he's quite happy for her to get ahead professionally and will applaud her every step of the way. But after a while, her need for constant attention will bore him and he will eventually decide that she is vain, conceited and impossible. If he wants to keep her, somehow he will have to soften up and make concessions, but is it fair to ask it of him? As for her, she will have to learn the economics of life and quickly; she must appear more sensible and practical if he is to give her a second look. Should they manage to stay together she is likely to be the dominant partner and he the convenient doormat. An unwise relationship.

LEO WOMAN WITH LIBRA MAN

She will attract him only if she dims her brilliance, which he's sure to find rather overpowering. She may be faithful and affectionate but a bit too demonstrative for the somewhat sensitive and shy Libran man. However, he will applaud her dress-sense, although her aggressiveness in business will unnerve him. At least both share a love of luxury – she may temporarily win him over if she spends a long lunch-hour with him window-shopping for cars and flatters him unmercifully. He is in love with someone new every week, so at some point he is bound to come across Miss Leo. The danger is that she may take him too seriously and sharpen her claws when he gets ready to move on. A good relationship for a sexual affair, but precious little else.

LEO WOMAN WITH SCORPIO MAN

There's no doubt about it, this is definitely one of those love/hate relationships, but fortunately one which normally burns itself out. Marriage would be most unwise between these fire and water signs. More aggressive than Mr Aries, more dominant than Mr Taurus, a Scorpio lover is, without doubt, the most difficult and yet fascinating of any. His sexual endurance is nothing short of phenomenal. She may need to take vitimin pills to keep up with him. The first thing liable to get in the way of their relationship is that penetrating eye of his. He is a born critic, and the last thing the Leo woman wants is to have her faults paraded in front of her. On a superficial level this partnership can work, if only for a while.

LEO WOMAN WITH SAGITTARIUS MAN

Both these are fire signs, so they are halfway to success before they begin. The Sagittarian man detests anything small (even his dog is likely to be a Great Dane) and will be intrigued by the way she can think and act "big". He will also appreciate the new people, places and interests she introduces him to. She will be impressed by the way he decides to pack a picnic at midnight to eat it in the middle of a snow-laden field: uncomfortable and wet – yes; and they may not actually get there, but the idea will appeal greatly. This is something of a dynamic duo, providing they can stay the pace, and they usually can.

LEO WOMAN WITH CAPRICORN MAN

The Leonine woman will find this man difficult to understand. He seems cool af first, but her ability to lend an aristocratic touch to his business image will warm him up fast. He will be attracted to her if he believes she can help him further his career, be it socially or at a practical level. And she's definitely a woman who commands the kind of respect usually reserved for celebrities or dignitaries. He won't be able to wait for his boss to meet her – an enormous compliment from a Capricorn man. What will attract her about him isn't quite so easy. He is so engrossed in his work and career, he certainly doesn't have time for changing his basic personality. However, if he is crazy about her then he'll try. The first thing he'll have to do is to rob his piggy-bank (which he will rebel against), take her out for an expensive evening, controlling all impulses to check the bill. Secondly, he should leave that cool reserve at home and respond to her natural warmth and fire. But all this seems a lot to expect from them both, and in general this relationship is best confined to the office or other work premises.

LEO WOMAN WITH AQUARIUS MAN

Love and sex to Mr Aquarius is his diversion, not his preoccupation, and she may feel that his attitude to relationships borders on the Victorian. He will expect her to be virtuous, faithful and patient enough to put up with all his little eccentricities. She will want him to be involved with her emotionally and in bed; he will be wrapped up in politics or some other cause. If they do actually manage to get together, then this could be an excellent combination of talents, but unlikely to be of long duration. Aquarius is also the sign of the truth-seeker, so there's no point her expecting him to tell her she is ravishing unless she actually is. As time goes on, she'll be less enamoured with his ability always to hit the truth button. A difficult relationship.

LEO WOMAN WITH PISCES MAN

Another of these fire (Leo) and water (Pisces) combinations, therefore a rather difficult one. The Piscean man will tend to throw a rain-cloud over her sunny disposition, and will overreact to anything he regards as a slight criticism, although she will feel she is offering constructive suggestions. These two just don't think along the same lines. Nevertheless he is not shy about commenting on her hair, clothes, make-up, housekeeping, even a book she reads. And sexually he is capable of initiating her into all sorts of erotic deviations which she didn't even know existed. Some Leonine women look around for slaves, and if that's the case then this is just the man for her. But the abolition of slavery took place quite some time ago now, and besides, Mr Pisces is far too sensitive a soul to be downtrodden in this way. An unwise relationship.

LEO WOMAN WITH ARIES MAN

Mr Aries possesses zeal, zest, vitality and that certain something in his temperament which she admires. She will love his spontaneity when he shows up at the strangest times to whisk her away to strange places to do wonderful things. In this relationship she can have the spotlight all to herself – once in a while, that is – but she must remember that he can be as theatrical as she is and needs equal time for applause and flattery. Because of their dramatic sense, they keep each other on their toes, staging arguments and fights – in public and in private – for the sheer fun of it. If anyone is going to handle the lady it is certainly this character and he doesn't even have to try.

LEO WOMAN WITH TAURUS MAN

On a physical level this is a great match. She loves to give, feel, bestow; he reacts by appreciating and warming to her touch. He is capable of being the most loyal mate. Even so, he'll still be jealous of her wide circle of friends, and upset when her regal approach to living eats its way through the bank balance. Maybe if they care about each other enough they will find some happy compromise; but more likely, though, they won't for both are extremely stubborn and fixed in their ways. He will think she should change and vice versa. Really this is only an ideal combination for a short sexual affair but not for marriage.

LEO WOMAN WITH GEMINI MAN

It may appeal to the Leo woman to be part of his all-female fan club for a short while – but only a very short while. He will be quick to tell her of his sexual fantasies and, while initially this may turn her on, she will soon tire of having to play-act. And, even more insulting, after a rousing session of love and sex, he is capable of departing from the scene at 2 a.m. in order to go for an encore with someone else. The Leo ego will come in for an awful bashing with this relationship. She must be a purring pussycat rather than a roaring lion if they are to last through the first week. He will need to control that roving eye; but as this advice is going against the grain of their true personalities, it's doubtful whether they can last the course.

LEO WOMAN WITH CANCER MAN

At last, she thinks, a man who will not only love and protect her but empty her ashtrays and wash the dishes as well. He is naturally sensitive, emotional and supportive. And she will be impressed by how suave he appears when she takes him to opening nights at the theatre or to the boss's home – the perfect escort and the most attentive lover. However, she is by far the stronger character, and if he sticks around, his individuality and personality are in danger of being well and truly squashed. He may be prepared for this, out of love for her, although when the first rosy glow of romance has died he is likely to withdraw into his shell where he will stubbornly stay put, no matter how much she kicks at it.

HOW WELL DO YOU KNOW YOUR LEO WOMAN?

Answer honestly the questions below, scoring 3 for every Yes, 2 for Sometimes and 1 for No, then add up your total.

1. If you attempted a sexual quickie, would you be in trouble?
2. Is she an expensive lady?
3. Does she like to dance?
4. Is she putty in your hands when you have flattered her?
5. Is she lazy?
6. Is she frightened of water?
7. Is she demanding?
8. Is she proud?
9. Will she tell you if you haven't satisfied her sexually?
10. Does she expect expensive presents on special occasions?
11. Even if she doesn't own a Botticelli, is she proud of her possessions?
12. Does she judge people by appearances?
13. Does she feel the cold?
14. Does she find financial budgeting difficult?
15. Does she envy her more successful or wealthy girlfriends?
16. Is she generous?
17. Careerwise, has her life been somewhat chequered?
18. Does she loathe housework?
19. Is she ambitious for you?
20. When she says no to sex, does she mean it?

(Answers)

1–30

If your relationship with your Leonine woman is relatively new then maybe you can be forgiven for such a poor score, but it doesn't bode well for the future. You seem to have got her all wrong. However, it may be that she is not true to her sign and that there are other influences at work. If so, they are likely to be earthly ones. Try reading the chapters on Capricorn, Taurus or Virgo. This may give you a greater insight into her character.

31–50

This is the ideal score. You appreciate all of your Leonine lady's fine qualities and are tolerant of her lesser ones. You are either very perceptive or have known her for some time. You seem quite able to cope with all her little foibles and your relationship is an extremely promising one. It takes quite a man to understand this young woman. She should hang on to you.

51–60

You have my admiration, you know your Leonine female inside-out and are still not put off. It could be that you are extremely soft in the head, or perhaps in the heart. Either way, you've certainly got your work cut out, but maybe you've decided she is worth it.

HOW WELL DO YOU KNOW YOUR LEO MAN?

Answer honestly the questions below, scoring 3 for every Yes, 2 for Sometimes and 1 for No, then add up your total.

1. Is he lacking in energy?
2. Does he like to see you in furs or silks and satins?
3. Does he regard your work as unimportant?
4. Is he extravagant?
5. Does he always get mixed up with the wrong friends?
6. Is he put out when you refuse him sexually?
7. Is flattery his Achilles' heel?
8. Does he enjoy the good things in life?
9. Does he roar when you flirt?
10. Does he try to dominate you?
11. Is he snobbish?
12. Is he intolerant?
13. Must you always look your best for him?
14. Does he find it hard to apologize?
15. Is he a flirt?
16. Does he place a heavy emphasis on sex in your relationship?
17. Is he a good host?
18. Is he self-indulgent?
19. Is he a snob?
20. Does he patronize you?

(Answers)

1–30

Either you are a hopeless judge of character or you are not dealing with a typical Leonine. This man is far too self-effacing, modest and emotional to be born under the sign of the Lion. If you're having trouble figuring him out, I suggest you read the chapters devoted to the water signs, such as Pisces, Scorpio or Cancer.

31–50

Not only are you involved with one of the nicer Lions, but you also seem to have him worked out pretty well. Mind you, it's doubtful whether he will enjoy being pigeon-holed in this way; perhaps you'd better admit to being a little puzzled on occasions. Nevertheless, you appear to have an excellent relationship.

51–60

You have my deepest sympathy. How can you possibly put up with being dictated to in this way? Perhaps you are the sort of person who neeeds someone to fill an empty gap where your personality should be and maybe it's time you found yourself before you take on this character. However, at least you know him well and are fully aware of what you are getting into.

Virgo (the Virgin)
Sign of the Doctor or Analyst

August 24 – September 23

The second Earth sign: Intelligent, shrewd, discerning, critical, practical rather than abstract
Ruler: Mercury
Colour: Grey or navy blue
Career: Teacher, psychologist, technologist, nurse, scientist, statistician, accountant, inspector
Famous Virgoans: Lauren Bacall, Anne Bancroft, Ray Charles, Greta Garbo, Sophia Loren, Queen Elizabeth I, Cardinal Richelieu, Margaret Trudeau, Twiggy, H. G. Wells

---

VIRGO MAN

The Virgo male is critical, discriminating, practical and evaluates life by facts and figures. He can't help himself; he must analyse, take to pieces, sift every minute detail. Most Virgoans also possess an extreme interest in hygiene and cleanliness. They tend to be rather reserved emotionally.

The Virgo male carries out tasks quickly and methodically. He plans, makes lists and then does. There isn't really an impulsive side to this character at all, unless it is the way he rushes headlong into business competitions. In all other areas of life he proceeds with wariness.

107

On a more personal level, he never leaves a sink full of dirty dishes. He straightens pictures, empties ashtrays, removes other people's cleaning tickets and gets twitchy if his lady's make-up is anything but perfect. However, he can over-organize his life if he is not careful, which may leave him with an impeccable apartment but nobody to share it with. He detests stupidity, vulgarity or carelessness and loses no time in letting people know – though he won't be listening if others tell him that he lacks perfection and therefore should not expect it.

When a Virgo man asks a female out, there's no point in her anticipating lavish entertainment. For this is Mr Practical and he doesn't throw his money away. He lives well within his means. The same could be said of the way he expresses his affections. A woman who falls in love with him may wonder whether he has even noticed. He is not exactly demonstrative, so don't expect a bear hug in the middle of a crowded street, or even a gentle peck on the cheek while dancing hip to hip. It is for this reason he is often labelled cold and aloof. But don't be fooled: when his passions are aroused, they will be white-hot with emotion, though he may not show it.

The Virgo man forms very few deep ties, for it takes a great deal to melt his heart. He has a knack for being able to sense faults in other people. He may have his own failings, but it's an unwise female who dares to point them out to him: she will find herself Virgo-less. She will have to learn to live with his criticisms. Indulge him and take heed, for he rarely criticizes unfairly. If he says that bright red lipstick doesn't suit her, or that her hair looks a mess, he's probably right.

Unfortunately he doesn't always balance the thoughts of others against the better side of their personality, and this can lead to him remaining a bachelor until quite late in life. This won't bother him to any great extent, he's quite happy to be on his own, rather than marry the wrong woman, and who can say he's wrong? For once he is trapped, he is not easy to live with. He has very set ideas on how the household should be run – a right old fusspot.

The Virgo man likes to impose his views on others and so he needs a rather special kind of mate. Few of us are prepared to put up with such a character for very long. However, should you be round long enough, you will find that his love is shown in many different ways. He may not have a glib tongue but he expresses his love in the small things he does for those dear to him. There won't be a diamond ring on their wedding anniversary – he may stretch to a bunch of violets – but he will remember. His crystal-clear memory will see to that. Loved ones should try to remember that his inability to express himself fully is as depressing to him as it is to them.

VIRGO WOMAN

The Virgo woman is adept mentally and also extremely good with her hands. When a fuse blows in her home, she will whip out her tool-box and go and mend it. Where her appearance is concerned, her clothes are plain and simple. She loathes ostentation of any description, but usually manages to appear neat and surprisingly sexy in the most unassuming of outfits. Often the slightly puritanical vibrations which she gives off are extremely exciting and challenging to the opposite sex, who long to turn this iceberg into a ball of fire. It's another matter entirely whether or not they succeed.

She is intelligent and critical of others – as well as of herself. Maternal instincts aren't that well developed and the idea of spending all day chained to the kitchen sink will definitely not appeal to her. Away from home she doesn't necessarily crave success, but she does like to keep her intellect busy. A Virgo woman confined to boredom and routine is not a happy sight.

Don't listen to people who accuse this woman of being a prude. Just because she has high moral standards doesn't necessarily make her narrow-minded. She enjoys sex, but if she really loves her man, then he will be safe to trust her with the most attractive man on the block. Promiscuity is just not her thing. She may keep a tight control over her emotions but they do exist.

The spinster aunt is another conception of the Virgo lady – you know, the traditional old maid – and there's some truth in this. For if the Virgo woman doesn't meet her ideal early in life she is highly unlikely to settle for second best. She'd rather be alone in an empty bed and lead an active life on the other side of the bedroom door. She is not a romantic soul either, so any suitor is discouraged from going down on one knee beneath the silvery moon to ask for her hand in marriage. She may accept, but it will have nothing to do with the moonlight. He will need to be careful; if he rushes in like the proverbial bull in the china shop, he will more than likely just end up in pieces among all the other broken plates. She doesn't really believe in the love-at-first-sight syndrome – so she very rarely finds it.

The Virgoan woman could learn to let her hair down on occasions, and see what happens; she would certainly profit from the experience. But that would be going against her nature.

THE HYDE SIDE

These types of Virgoans are critical, pedantic, fastidious, interfering, overly modest and they suppress all emotion and feelings. Because they find fault with every possible advantage to life, they are unable to progress and, not surprisingly, are impossible to please. This type is particularly good at destroying plans and ideas without offering any alternatives, and as a result failure is a constant companion. Of course, it's never the Virgoan's fault. Good heavens no! Circumstances were to blame. Downfall is always attributable to someone or something being against them, since these Virgoans can never face the fact that they are responsible.

Friends cause no problem in their life, mainly because they haven't any . . . well, not many anyway. These types tend to have a rather depressing effect on people and only those capable of overlooking the petty fault-finding will become their companions.

Sexually, there's no one quite good enough. Well, let's face it, who likes to be criticized as soon as their feet are off the floor? Such characters are the original passion-killers, running at least three lengths ahead of army socks and flannel nightshirts.

They suffer from a special kind of stubbornness. Despite the catastrophes happening all round them, they couldn't possibly have anything to do with them. One thing is for sure, the old adage "you can't teach an old dog new tricks" is especially pertinent here, for the older this Virgoan gets, the more difficult he or she is to change. Therefore, this type is one for catching young or for forgetting about.

HOW TO CATCH AND KEEP YOUR VIRGO MAN

Before any woman goes off Virgo-chasing, she should ask herself one question, and seriously: "Do I really want him?" The Virgoan male is not the easiest character to live with. In fact, he can be downright impossible. Many would accuse him of being petty-minded, mean and of attempting to impose his code of behaviour on other people, and they are probably right in doing so.

But if you are determined that this is your man, then you must attempt to be as perfect in all as can be realisitically contrived, for he will usually only settle for THE best. It takes a lot to melt his heart and he has to decide that he likes a female before he allows himself to fall in love with her. He is extremely critical.

His woman must be an economics expert, not desirous of great wealth or luxury, simple in her mode of dress, and ready to devote herself to him. Neither can she expect him to woo her with words of love. Instead, Virgoan devotion is shown in the small things he is happy to do for his loved ones, and no one looks after or tends to the sick with such care and tenderness as does this man. His mate will never have to worry about financial security, for no matter how little this man earns, he always makes it stretch and still has some to save. He may well be attracted to a career woman, for he is happy to work in partnership towards their mutual objectives and does not subscribe to the old-fashioned view that a woman's place is in the home.

The Virgoan man is usually keen on some form of physical exercise. He likes to keep fit, so any woman interested in him would be wise to discover his particular sport, even though it may only be walking. He has also been known to acquire some pretty strong ideas about health, hygiene and food. This is the sign of the vegetarian.

If the Virgo-chaser has not already been put off, let me add that this man is a nagger. Still interested? Well then she probably deserves him. With this much stubbornness in her nature she possibly belongs to the sign of Taurus, and if anyone can handle him then she can.

111

VIRGO August 24 – September 23

HOW TO CATCH AND KEEP YOUR VIRGO WOMAN

Flighty or irresponsible males should be wary of this female, for Virgoans are all common sense and not easily persuaded to a light-hearted fantasy trip. She has the annoying habit of always expecting others to live up to the standards she imposes, and if they fall short of her expectations, they are met with little mercy. She has a natural talent for seeking out weaknesses, and her critical eye means that she can undermine the strongest of men.

Financial and emotional security are equally important to the Virgoan female. She is also a perfectionist. So whoever wins her heart indeed has triumphed. She does not like hairy or unkempt men; she usually has a positive obsession about cleanliness and maybe some strange ideas on health and hygiene. She will be attracted to any man who vibrates vitality and good health, who has a clever head for monetary affairs and is loyal. A paragon of virtue, in fact. She is not impressed by ostentatiousness in any shape or form and suitors buying her presents should make sure these are simple and practical.

A Virgoan woman is highly intelligent and extremely active. Don't expect her to be content and happy living in a purely domestic environment. She needs to go out into the world and exercise her own individuality. Neither is she the maternal type; although children will always be looked after, their every need catered to, this will be tackled with a certain amount of detachment. Some accuse her of frigidity, for she displays her love in her own way. And when she worries and fusses over the smallest detail, she is, in fact, showing how much she cares. It is quite clear then that only knights in shining armour need apply.

HIS IDEAL PARTNER

The best way to sum up this character's ideal partner is to say that she must be perfection personified. Forming any kind of relationship can be, in a word, difficult. Usually his best bets are found under the signs of Capricorn and Taurus, though a coarse Capricorn or a tawdry Taurean doesn't have a snowball's chance in hell with him. But on the surface, these two signs

112

share his common-sense attitude to money, thus eliminating one constant source of friction. Neither the Goat nor the Bull are given to flights of fancy; they keep their hooves firmly on the ground and this is all-important to the Virgin. He doesn't mind the odd fairytale romance, but there's no point in admirers expecting him to believe in castles in the air.

Mr Virgo is not the most promiscuous of characters. He doesn't bed-hop simply for the sake of gratifying his needs. I'm not saying he is a prude; but if you held a sex orgy purely for Virgoans you'd spend a quiet evening on your own. His ideal partner is kind and understanding, and will not decide overly quickly that he is cold and sexless. For although sex isn't at the top of his list of priorities, you will find it about one-third of the way down. He finds it difficult to express his love verbally, but his thoughts and actions, presence of mind in a crisis and his Florence Nightingale attitude when a loved one is ill make up for this.

Furthermore, his ideal mate will fuss over his health. Virgoans are notorious hypochondriacs and a medicine-chest full of patent pills and potions will set his mind at rest. She must learn how to treat a common cold like an advanced stage of malaria, and a simple sprained ankle as a multiple fracture.

Career-wise, his perfect mate will give him a gentle nudge occasionally – and *gentle* is emphasized: a hearty kick in the seat of his pants will only lead to rebellion. He knows where he is going but he sometimes needs someone else to pay his fare and put him on the right train.

Virgoans loathe dirt of any description. In fact, they have a deep-seated abhorrence of it. Any female with dirty fingernails or who doesn't smell one hundred per cent clean had better look somwhere else for a mate or stand downwind. This man's home will need to be spick and span, clean and germ-free. He may forgive the former but never the latter. His woman will also be expected to be faithful to the letter. He is no Don Juan and a *femme fatale* leaves him quite unmoved. Insincere, pleasure-seeking or loot-hunting females had better forget him.

To get through to this self-styled god of gods, this angel in angel's clothing, this clean, clinical, sometimes antiseptic creature, you'll need to be yourself, for better or worse. He may find it difficult to accept the worst part but he will certainly appreciate any female being totally honest with him. And when his ideal mate moves into his perfect life, shares his perfect house, she had better remember to take her toothpaste and a bar of soap.

HER IDEAL PARTNER

Like her male counterpart, the Virgo lady is discriminating. Not surprisingly, then, it's difficult for her to find true happiness. However, when it does come, it's likely to be in the shape of a Taurean or a Capricorn. She likes her ideal man to be practical, with strength of character. Males born under any of these signs will fit in with this, so long as they are typical. Even then, the gross type of Taurean is not her cup of tea, nor the mumbling Capricornian, who'll only send her running for a phrase book on common slang.

The Taurean is, of course, more highly sexed than she is, but he should be able to knock down her inhibitions and awaken her dormant sexuality. She may not like it, but she recognizes the fact that she needs a man who will tell her when to shut up. Sensitive, emotional or artistic types should give this lady a wide berth. Her level-headed attitudes to life and her ability to grind such characters into the dust with her nagging could destroy them. Her ideal man will not be afraid to stand up to her and put her firmly in her place, when the need arises. At the same time, she has the strength of will to carry him through a rough patch.

She's not attracted to the Don Juans of the world and pursuers with a smarmy tongue had better leave it at home; it's not needed with this lady. She rarely mistakes gaiety or fun for anything but irresponsibility.

Apart from this, the Virgoan has a very low opinion of the opposite sex. She finds it difficult to believe that anybody could be stronger or more practical than she. So you can see it's going to take quite a character to show her the error of her ways. Lastly, once happily mated the finer side of her character emerges, you'll be glad to hear. Eventually her husband may even get used to following her around the house with a vacuum cleaner. Hopefully anyway.

SEXUALLY (MALE)

Friendship nearly always comes first with this individual. Not the back-slapping "Hail, fellow, well met" kind of friendship but a slow growth that has to be nurtured. Give it constant attention as you would a potted plant, and it will reward you with beauty all of its own. This is what Virgo love is like. And he's prepared to wait a long time for anything he considers worth having. Self-sacrifice comes naturally to him. Whirlwind romances are just not on. The opposite sex should never expect to be swept off their feet and dragged by their hair to the nearest registry office.

Mind you, his willingness to wait can have ulterior motives. The Virgo man has an active mind and a keen intelligence and, rather like the Geminian, enjoys teasing himself, almost to the point of masochism. Therefore, the more he wants a female, the more he decides to put off the inevitable. He is capable of building the wildest dreams around the woman of his choice, and, of course, this sometimes leads to disillusion when things don't turn out as he hoped. But if all is well in his dream world, a swift romance will follow.

And when he meets the right girl, she will have to be on her guard, for her imagined perfection could make him feel inferior. He is quite capable of believing that he's not worthy of such a lover, become slavelike in her presence and take up a position of doormat.

The Virgoan's highly critical attitude could be the biggest drawback in his love life. It wouldn't be so bad if he could sometimes keep his opinions to himself, but, regrettably, he finds this impossible. His thoughts on her inadequacies are aired in a sarcastic and blunt manner. And she doesn't have to commit an enormous *faux pas* for this to happen. The least little thing can set him off. She may be wearing her sexiest outfit, be spotlessly clean, reeking of French perfume and making considerable progress with him, then all of a sudden she sneezes. When this happens, there are no ifs or buts, it's the end.

That every Virgoan male follows the Virgin rule is a complete fallacy, but because of his active mind and his inability to find the ideal mate, he tends to seek fulfilment in other directions, displaying a seeming lack of interest in things sexual. That is until he finds himself in the presence of someone who looks as if she just might be the one. If he is lucky enough to meet a partner who can constantly surprise him without appearing to be insatiable, he might just be able to increase his liking for the carnal side of life. In order for this to happen, she will need to play on his love of anticipation, fantasy and possibly masochism.

Ladies who have set their heart on a Virgoan man should be warned that there is no point in flaunting sex at him at the first meeting. They must endeavour to establish some kind of mental rapport. The physical conversations come later. If he shows a total lack of response, there's little a woman can do about it except look around for a more receptive target.

SEXUALLY (FEMALE)

The Virgoan woman invariably waits for her man to approach her. And then if she does invite him in for a nightcap, that's exactly what she means. One drink and he'll be on his way, without even a kiss on the porch – not unless they have been out before.

She likes to be given time to weigh up her man and to find out what it is that makes him tick. And woe betide him if he doesn't live up to her ideals. She is not attracted easily and she takes her sex life seriously; when she can fit it in, that is. A couple of weeks with a healthy sex maniac, regardless of compatibility outside the bedroom, might do wonders for this girl and make her realize exactly what she has been missing. The only drawback to this is that, once she has been awakened in this direction, she will set all her standards by the demon lover who actually turned her on. And finding another lover who can measure up will give her more cause for concern. The fact that Miss Virgo can go without sex for a considerable length of time is in itself a form of masochism, which could be one of her kinks, albeit subconsciously. The fact that she professes to have to know the person better is also a sign that she likes to tease herself.

She does, however, need a patient lover; it's no use any man throwing her over his shoulder and heading for the nearest bed. She will wriggle free before he has had a chance to pull back the covers. But once they do get to know each other, her puritanical image flies out of the window and a passionate animal emerges instead. Mind you, when this occurs, he'd better keep it to himself, for she would rather forget it. However, if you've known your Virgoan for some time and feel you know her well, it's probably permissible to tease her about this side of her character; for the most part she will take it in good humour, if you have chosen your moment carefully.

HOW TO END THE AFFAIR

Since you are reading this section, presumably your Virgoan hasn't turned out to be as perfect as he or she thought. Well, let's look at the bright side; it doesn't take much to get rid of this character, for Virgoans have a clear picture of everyone they are involved with, and that includes a mate. All one need do is discover what the image held of you is, and then go completely the other way, destroying any preconceived ideas. A disillusioned Virgoan can break the three-minute mile when it comes to making an exit.

Good with money, are you? Well, don't be: become a spendthrift. Chuck it about, especially if the money happens to come from your Virgoan. Spend, spend, spend. Sexually discriminating, are you? How wrong can you be. Treat your Virgoan to some of your past escapades. Fidelity? What's that? You do what you do, when you want to and where. Phrases like this will soon shift the unwanted mate.

There are other obvious ways. Forget to bath for at least a week. Wear the same clothes every day. Better still, contract a disease. Any one. The more contagious the better, preferably sexual. Lose your toothbrush and forget to buy another; halitosis is a real Virgo-beater.

It is better to make a clean (as in snap) break with the Virgoan. This type won't bother to pester you or your relatives once the exit has been made. Now you have fallen from your pedestal, you are yesterday's news so far as he or she is concerned. There's a chance the actor or actress within will really triumph – who knows, you may even win an Academy award – while you are relieving yourself of this tiresome mate.

ATTRACTING THE SUN SIGNS

VIRGO WOMAN WITH VIRGO MAN

Well, here he is, your Mr Perfect. Careful, correct, pertinacious, he notices all those tiny details you take so much pride in – how your white suit never wrinkles and your manicure is perfection itself. You in turn will marvel at the fact that his white denims always appear absolutely spotless and at how marvellously organized his apartment is. However, with all this mutual admiration going on about a side of life some people would consider not so important, you may never get around to anything deeply serious. Things could start to get a little sticky when he does actually find something wrong with you. A Virgo woman is not used to being talked to like that. Despite all this, there's no doubt you two do have a lot in common and if you can keep a sense of proportion in your relationship and worry about the more important things, then there's a good chance of it working out, especially on a business or friendship basis.

VIRGO WOMAN WITH LIBRA MAN

He's enchanting, isn't he? Marvellously considerate, totally romantic and really knows how to treat a woman. The Libran man's passions are as emotional as they are physical. She'll need to watch her sharp tongue, and her tendency to nag about his easy-going attitude to life won't go down well. If she doesn't want to lose this lamb of love, she should shake him a perfect Martini and relax. It's not impossible to imagine this relationship existing; for how long, though, is the burning question. She won't appreciate the lazy side of him. The Libra man likes to spend his money on things that the Virgo woman considers unnecessary, such as fun or enjoyment. He in turn won't understand why the ashtrays have to be emptied every time they are used, and if she has straightened that picture once, she must have straightened it a dozen times in the space of one day. If they are typical of their signs, this is an extremely unlikely union.

VIRGO WOMAN WITH SCORPIO MAN

If this relationship is based on sexual attraction, then it may just work, so long as these two critics of the zodiac both leave their sharp minds outside the bedroom door. Heaven help the pair of them if they should allow them to enter. You'll be fascinated by her intellect; and what he calls her "mystery", others describe as aloofness. He will want to know everything about her but, if she is wise, she will keep some information back. He must be on his guard not to scare her to death with his passion; she is not used to it and has little idea what to do with it. In general this is a great business partnership but not really a viable personal one.

VIRGO WOMAN WITH SAGITTARIUS MAN

The Sagittarian man usually wants a friend as well as a lover, and that's OK by her. But he will want someone he can take to the Andes or Outer Mongolia on the spur of the moment, and this she may not appreciate, for the Virgoan woman needs to plan and organize. Such spontaneity is likely to throw her totally. Furthermore, his lack of concern with detail and his constant urge to move on doesn't bode very well for the Virgoan. To her, detail is of the utmost importance; it's not worth doing anything unless one does it well. Conversely, the Sagittarian believes in having a go at everything and doesn't expect to do anything in any great depth. Not a satisfactory relationship.

VIRGO WOMAN WITH CAPRICORN MAN

This is one of the zodiac compatibles, and the chances of them living happily ever after are very strong. She'll love his cautious practical side, encourage his ambitions and respect his financial ability. He'll remember that anniversary of their meeting and bring her sensible presents; she can feel free to ring him up about tips on the Stock Exchange or investments. She could even become quite romantic – as much as she is able to, anyway. She may even serve him freshly squeezed orange juice

119

in a silver goblet every morning. Totally out of character, but she will love the way that he can make her do things she had never thought of before. An excellent union.

VIRGO WOMAN WITH AQUARIUS MAN

It's difficult to imagine these two together in the first place. Eccentric, chaotic, disorganized as he is, Mr Aquarius may bring too much confusion to the relationship for her Virgoan system to bear. She could try offering him practical suggestions in order to make his schemes for advancement at work into realities, but will he listen? It's doubtful. He needs his freedom to come and go. She'll have to accept the fact that this is Mr Surprise. She must try never to pin him down or ask where he's been all day; if she does, it will be the end. An unlikely relationship.

VIRGO WOMAN WITH PISCES MAN

This man's an absolute delight, although not necessarily with her, for after all he is her opposite sign. She must make sure that she never lends him her American Express card for he will tend to go on spending binges whenever depression hits him, which can be every other day. Self-indulgent as he may be, he is invariably generous, especially with her, both in and out of the bedroom. But she'll never understand his romantic instincts, his sentimentality and his need for fantasy. She may even resort to patronizing him, which would be the worst possible thing to do. If she can't accept this gentle soul as he is, better to leave him alone. A good business relationship.

VIRGO WOMAN WITH ARIES MAN

Apart from being extremely dictatorial and bossy, the Aries man is impulsive and fiery; he is also invariably late and impossibly impetuous. If you stay with him at a hotel and ring down for room service, he'll let the man in while he is only wearing his socks. This may shock her rigid, though he will no doubt find it fairly amusing. Senses of humour vary quite considerably. He has a penchant for sick jokes and frequently lets rip with rough language, but he'll get little reaction from her, apart from a slight blush. She likes to fuss constantly over her man, and this will only irritate him. After the first sexual encounter, it may be painfully obvious to both that they are poles apart, and ideally that's the way they should stay.

VIRGO WOMAN WITH TAURUS MAN

A highly successful relationship. He's not everybody's cup of tea, but he certainly is hers. She will ably and willingly take care of his plants and aquarium. Both parties prefer to spend the lunch hour picnicking in the park or making a deposit in a joint savings account. She will control her fits of snappish criticism if she wants to keep him and he'll try hard to control opinionated behaviour, even though he knows he's always right. An excellent partnership.

VIRGO WOMAN WITH GEMINI MAN

He enjoys and respects her sense of humour, which can range from the witty to the sarcastic – but he's not that sensitive. She, on the other hand, will have a tough time keeping up with his erratic lifestyle. Although Mercury rules both, she may be too orderly to cope with his constant changes of direction. There are many differences between them, though both are intellectuals and may have so much to discuss and analyse that they won't notice the basic emotional differences between them. A good friendship.

VIRGO WOMAN WITH CANCER MAN

At first sight his home looks as though it's out of Homes and Gardens or the Ideal Home Exhibition: the worktops are immaculate, ashtrays emptied and the table positively gleaming – but his cupboards, dresser drawers and hidden places will be in complete chaos, with dust and dirt lurking in every corner.

121

Mind you, she has a penchant for tidying and, no doubt, will offer to straighten out his sloppy living arrangements, before they even begin to get to know each other. This won't be appreciated. He is quite content with his overloaded nest, and won't take kindly to having it rearranged. He is also a water sign, highly emotional and extremely sentimental; just the sort of softy basically she should avoid. She'll have to soften up a good deal if this partnership is to stand a chance.

VIRGO WOMAN WITH LEO MAN

Initially, all will go well. He'll respect her for not throwing her adoration at his feet, and she will love his humour, success and immaculate wardrobe. What she must try to do is think of him as King of the Jungle – and never mistake him for a tame pussycat. A typical Leo temper smoulders underneath all that cool, ready to erupt at any given moment, especially when confronted with a sharp tongue like the one she owns. He needs flattery and she'll give him criticism. She needs security, he gives her financial uncertainty. If this is one of those rare times when Miss Virgo is really prepared to give all, then it might just work, for she might be happy to allow him to be boss and try to adapt herself to his way of thinking, but it's a bit of a long shot.

HOW WELL DO YOU KNOW YOUR VIRGO WOMAN?

Answer honestly the questions below, scoring 3 for every Yes, 2 for Sometimes and 1 for No, then add up your total.

1. When eating out, if the cutlery were dirty, would she send it back immediately?
2. Does she need financial security?
3. Would she refuse to make love to you if you had just come in from mending the car, covered in grease?
4. Is she a nag?
5. Is she critical?
6. Does she think sexual standards are slipping?
7. Would she straighten a picture at a friend's house?
8. Is she as capable as you of admiring a pretty girl?
9. Is she a hypochondriac?
10. Does she have an overloaded medicine cabinet?
11. Does she infuriate you by constantly splitting hairs?
12. Is she a worrier?
13. Would she find difficulty in making love in a bed that hadn't been made?
14. Would you embarrass her if you expected her to make love on the floor?
15. Does she tend to think that most people are fools?
16. Does she have unusual allergies?
17. Does she refuse to make love to you if you haven't bathed?
18. Does she have a sharp tongue?
19. Is she well organized?
20. Is she interested in food from the health point of view?

(Answers)

1–30

There's no way you can have been with a true Virgoan woman for any length of time and know so little about her. You would obviously be a complete fool and then she wouldn't have put up with you anyway. One can only assume that either your relationship has been of short duration or she is not typical of her sign. If the latter is more likely, I suggest you read the chapters devoted to Sagittarius or Gemini. She is far more easygoing than a true Virgoan, so other influences must be at work.

31–50

You seem to be involved with a Virgoan with more of the sign's better characteristics and fewer of the more undesirable. You know her relatively well, a fact that she no doubt appreciates, for you seem to accept quite magnanimously the faults she does have. If you've only known her for a short while, then things look really promising.

51-60

Extremes are usually undesirable and, regrettably, you seem to be involved with a Virgoan lady with more than her fair share of this sign's faults. If you know her so well, there must be something masochistic about your own personality. Perhaps you too are a Virgoan. It takes a brave or perhaps foolhardy man to put up with this young lady.

HOW WELL DO YOU KNOW YOUR VIRGO MAN?

Answer honestly the questions below, scoring 3 for every Yes, 2 for Sometimes and 1 for No, then add up your total.

1. Does he feel he is unusually unlucky in his profession?
2. Is he strongly aware of physical fitness?
3. Would he rather be himself than like James Bond?
4. Does he think there's too much fuss made about sex?
5. Does he get upset over little things?
6. Is he careful with money?
7. Does he suffer from skin rashes?
8. Could he go without sex for a month?
9. Does he seem to lose interest in sex when your hair needs washing?
10. Would you be embarrassed to cry in his presence over a silly romantic film?
11. Does he need a close male friend?
12. If, due to the influence of alcohol, you got a little silly in front of a friend, would he go around apologizing?
13. Does he loathe so-called trendy clothes?

14. Would he cancel an evening with friends if, just before you were leaving, he started to develop cold symptoms?
15. Can you rely on his faithfulness?
16. Does he criticize more than he praises?
17. Do male homosexuals embarrass him?
18. Is he a little bit too clinical about sex?
19. Is he quick to see fault in other people?
20. Does he always bath before bed?

(Answers)

1–30

It's hard to imagine anybody being this unobservant, especially someone involved with a Virgoan. It is possible, of course, that he is not typical and that other influences are at work. If you are having trouble understanding him, then I suggest you read under one of the water signs such as Pisces, Scorpio or Cancer.

31–50

You seem to be tied up with one of the nicer types of Virgoans, and you appear to have a pretty good understanding with him. If you are not in a steady relationship, it's likely that you will be in the near future. He appreciates someone as realistic as you.

51–60

Of course you are sure he's faithful to you – who else would put up with him? Probably no one. You seem to be unfortunate enough to have somehow got yourself tied up with one of the nastier Virgoan types. And even though you may recognize it, for some reason you stick around. Are you sure you know what you are doing? You've only got one life – are you sure you want to be this unhappy?

Libra (the Scales)
Sign of the Artist or Poet

September 24 – October 23

The second Air sign: Charming, kind, easygoing, diplomatic
Ruler: Venus
Colour: Indigo blue
Career: Diplomat, connoisseur, beauty specialist, hairdresser, valuer, social worker
Famous Librans: Julie Andrews, Brigitte Bardot, Truman Capote, Johnny Carson, Jimmy Carter, Montgomery Clift, F. Scott Fitzgerald, Gandhi, George Gershwin, Buster Keaton, John Lennon, Franz Liszt, Groucho Marx, Pierre Trudeau, Oscar Wilde

---

LIBRA MAN

The Libran male is intelligent and capable of balanced judgement. But all Librans are inclined towards indecision, being too easily influenced by the opinions of other people. However, at least for the most part their thinking is along cheerful, optimistic and compromising lines. There's a natural desire to be diplomatic and co-operative, for this is the sign of partnership, and because Librans will do anything for peace and harmony, they are often misunderstood, criticized or called cowardly.

127

What other types fail to realize is that the Libran is completely unsettled in any environment of discord or conflict. He is idealistic, a perfectionist at heart, possessing an excellent evaluation of harmony, art, beauty and form. He has considerable charm and powers of persuasion, so much so that he can convince anyone that violets are daffodils.

One of the strongest characteristics associated with this sign is his keen sense of justice. He will fight for the underdog with a ferocity that will bely the rather lazy side to his character. He cannot bear to think that one person is taking advantage of another. This type of mind is also somewhat naïve, but when he discovers he has been taken for a ride, he'll never actually come to blows, for physical violence is abhorrent to him. His love of beauty reveals itself in his taste for the arts, his attractive surroundings and, most of all, his love of women. His diplomacy and charm will put any politician in the shade, but ask him to make a snap decision on any subject or issue and he'll be stumped. It will take him at least a week to decide whether or not a blue tie goes with a black suit; and when he has eventually decided that it doesn't, he'll probably change his mind, wear a black tie with a blue suit!

Even the strongest member of this sign suffers from indecisiveness. He will often waver between one side and the other of a question, his mental scales weighing up the pros and cons. He is also a social butterfly. It's hard for him to lead a secluded or reclusive life. A Libran without people is as much good as a car without fuel. He enjoys social intercourse and all that goes with it. The ideal evening for him will be good food and drink (and lots of it) with his closest friends (lots of them). The problem is that he never knows when to stop, for when it comes to the social round, he has incredible stamina, wearing his loved ones down to burnt shells of their former selves.

Observing a Libran in this context, some people find it difficult to understand how he ever earned the title "lazy". But watch him during one of his quiet times and it will be little wonder. He has the capacity to work like a neurotic bumblebee, yet when all the honey is in the hive, he will sink slowly but surely into an utterly apathetic phase. Trying to shift him at this time is like trying to push over the Empire State building with bare hands. He will be immovable and able to come up with a myriad reasons just why he should rest and take things easy.

This character's susceptibility to the moods of his partner is reflected in his everyday behaviour. When his personal life is running smoothly, he will be the life and soul of any gathering. But when his wings are clipped, he is a sorry sight. He is quite capable of walking out of crowded restaurants and theatres. He won't be lost for good, but he will be located on the pavement breathing great gulps of fresh air. Humanity *en masse* does not please him greatly and he may suffer from mild claustrophobia. While he enjoys socializing, he doesn't like to feel encumbered.

Remember, love is of paramount importance to him, and even in old age he rarely loses interest in his mate. A Libran in love attempts to achieve something of his ideal, and although he may recognize even the smallest failing in his mate, he will not argue over it for fear of disturbing the balance.

LIBRA WOMAN

The Libran female is sympathetic, kind and affectionate. She is considerate of other people's feelings and, being peace-loving, tries to live in harmony with her fellow humans.

Social relationships are important to her, but above all she needs a mate for true fulfilment and happiness. If one marriage doesn't work out, she'll be swift to enter into another. But even when single, she is not without an alter ego. She is very dependent on the approval of other people and likes someone around who appreciates everything she says and does. This is a beauty-loving and artistic type. Her sense of proportion, line and colour are superb. She is very particular in her mode of dress, likes slinky silks, smooth satins and delicate lace and will always smell like a freshly opened bottle of the most expensive Parisian perfume. She also values music and other cultured entertainments. Being fastidious, she dislikes messy or dirty work. She is very courteous and refined. Good manners are important to her. She exhibits them herself and expects them from other people. She loves ritual when it is tastefully done, but is repelled by a coarseness or vulgarity. If forced to live in uncongenial environments, she retires into her shell.

This woman shares many of the male Libran's characteristics. Her logic and powers of debate sometimes make other people feel a little under-educated. She will enter a debate at the drop of the smallest topic but when a fellow debater becomes angry, coarse or aggressive, she will be off.

The Libran's frank and open admiration for the opposite sex may make members of her own sex a little green-eyed on occasions, but in general leads to popularity. She makes an excellent wife and lover and revolves her entire life around her loved ones. Those girls born under this sign learn early in life that self-sufficiency just isn't for them; only with one man can she find true expression, even though his identity may change with alarming regularity.

The Libran woman is all-female, and this leads men to believe that she needs protection – an image she will try hard to perpetuate. She is not at all interested in burning her bra or learning to drive a ten-ton truck, yet in moments of emergency she can fill a man's trousers admirably. But in general, she learnt a long time ago that it is far easier to get her own way through feminine wiles and that a bat of an eyelid or a wide-eyed look can go much further than a gruff voice or belligerent attitude.

When she has a professional life, she is usually attracted to the trades which allow her to express her love of beauty. You won't often find a child of Venus working in the butcher's or the hardware store. She is more likely to be connected with modelling or design.

Her impeccable taste will be reflected in her surroundings. However humble her apartment, it will be attractively decorated. She can turn the ugliest of rooms into a sheer delight. Not for her cold linoleum or ancient curtains. Living in squalor unbalances her scales and can make her mentally and physically ill.

Lastly, the typical Libran girl has no wish to be a millstone around her partner's neck. She will never drag him down into the mire and will always be around when needed. He will never complain that she doesn't show her affection for him, for she is as loving as a dependent bunny rabbit. She has no greater wish than to share her mate's burrow.

THE HYDE SIDE

Weaker Librans are shallow and flirtatious, indecisive, too

easy-going, untidy, frivolous and will sit for days on a fence, rather than make a decision. These characters are far too obliging for their own good and find it almost impossible to say "NO". Not surprisingly, they tend to attract complications. They cannot understand how they manage to go from one scrape to another, not realizing that it usually stems from mistaken kindness. A tendency for them to escape from things ugly and inharmonious can make life rather difficult, to say the least. One cannot realistically expect to live for ever amidst beauty and harmony. Not surprisingly then, as soon as life becomes the slightest bit unpleasant, these types are quite likely to leap from the vegetable patch in search of a new rose garden.

While the stronger type of Libran is sometimes guilty of indecision, these characters couldn't make a decision if their life depended upon it. The "umming and arrhing" are painful to observe. Give them three different ways in which to solve a problem and you reduce them to a gibbering heap. They will then try to convince you that they are in fact searching for perfection. Don't believe a word of it.

Weaker Librans also have deficient memories. Despite declarations to the contrary, it is virtually impossible for them to suffer from a broken heart for very long. You'll catch them rubbing a red eye for a couple of minutes – that is, until a new perfume or fresh pair of big shoulders come along, at which point they recover in record time. Add to this a tendency to live always in the present, caring little for what the future holds or what has hurt them in the past, and you can see why the Hyde side of Libra doesn't lead an easy life.

But it's rare to find a really bad Libran, for there is no real malice in these types. Label them "unfortunate" if you will, but in this particular instance the right mate could be of invaluable assistance. As with all other Sun signs, it is unusual for anyone to be all good or all bad, more likely a fair mixture of the two. But good or bad, one should never take Librans' attitude to love seriously until one has got to know them better. They love to play at being in love, and the rest of us must learn to differentiate between the game and the real thing – not easy.

HOW TO CATCH AND KEEP YOUR LIBRAN MAN

This man is the complete antithesis of a Virgoan male. The Libran is interested in females, fun and fashion, possibly in that order. There are several ways of attracting such a character. If you possess physical beauty, then you are halfway there, for he is rarely lured by anything else. But the object of his affections still has to display refined tastes in all directions. If this is impossible, then desperate members of the opposite sex can always appeal to his keen sense of justice; he is always willing to help the underdog, so any female chasing him can make him stop in his tracks for a moment by asking his advice about some problem she is experiencing. He will immediately don his shining armour, leap on to his white horse and attempt to solve all her difficulties.

It's pointless trying to be practical with the Libran, who lives and believes in a constant love story. This week it will be one member of the opposite sex, next week someone else; his charm makes it extremely difficult for women to deny him. Nevertheless, although it is safe to ride along with him on his sea of fantasy, for the sake of self-preservation it is also wise to keep something back.

As previously mentioned, appearances are extremely important to this male. He'll notice anything new, even down to a new shade of lipstick, and if he doesn't approve he won't hesitate to say so. But there are compensations. The Libran man is something of a dream lover, though he does of course have his drawbacks: indecision and the inability to say "No" to anything he decides is a just cause. The latter can result in him being constantly on call to those in trouble – who, infuriatingly, are usually attractive women, but this must be accepted for he abhors disharmony and discord. He will simply walk away and will be lost for ever. As far as his irritating inability to reach a decision is concerned, it is really a matter of getting to know your Libran, for in most instances he will be glad to have this task lifted from his shoulders. Provided that decision works out well, all will be sweetness and light; but when things go awry, he will unjustly accuse this female of making a mistake. Such a character is attracted to the physical perfection of Bo Derek, so the woman determined to attract a Libran man must make the best of the attributes nature has given her.

HOW TO CATCH AND KEEP YOUR LIBRA WOMAN

This is one of the most charming females under the zodiac, every inch female, right down to her toenails. The problem with her is her tendency to fall in love in record time. One man is favoured this week, someone else the week after. Each affair is intensely romantic and, while it lasts, her man is loved with all of her heart. Any male who attempts to keep a Libran female to himself is asking for trouble. She is a sociable animal, who adores the opposite sex and cannot devote herself completely to one man.

She is attracted to sophisticated people, so will be drawn to a man who is charming, well dressed and can converse on the arts. For while the Libran female is not necessarily an authority on the aesthetic side of life, she usually wishes to be and is ready to learn. Never try to hold a Libran female to her declarations of love; they must not be taken too seriously. She is completely devoid of jealousy, for she hates discord and tension. Should a man manage to make her jealous, then he has been truly accepted.

While not exactly clinging, the Libran female has an inborn need to revolve her entire existence around her man, and naturally she expects the same from him. It is therefore crucial that he always makes her feel she is the most important thing in his life and that without her he wold be absolutely lost. Because of her devotion, she is always trying to think of new ways to please and keep her man happy. But if this goes unnoticed, she will soon become disillusioned and begin to look for a more grateful and receptive audience.

Once she has committed herself to a man, he should make it a habit to notice anything new there may be about her, however small, for she'll be deeply hurt if her efforts go unrewarded. She is also a sucker for sentiment and makes much of a special anniversary and will find any excuse to give a small gift. This is another side of the character that the aspiring male will need to develop. If he can make their relationship as much of a love story as can be contrived, he will be sure to keep a strong hold on this woman's emotions.

HIS IDEAL PARTNER

Generally speaking, women born under the signs of Gemini or Aquarius have the best chance of bringing true happiness to this man. Mind you, catching him is one thing, getting him to march up the aisle is something else, for this requires a decision – something the Libran detests.

His ideal mate will be capable of joining in his active life outside the home, somebody who can socialize and mix with a variety of people. Wilting roses or shrinking violets had better stay put in the flowerbed. Furthermore, females with intense natures who love nothing better than a good fight had better leave this character be. Such passion will only upset his equilibrium and put his scales out of order, for he dislikes emotional outbursts.

His ideal partner will possess a similar disposition to his own. The Cancerian, for example, who takes every work or gesture seriously, would drive him up the wall. Mr Libra is strongly attracted to the opposite sex. Put him in a roomful of pretty women and note his reactions. Charm oozes from every pore in his body. He flits from one to another like a sex-starved butterfly, collecting fuel for his ego. He does appreciate that this is a two-way operation and he will give as much as he gets. The right woman for this man will be fortunate indeed. To be close to him is like having the sun in your pocket twenty-four hours a day and more.

His ideal mate will be expected to provide a beautiful home, but mustn't get upset or angry when he doesn't spend all his time there. She must be prepared to put on her make-up and go out at any given time, looking like a princess and behaving like a queen at the drop of a smile.

A Libran well matched is a happy and well balanced creature. (It's those scales again.) But he'll suffer considerably when involved with the wrong woman. Because of his tendency to play at being in love from a very early age, a subject of this sun sign is likely to be much married, unless common sense is brought to bear at some point. The lady who captures this man must be able to put up with his indecision and his carefree if meaningless flirting, but she will have discovered that it's worth it.

134

HER IDEAL PARTNER

As with her male counterpart, this lady's ideal man is likely to be found under the sign of Aquarius or Gemini. For men born under this sign tend to be intelligent and hate ugly scenes or shows of temperament just as much as she does. Any man who believes that a good row clears the air, or that the occasional left hook will keep his woman in place, is a definite non-starter. Neither is she generally attracted to the home-loving man. She has no wish to be a baby-machine or a dishwasher. One child, two at the most, will be enough for her to cope with. Her maternal instincts could never be compared with the old woman who lived in a shoe. Her ideal mate will never take her for granted and will never allow her to forget her femininity. This isn't much to ask when you consider just how much he is prepared to give her in return.

She is clear-minded and will always listen to her man's side of the question. Miss Libra is always six of one and half a dozen of the other. There's a good reason for this. This way she can always avoid making decisions on the wrong judgement. She is usually very popular with both sexes, due to her charm and diplomacy, and this characteristic must never be squashed (in general, Scorpions or Taureans tend to be the ones to do this).

It's a case of "little things mean a lot" to this girl. It's perfectly all right for her man to be out of work for a week here and there, for she will rally around and keep the home fires burning, but he had better never forget to notice her new dress or hairstyle, unless he wants a weeping willow on his hands. Illogical? Maybe. But that is how she is. Any man who can't see and accept this side of her character is certainly not her ideal mate.

SEXUALLY (MALE)

Any female will need her wits about her when entering the sexual phase of a relationship with a Libran man. He knows exactly the right things to say at the right times. He can sweep her off her feet with his verbal expertise and before she knows where she is she will be chuckling by his side on the mattress. All good intentions and New Year resolutions not to give in will crumble in the face of his smooth and winning ways.

One thing to bear in mind is that Mr Libra never goes out looking for sex; he's on the look-out for Romance with a capital R. It doesn't take much for a woman to be kidded into believing that this is the first time he's ever felt so strongly. But it will be up to her to keep the romance burning brightly, for once the flames start to flicker . . . it's bye-bye time! The Libran man will spend hours telling his woman that she is the only girl in the world for him, that she is the most beautiful creature it has ever been his good fortune to be with, and from him the lines do not sound hackneyed. Always bear in mind, though, that he is far more stimulated by the romance of a situation than the basic sex act. It's of secondary importance to consummate an affair. When it comes to making love, the time will have to be right and the experience itself something beautiful. He should never be rushed. He likes to take his time, and impatient females should probably forget it.

Those who enjoy a sweet flight into fantasy, if only for a while, should form a queue on the right-hand side of the page. There's no need to worry about any deviations. He won't get out the thumb screws or the iron manacles from his closet: he doesn't go in for sadism or masochism. He is romantic through and through.

One more thing: any woman wishing to keep her Libran happy will have to subscribe to the old idea of the man as the leader. An emancipated woman is not in the least bit attractive to him. If she has burnt her bra, she may also have burnt her bridges so far as he is concerned.

SEXUALLY (FEMALE)

The Libran female is in love with the entire male population. When she swears undying devotion at the drop of a proverbial hat the opposite sex shouldn't panic, just relax and enjoy the attention they are getting while it lasts. As soon as they have fallen under her spell, she will be looking for another mountain to conquer.

She must be approached and handled in the correct way. She likes to feel she is the most desirable woman around and the relationship must be maintained on a romantic level. She gets a kick out of being told of her attributes; you just can't lay it on thickly enough. But she is a woman who puts herself into problematic situations through her inability to say no.

Basically she is against any kind of deviation, but if it turns her man on, she will be only too happy to oblige, though later on neurosis and resentment may set in. She prefers one partner at a time, and for each relationship to be run along physically conventional lines. The Libran female is also proud of her sexuality. Some men may even call her a tease – the girl with the neck-line that little bit too low, or the one who shows a little bit too much thigh when she bends over to change the record. In consequence she is often mistaken for an easy lay: not true. She simply loves to show the world at large what she is. It gives her a feeling of power. Knowing that men are drooling over her gives her a buzz, and she naturally picks out her best features to make the most of them. A word of warning, though: just as this lady is not an easy lay, neither is she into sex in the back seat of the car. Any man with this particular penchant, had better find himself a co-operative female garage mechanic.

HOW TO END THE AFFAIR

Many Librans rightly believe that they are God's gift to the opposite sex, and this vanity makes it difficult to extricate oneself from a relationship with one of them. The best thing to remember is that if the tables were reversed she would go without giving you a second thought.

If you are female and attempting to offload a Libran man, then you can turn him off by going to bed in rollers and curlers and a mud pack all over your face. Or borrow Aunty's red flannel nightdress and bed socks if need be. Try doing your daily exercises in front of him while you are stark naked; he doesn't like to be confronted so basically with a human body. Drop a few four-letter words around. Meet him in over-crowded places. Anything which will belie your femininity will send him on his way. If you wish for a quick break, utilize all the above and then introduce him to a feminine friend. The rupture in your relationship will certainly be mutual.

Similar ploys can be used by the male attempting to lose a Libran woman. If spending the night with her, let her know that you haven't changed your socks for a week. Don't, in any

137

circumstance, brush your teeth before retiring, and forget to use your deodorant. Body odours and bad breath can be guaranteed to put her off. She may forgive you once; twice or three times? Not a chance. When you believe she is at last loosening her grip, forget to shave. Rub your bristly chin against her cheek a couple of times and you'll be out of the door so quickly she'll have to send your clothes on to you. If your Libran still won't let go – and this applies to both male and female – try getting a bit physical. I don't mean black her eye or scratch his eyes out. Just look as if you are going to. Not many Librans like to have claws shown to them. All this and your Libran is still around? Then you must be married already.

ATTRACTING THE SUN SIGNS

LIBRA WOMAN WITH LIBRA MAN

If both parties here are typical of their signs, an excellent relationship can result. Two Librans in harness make for a perfect combination. He will like the way she thinks, and she will appreciate the things he does. Naturally, both will cast a roving eye outside of their home on occasion. But each will understand why the other did, so – not to worry. Such an arrangement wouldn't suit everybody and the biggest draw-back to it could be that while he or she is indulging in a quick flirtation on the side, something more serious may develop. But it's a chance that this couple may just be prepared to take.

LIBRA WOMAN WITH SCORPIO MAN

Her beauty, honesty and sense of fair play are likely to appeal to his good judgement. But the inescapable truth is that he will dominate. "So what?" she might think for a while, for she will be provided with the security and safe haven that she needs. After a while, though, it may become something of a bore. Moreover, he is notoriously jealous and her roving ways won't suit him one little bit. Sexually, he's a good teacher and she's a willing pupil. In the short term, he will be supportive and sympathetic; in the long term she will begin to suspect she has

138

bitten off more than she can chew. Loathing any kind of confrontation, she will run when he wants all-out battle. Ideally, then, a brief sexual affair may be fun; anything else – nothing short of disastrous.

LIBRA WOMAN WITH SAGITTARIUS MAN

She will definitely be attracted to this exciting devil-may-care character and his exhilarating ways. But she may not be able or want to cope with his madcap life. He in turn is attracted to her social scene, but will have no deep desire to settle down. Jealousy is an alien emotion to her except in this particular instance; as she becomes more possessive, he will try to escape what he believes is bondage. While flirting to her is a game, she may find it difficult to deal with his continuing adventures. An ideal relationship if based on friendship.

LIBRA WOMAN WITH CAPRICORN MAN

This man can provide the stability and luxury that she desperately desires. There's a good chance of permanency here if she can stifle an inclination towards boredom. She also needs to remember that his views on sex tend to be much more liberal before marriage than after. She must ask herself whether she can really live without a few fireworks, and he must decide whether he needs the calm tone of his life disturbed in such a startling way. He may relax a little in her company but will always put his work first and her second, which will be a bitter pill for her to swallow. He will love the way she can wheedle her way around his boss, she'll love the way he can efficiently tackle her tax return. Is this really all life is about?

LIBRA WOMAN WITH AQUARIUS MAN

These two together are capable of a detachment like no other zodiac sign. Each will occasionally need to seek seclusion but will understand the other's need and won't question it. They both love peace, beauty, society and equilibrium. While this

139

can be a perfect partnership, the only danger to it is that, since they both need solitude, it will be all too easy for them to shut one another out completely, although in general this is a problem which could hardly be described as being insurmountable. It's a relationship which can work at all levels.

LIBRA WOMAN WITH PISCES MAN

There'll be a tremendous amount of affection and romance between these two, though it may not last over-long. He is sociable but chooses his friends painstakingly, whereas she can get along with practically anybody – something that he finds a little superficial. His ideal evening is dinner for two by candlelight, when she can be intimately totally his. Conversely, she prefers to spread her talent and wit as well as affection over a wider field, with the result that there may be many times when she will be wiping away his tears and feeling guilty. Conflict may wrench these two apart. Don't forget she possesses a keen sense of justice and will no doubt realize that what she is doing to the Fish can hardly be called just.

LIBRA WOMAN WITH ARIES MAN

She is well balanced – he's fiery and impetuous. She loves beauty, comfort and tranquillity. His passionate nature requires action. Her ruler is Venus and his is Mars, planets which respectively embody the zodiac's ideal female and male characteristics. In other words, each has what the other needs and wants. With his passion and her passionate response, these two could make sexual history, and this is the level where the relationship should remain. When it comes to anything else, he is an egoist who must always be put first; she believes in sharing and expects devotion in a totally different way. To him, music and candlelight are all right on special occasions, but otherwise he requires much more action. Not an impossible relationship but certainly not an easy one.

LIBRA WOMAN WITH TAURUS MAN

These two have certain things in common, both being fascinated by beauty (so he should appreciate her) and the people who create it. Unfortunately, this will not be enough for a solid relationship. In her anxiety to please this man, she could find herself overlooking his stubborn side and his possessiveness. Mind you, with him for a lover, she could experience initial happiness, for he is highly sexed. Later on she is sure to feel he should be a little more adventurous. If they are to survive, she'll need to lighten his earth-bound behaviour with her whimsical nature and she shouldn't be surprised or disturbed when he doesn't find her jokes funny. A tricky partnership.

LIBRA WOMAN WITH GEMINI MAN

This is a partnership of two Air signs, therefore one of the ideal ones under the zodiac. Her flights of fancy are great for both of them, but he is more light-hearted and more superficial. She has to recognize the fact that he is a tease and a flirt, while her flirtations are backed up by solid caring. His are merely for the fun of flirting. His moods go from high to low and she valiantly struggles on in the middle, attempting to keep a balance. She won't be able to, of course, but because these two are so well suited, it won't prevent her from trying. A good relationship.

LIBRA WOMAN WITH CANCER MAN

She loves her freedom and he's too wrapped up in her home and family interests to understand her social expansiveness. However if they do hit it off and if she can bear to have her wings clipped permanently then he'll provide the devotion that will keep her serene and secure. She may try, initially anyway, to be more domesticated; he in turn may try to be more gregarious and outgoing. But when two people go against their true characters, it can only be a matter of time before something snaps.

LIBRA WOMAN WITH LEO MAN

He demands flattery, attention and love, and so does she. He will adore having a beautiful feminine Libran as his mate, so long as people admire his taste in choosing her, rather than admiring her for choosing him. She may regard him as conceited, but if she wants to attract and keep him, she will have to put up with his endless preening. Whether this relationship works out or not depends on how deeply they love each other. If they can both learn to give attention rather than sit back and expect it, then they may have a chance.

LIBRA WOMAN WITH VIRGO MAN

He is sure to feel that she is incredible, gorgeous and unreachable. On the other hand, she will see him as steady and reliable. Problem: she absolutely hates to be criticized, and he must find fault. This union doesn't have a spectacular outlook – Librans loathe details; Virgoans thrive on perfection. She will need to develop a very tough shell if she is going to survive his sharp barbs and he will need to learn how to shrug his shoulders when she overlooks a minor point which to him is of paramount importance. In general, though, there's too wide a gap for anybody but Superman and Superwoman to fill.

HOW WELL DO YOU KNOW YOUR LIBRA WOMAN?

Answer honestly the questions below, scoring 3 for every Yes, 2 for Sometimes and 1 for No, then add up your total.

1. Do aggressive men repel her?
2. Would it be impossible for her to live without love?
3. Does music influence her mood?
4. Does she like to dance?
5. Does she have difficulty in saying no?
6. Does she enjoy being female?
7. Do silks and satins turn her on?
8. In her view, should sex always be romantic?
9. Does she think that all men should be gentlemen?
10. Is she indecisive?
11. Do quarrels unnerve her?
12. Are other women jealous of her?
13. Does she have trouble getting on with her own sex?
14. Does she always remember special anniversaries?
15. Would she like to be glamorous and famous?
16. Is she sensitive to her environment?
17. Does she think jealousy is a wasted emotion?
18. Does the thought of motherhood depress her?
19. Does she think sexual relationships are a waste of time?
20. Is she ruled by her heart rather than her head?

(Answers)

1–30

She's far too conservative, practical and realistic to be a true Libran. If you have known her for any length of time, you'd be wise to turn to the Earth chapters, such as Taurus, Virgo and Capricorn, as these influences are sure to be strong on her chart. If your relationship is only just beginning, then there's hope for your, though you appear to be totally on the wrong track when it comes to understanding her, but maybe this is a ploy on her part.

31–50

You are lucky enough to be involved with one of the nicer types of Libran. You've a prize there, but hang on to her. It's likely that you've known her some time, as you appear to understand her fairly well. If not, you are an absolute genius and on the right track if seeking a long-term relationship.

51-60

I'm afraid you appear to have found one of those frivolous Libran females, and you seem to be totally aware of this fact. You are really the sort of man who prefers a child bride, rather than a complete woman. Better check that she's not getting fed up with being patronized.

HOW WELL DO YOU KNOW YOUR LIBRA MAN?

Answer honestly the questions below, scoring 3 for every Yes, 2 for Sometimes and 1 for No, then add up your total.

1. Is he indecisive?
2. Has he difficulty in saying no?
3. Has he a good eye for colour?
4. Is he easily imposed upon?
5. Are there times while making love with him when you want to say, "Oh, come on, get on with it"?
6. Does he loathe sport?
7. Is he lazy?
8. Is he a "woman's man"?
9. Has he had a complicated love life?
10. Is he romantic?
11. Is he a terrible judge of character?
12. Does he care what people think of him?
13. Does he like to dance?
14. Is he a flirt?
15. Does he run away from an argument?
16. Does he have a sense of occasion?
17. Is he diplomatic?
18. Does he flirt with your girlfriends?
19. Does he like his food and drink?
20. Does he prefer to take the lead in sex?

(Answers)

1–30

Either you know very little about this character, and perhaps you've not been very long together, or he isn't typical to his sign, which is more likely to be the case. Try reading under one of the earth signs, such as Taurus, Virgo or Capricorn; there you may find your man and may actually begin to know him a little better. If he swears he is typical of his sign, then you are in trouble!

31–50

You are lucky enough to have got your claws into one of the nicer Librans. and you are the type of girl who seems to be able to appreciate this Mr Superman. If yours is a new relationship then it has a fair chance of lasting. If he's been in your life any length of time, then you must be one happy lady.

51–60

You seem to have here the kind of Libran man who has all this sign's faults as well as its virtues. but you seem able to cope with them. It's to be hoped that you are a practical lady. This character of yours appears to live in a perpetual world of bluebirds and rainbows. He is also extremely self-indulgent. You are clearly the type who likes to do a bit of mothering. But don't let him ever find out, or he'll be off.

Scorpio (the Scorpion)
Sign of the Researcher or Analyst

October 24 – November 22

The second Water sign: Magnetic, persevering, determined, perceptive, forceful
Ruler: Pluto
Colour: Burgundy
Career: Surgeon, soldier, detective, psychologist, undertaker, physicist, butcher, scientist, lawyer
Famous Scorpions: Richard Burton, Prince Charles, Charles de Gaulle, Indira Gandhi, Art Garfunkel, Billy Graham, Robert Kennedy, Marie Antoinette, Pablo Picasso, Leon Trotsky

---

SCORPIO MAN

The Scorpio male usually displays intensity of expression, of thinking and of feeling which springs from inner depths. They may be seen as strength of will, an undeniably magnetic quality, penetrating eyes, or the passion of power, of conviction. That purposefulness is not always evident, yet it is there – subtly concealed perhaps, rather like the Scorpion – a potency which is restrained until ready to strike. His emotional energy needs to be harnessed constructively. But when those deep passions of his erupt, it's enough to put Vesuvius to shame. There are times when he'll seem even stronger in his silence, for then he can be quite intimidating. Those around gingerly tiptoe

146

about, awaiting the inevitable explosion. For on these occasions he is not pleased – not pleased at all, and somebody is going to pay.

The Scorpion is renowned for those eyes, as well as for his critical faculties. Next time you meet a man who looks through you and says exactly what he thinks of your new outfit, don't dismiss him immediately; you may be passing up the opportunity to get to know one of the most fascinating of the male species.

Scorpio man has an extreme love of power. Nothing put on this little globe of ours cannot be conquered. He is ambitious, and will be completely ruthless on the way to the top. Will he reach the dizzy heights he sets for himself? You may as well ask will tomorrow follow today! Of course he will. Many a self-made man was born under this sign: Charles de Gaulle, Pablo Picasso, to name but two.

He cannot do things by halves and when in love, there's nothing he won't do to please his mate. She had better feel the same way. He will expect it from her. He has a keen affection for those he loves and likes. But he doesn't dole out that affection to just anybody. His loved ones can regard themselves as something rather special. Although he is quick to recognize that beneficial partnership, he won't jump in with his eyes closed. He will wait to see how things develop, unwilling to take any chances.

Whether loving or hating the Scorpion, people find themselves irresistibly drawn to his magnetic personality. He is difficult to overlook. Furthermore you'll be wasting your time if you try to hide your feelings for him. He can sense what other people feel from across the room. And if his opinion is unfavourable, he is likely to go out of his way to antagonize the offending person. He enjoys a good argument. While it is true that the Scorpion says exactly what he thinks, when it comes to his profound emotions, he has difficulty in expressing them. At times he is totally unsympathetic, but when someone is in trouble, he can be a tower of strength.

His small circle of intimates will probably date back to the time when he was climbing trees or fishing for tiddlers in the river, for he doesn't make friends that easily later in life. The Scorpion man suffers from jealousy, which he tries desperately to control, not always succesfully. He likes other people to know

147

of his successes. Status symbols are a must. Expensive gifts are showered on loved ones, lest they should ever forget that he has "made it". He craves respect and admiration, likes to be held in awe; let's face it, don't most of us feel a little uncomfortable in his company, with that eagle eye of his turned upon us? However, he is none too pleased when the same tactics are used on him. It's safe to say that he cannot take his own medicine and becomes extremely stubborn when criticized.

The Scorpion male keeps his lady love busy. It's highly unlikely that she'll have time to run a second relationship, not to mention the ugly scenes it would cause, should he ever find out. This is a time-consuming personality. He is bound to have his enemies; all Scorpions do. But anyone crossing this man is brave to the point of stupidity. He'll never forgive or forget. Those getting on his wrong side had better beware; mercy is not a word he normally uses or practises. Remember, he has that sting in his tail and when he uses it he doesn't mess around.

SCORPIO WOMAN

Naturally the female of the species shares many of the characteristics of the male. She too is cautious in giving friendship, but fiercely loyal once she has. In passion, forcefulness and intrigue, her dynamism knows no peer. The Scorpio vitality is at least partially a sexual energy that is channelled into every project she undertakes. She marches into battle bravely and is somewhat intolerant of weak humanity. Physically, she may not be the best looking female of the zodiac, but she is certainly the most magnetic. If you run into a pair of hypnotic eyes at a party, you can bet they belong to a Scorpion.

Being such a strong personality, the Scorpio woman doesn't find it easy to come by lasting personal relationships. She often finds herself saddled with weaker characters that she can wrap around her little finger – or any other finger if she wishes. If she does finally meet her match (you'll have a hard time getting her to admit that you are her equal), she becomes all jealousy and possession. Some members of the opposite sex find that this makes them feel important, while others would strap on their running spikes and zoom off in the opposite direction.

She isn't exactly the easiest person to live with. She tends to be critical and exacting. It is most difficult for her to make allowances for the weaknesses of others, and matters of principle are taken well out of proportion. But despite her strength of character, she is all woman, passionate, sensual, with a large capacity to indulge in and enjoy love. Anyone she really cares about will have felt her soft and more tender side, which is reserved exclusively for them. The rest of us come up against an aggressive, sharp-tongued shrew.

When she slips in motherhood, she becomes efficient and loving, tending to be too possessive and expecting too much from her offspring. Often she places before them almost impossible objectives. Nevertheless they will always sense her deep emotional love for them and they will always feel secure.

One of the most attractive things about her is that she can make her man feel that he is the only one in the universe, but he had better not dare cast an approving glance at any other woman while in her company, or his Scorpion mate will literally scratch his eyes out.

Despite her individualism, she likes nothing more than to see the one she loves get on in life. She is ambitious for him, using all her assets to push him forward to the heights where she knows he belongs. Any foolhardy person attempting to get in the way will soon feel the rough side of her tongue and will be nursing their bruises for weeks.

Scorpio woman has strong appetites. What she likes, she likes a lot of, and this includes sex. What she doesn't like, she won't have any truck with; and this includes people. Like her male counterpart she has a small and intimate circle of friends, and nothing is too much trouble for them. She is not gregarious, takes her time to forge true friendships, and does not have many acquaintances. She is an extremely exclusive female and needs an extremely exclusive type of mate. Her man must be unique.

THE HYDE SIDE

The lower type of Scorpio is sly, secretive and cunning, possessing diabolical and uncontrollable passions. When they feel they have been offended, they are underhanded and treacherous, lusting after revenge. They fly into a rage at the slightest provocation. Scorpions are the most vindictive enemies in the zodiac and can frequently blackmail people into doing their bidding because others are afraid of their fearsome personal vengence. Their armouries are stocked with ways to repay those who have trespassed against them, and they are very slow to forgive. They are intensely selfish and possessive. There is a gross sexual appetite as well as over-indulgence in food and drink, and once aroused, jealousy is all-consuming.

Add to this a brooding resentment, destructiveness, stubbornness, suspiciousness, capacity for being deliberately cruel and you have a rather unpleasant mixture. Instances which might create mere dislike in those born under different signs, create in these types violent anger and even hatred. The stronger Scorpio never forgets a wrong, real or imaginary. Furthermore they take great pleasure in uncovering the weakest aspects of others. This is where the sadistic, cruel streak is evident. Critical of others as they are, in later life it's quite likely that these characters will turn their sting inwardly, becoming extremely bitter and self-destructive, but not before they've tried to destroy those around. It's hard enough to like these types, let alone love them. Arguments and sarcasm are not characteristics which encourage affection or endearment, unless you happen to be Lucrezia Borgia.

The splendid Scorpion inclination to self-improvement present in the better subjects of this sign turns to avarice and greed in these more negative characters. They are covetous and envy everyone they meet. If they cannot be successful any other way, they may take up crime in order to get things they think they desperately need.

After this doom-laden prognosis, it is nice to bring in a little sunshine, for, as with every sun sign, no Scorpion is all bad or all good. Nevertheless, those around have their hands full.

HOW TO CATCH AND KEEP YOUR SCORPIO MAN

As has previously been mentioned, this is a sign that inspires either love or hate, but fortunately for Scorpions some of us will love them. One of the many reasons why the Scorpion is able to arouse so much passion in all of us is because he is such an overwhelming character. His dislikes and likes are keen and all-absorbing and anyone with a sense of freedom or justice cannot help but be offended by this.

Jealousy and possessiveness are an integral part of him and it's no good any woman aspiring to change him. If she tries persistently to do so, she will only drive him to his other love, namely the bottle. Ideally, the Scorpion should find himself a weaker mate, for he likes to control people and a stronger personality will clash violently with him. A hopeful female must take on the appearance of a helpless wench, which will arouse the protective instincts within him; she must be prepared to be guided by him in everything, and perhaps above all be wise enough to accept the fact that, if she is not careful, her own identity will be lost in close proximity to such a man. If she can put up with all this, then she will have found a devoted lover, who will never cease to show his gratitude in his own way and will be a strong rock to lean on.

Aggressive or assertive women should run as fast as their legs can carry them when approached by the Scorpio male, for they can only be letting themselves in for a lot of heartache.

HOW TO CATCH AND KEEP THE SCORPIO FEMALE

This is an extremely attractive lady, who draws men to her like pins to a magnet. She is passionate, sensual, magnetic.

There are, however, certain disadvantages that go along with the Scorpion woman: she is intensely possessive, jealous and has very strong likes and dislikes. And where these are concerned she can be immovable. When hurt, she is capable of bearing malice for an unbelievable length of time, and should a chance arrive for her to effect some kind of revenge, even if it be in a decade's time, then be certain that she will take it.

All Scorpio-chasers should be wary about frolicking with the feelings of a Scorpio. They will need to appear capable of an enduring and faithful love, for this female will not take a back seat and needs to play a prominent role in her man's life. She can be totally unreasonable at times, completely lacking in tolerance with people she cannot abide. The man in her life will need to accept that; she cannot be made to change; if he wishes to oppose her in any way he would be wise to wait until he has managed to arouse her passions and love; otherwise a very bitter quarrel will ensue which she will never forget. This woman's mate will have a lot to put up with but he can be certain that once he has won her heart, she will love him with every fibre of being and defend him against the world.

Anyone looking for a light-hearted interlude with her is likely to find himself fairly stung and will desperately regret the day he ever set eyes on her.

HIS IDEAL PARTNER

The Scorpion believes nothing is impossible. He knows exactly what he wants. Ladies who attract this character will have probably been checked out more efficiently than by the FBI. He doesn't date or become involved with just anybody. He senses a female's failings within the first half-hour; and if her score is nought with him, she can be quite certain that he won't be round again.

His ideal partner is likely to be born under the sign of Cancer or Pisces, which signs have the greatest chance of giving him true happiness. The Crab and the Fish possess a knack of controlling this fearsome character, for they are sensitive, emotional and sympathetic.

Mr Scorpio works hard all day and therefore he needs a calm and serene influence in his home. His ideal partner will put the dogs out in the yard and hide the children from view until he's had time to unwind. He is not the type to see the joke when he slips on the old roller-skate.

One of the main qualities his partner will need is satisfaction, with him and him alone. Sexually speaking, she will probably be too well looked after to need to look anywhere else. His ideal mate accepts his jealousy and knows that this green-eyed monster can be activated if she even speaks overlong to a local store-keeper: no point in protesting that she was only checking on the price of beef, he won't fall for that. It's very easy for him to imagine that she is being unfaithful. This sort of behaviour on his part would easily send a Gemini or Libran screaming out through the door. A Cancerian or Piscean, on the other hand, will just deal out an extra dose of love and calm his insecurities.

His ideal mate will understand that the Scorpion male must

be the breadwinner in his own household, and she must not mind too much dropping whatever job she might have. Members of the opposite sex who are militant feminists or career girls should stay well away. He would never be happy with the woman bringing home the wages and the competition in his domestic environment will only add to what he already has at the office.

His ideal mate will have an inexhaustible supply of love and infinite patience, and she will need to be highly sexed. (Anyone who is shaky in this direction had better get in some practice.) Total devotion is another prerequisite. Many of us will think this is a lot to ask. So far as this man is concerned, the opposite sex is either accepted or rejected. She has it or she doesn't. Strangely enough, Scorpion men frequently do find the kind of women that make them happy. Mind you, there is a slight possibility that his wife is too afraid to battle his authority and seek a divorce.

HER IDEAL PARTNER

No male should ever truly believe that he has made it with a Scorpion woman, not for a few years anyway. He should always bear in mind that she can be repulsed by him just as suddenly as she was attracted. This can be quite traumatic for the man who has fallen under her spell – just ask anyone who has been turned down at the eleventh hour by this female. It can take at least six months to become de-hypnotized. When that glassy look has finally left him, he will still be in the dark as to what caused the metamorphosis.

The answer is easy. It all stems from her keen love and hatred for her fellow man. She finds it totally impossible to be indifferent. And when the glitter has worn off the relationship and she gets down to the bare nitty-gritty and uncovers all sorts of idiosyncrasies she cannot accept, she will be off. She won't waste any time trying to regild their relationship.

Sexually, this female is stimulated by passion and emotion, and her ideal man will appreciate this. Happiness is easier for her to find with subjects born under the signs of Cancer and Pisces, who are able to understand the passionate and sometimes violent Scorpion. They realize that her sudden outbursts

153

are usually the result of her insecurity and will be able to reassure in the most convincing manner. The superficial Don Juan types that attract her fellow sun signs will hold little or no appeal for her. She possesses a strong desire to dominate all who enter her life, although at first her unsuspecting mate may not realize this and may go along believing she is a pushover. Yet there may come a day, once the confetti has been brushed from his hair and their lucky horseshoe removed from the car, when he receives a shock to his ideas. But after the battle is over, and he's licking his wounds, perhaps he should remember that he was warned.

No matter how close a man gets to his Scorpio lady, there's always a part of her that he will never be allowed to see. Her private thoughts and feelings will not be confided to anybody. This must be borne in mind before her mate is tempted to begin digging around her mental closet. She will appreciate the man who accepts the fact that he must stay on the other side of her "no trespassing" sign. There's no point in asking what it is she would like to keep hidden away. Only she knows that, and she isn't telling. This doesn't mean that her ideal mate will be allowed to have any secret skeletons. Far from it. She loves to hunt around and can be unreasonably suspicious. On her side of the dressing-table, the drawers will be bolted, but she will expect her mate to unlock his. Refusal will be taken as an admission that he has something to hide. Her ideal mate will hand over the key along with his heart and be happy that he has a mate for life.

If you want an easy time, better escape while you can, but deeper members of the opposite sex may appreciate the fact that she is one hundred per cent devoted, loving and (basically) on their side.

SEXUALLY (MALE)

Perhaps it would be wise to state straight away that members of the opposite sex need to be careful before they tangle with this hot-blooded creature, unless they have an A-plus in sex. He likes to know exactly where he stands in a relationship and he cannot be fooled. He will see through the virgin pretending to be the woman of the world or vice versa; such a ploy could be disastrous, not to mention extremely painful. He expects honesty. Those who attempt to tease or play with his affections will lose out, for he will simply walk out of their lives, never to return. Luckily for him, he has splendid intuitions, and can generally sense whether or not his intentions are welcome, so unnecessary problems are nearly always avoided. But once rebuffed, he doesn't come back for more.

As his approach to sex reflects his other excessive appetites, he is passionate, emotional and sometimes a violent lover. Ladies with masochistic tendencies will quickly discover this is just the sort of chap for them. But he will never involve his woman in anything he doesn't think she will enjoy. There's a slight sadistic streak in most Scorpions. His lady should note his reactions when she dons a leather skirt, and had better be careful where they are at the time, for he pays no attention to time, place or even children. He'll find some way to make love to her – but immediately. This can of course raise a few problems! And a few eyebrows. But it does introduce a certain amount of excitement which many members of the opposite sex may like. The relationship may be short-lived; it is even possible it will end up in gaol. But one thing is for certain; it will be an unforgettable experience.

This man is all male and knows how to show it. One thing that most women adore about the Scorpion male is that they don't have to spell out what they want or need from him. That penetrating gaze of his will have summed her up on the first meeting. He'll know exactly how to behave and what is expected, and what female can ask for more?

SEXUALLY (FEMALE)

No man in his right mind plays around with the affections of a female Scorpion, unless he is asbestos-clad and armour-plated. She can store viciousness and hatred for years, until an opportunity for revenge presents itself. Once her blue touchpaper has been lit, he had better stand well back – preferably on the other side of the world. If he can't run that fast, he could try mellowing her with a stiff drink; there is just a chance that he will dampen her fuse enough to stop it running its full course, but don't bank on it.

Her sexuality depends rather a lot on circumstances and age. For example, if she has had a few bitter experiences at the hands of other men, then her sting may have been turned in upon herself. She will have become neurotic, perhaps a heavy drinker. Ideally this type should be given a wide berth, unless a fiery male is in the mood to do a spot of rehabilitation.

If younger, and less experienced, she will simply be aware of her strong sensuality. And don't be surprised if she isn't a lily-white virgin; that's something she doesn't hang on to for over-long. Once affection has been given and reciprocated, it is difficult for her to practise restraint. She is not the sort to be satisfied holding hands in the back seat of the car or cinema. She wants the real thing, at a very early age. Nor is she the most subtle creature, either, when getting her satisfaction. If she is lucky enough to find the right man first time, one who can show her what love-making is all about, then her sexuality will be fully developed. Yes, this lady demands rather a high standard when it comes to making love. One can advise a Scorpio female to have a little patience with men who can't quite measure up to her standard, but she is unlikely to listen – unless there is a psychological reason for his problems. But then she will get immense pleasure in knocking down his mental barriers. Not for his sake, though, but for her own.

Being a sexy lady, she is willing to explore any avenue in the quest for gratification. In the right mood, she is quite happy to reverse roles. Give her a couple of drinks and the appropriate atmosphere and she will ravish her man as he's never been ravished before – no holds barred. On the other hand, if she has absolutely no intention of making love, she will soak up all the liquor any aspiring male can pour down her throat and then merrily wave goodbye, leaving him gibbering under the table. If she is not interested, she's not interested and you'd better believe it.

Although, sexually speaking, she is strong-charactered, she is also a bit of a romantic. She may be dying to consummate a relationship, may have been fantasizing about it for weeks, but fierce pride will stop her from making too obvious a move. Nevertheless, most men get the message loud and clear from those intense eyes.

She is a tough one to please, though, and while the effort is worth it, any sensible male who suspects that he can't live up to her expectations should make a quick exit.

HOW TO END THE AFFAIR

In a word – difficult; one could almost say impossible.

First, advice on how to dislodge the male of the species. If he is convinced that you are his soulmate, then you are in for a difficult time. Prepare yourself for fisticuffs and even a stay in hospital. You will have gathered that this is a procedure which needs caution and patience. Don't expect him to let you walk away with a smile and a hasty goodbye. You won't get any further than his outstretched arm, and that will probably have a fist attached to the end of it.

Although he is passionate and makes his mind up quickly, he will not actually make any drastic moves for some time. Therefore, try applying a little pressure, but go easy. If he has mentioned some kind of commitment like marriage, be one step ahead. Ask him when you can get the banns read. Stop him in front of furniture shops and coo over kitchenware. Take him with you to pick out the wedding dress. If he thinks you are desperate to surround yourself with the trappings of marriage, he will begin to have second thoughts. Whatever you do, don't let him find out that you are madly in love with someone else. This could be quite unpleasant – for you. Disillusion him slowly. If he still refuses to name the day, offer an ultimatum. You can be pretty sure that the relationship will die on its feet there and then. If you are naturally affectionate and lavish with hugs and kisses, put a blockade on them. Forget any verbal reassurances of love and make him feel insecure, without actually showing interest in another man. Be enigmatic about the whole thing.

Apply similar tactics to the female Scorpio. Never in any circumstances give her the slightest inkling that there is a rival in the background; not only would you receive a few scratch marks to ruin your good looks, but your intended would share in your misfortune. For when Scorpio ladies are unpleasant, they seethe with revenge and malice. A sure-fire winner when you are trying to loosen her grip is to deny her appetites, sexually in particular. Make excuses as to why you cannot possibly stay the night and make love. Two or three weeks of this behaviour and she will believe she is losing her touch. It won't be long before she is asking what is wrong, what happened to that sexy man who, at one time, could not leave her alone? Tell her you can't keep up with her between the sheets: it is exhausting you and sapping your vitality. She will soon be on the look-out for a more virile companion. She needs enthusiasm to keep her company in bed. No weaklings for this lady. Maybe your male ego can't take this kind of advice, but do you want to be rid of her or not?

HOW TO ATTRACT THE SUN SIGNS

SCORPIO WOMAN WITH SCORPIO MAN

An explosive combination. Both partners are excessively unsure of themselves, and therefore jealous. If they don't kick each other first, the intensity of the relationship – both intellectually and passionately – can be the most extraordinary experience they've ever known. It's satisfactory for a short sexual affair, but a lengthy relationship promises to be hard work, nerve-shattering and exhausting. Both are extremely critical and demanding, but aren't too happy to be on the receiving end of their own characteristics. It can't be long before they tear each other to shreds. Mentally and emotionally a possibility, certainly, and – who knows? – even physically.

SCORPIO WOMAN WITH SAGITTARIUS MAN

Initially she may find his innovation and his sillinesss very attractive. Conversely he will be fascinated by her depth of passion. However, their compatibility will grind to a resounding halt, since fire and water don't mix particularly well. He is blatant, sometimes undiplomatic; she is subtle. He is superficial, prefers to play the field where the opposite sex is concerned; she is deep and loyal. If both partners are typical to their sign, then the best advice one can give them here is to forget it. There's no way this will ever be more than a one-night fling.

SCORPIO WOMAN WITH CAPRICORN MAN

These are two extremely strong personalities, possibly the strongest under the zodiac, so this coupling could be akin to a clash of kings – Scorpio is forceful and powerful, Capricorn is tough and single-minded. Mind you, they are well mated on the sexual level and where strength of character is concerned. Both insist on loyalty. But both tend to demand the last word in everything. He'll expect a perfectly kept home, but will also expect to retain the right to stay away from it while he attempts to move up the ladder of success. She's all female and demands plenty of attention, and with this character she is just not going to get it. A possible business combination, but little else.

SCORPIO WOMAN WITH AQUARIUS MAN

Relationships are never wishy-washy for this woman, and the unpredictable Aquarian lover will drive the solid Scorpion into the funny farm. Certainly she will admire his humanitarian instincts, but she will wonder why they are always expressed outside of their home and relationship. His detachment and physical reserve will lead the passionate Scorpio woman to believe she is living either alone or in a monastery, neither of which would much suit her. The more she demands, the less he will give her. Too much of a compromise is needed for these two to make a lasting go of it.

SCORPIO WOMAN WITH PISCES MAN

When the Scorpio woman likes, she likes a lot, and this is a combination almost guaranteed to result in love. She can even adapt to the fact that when she attempts to get a decision out of the Fish, he sticks his head in the sand. But love for her will probably make him brave enough at least to make the gesture of a decision from time to time. Certain things must be understood, however. He always seems to be swimming upstream and down at the same time, whereas she always knows exactly where she is heading – not surprisingly she is likely to be the boss, and he won't mind at all. They are both very possessive, so if they decide to possess each other, they are likely to hang on in there for life. An excellent relationship.

SCORPIO WOMAN WITH ARIES MAN

Although these two can be compatible on a sexual level, in reality they are two dictators seeking to control each other. About the only way this duo can make the relationship work is if they can manage actually to enjoy the constant battling, to say nothing of the making up. But he's an egoist and a "me first" and he expects his woman to be content to play second fiddle to him. He's picked the wrong lady here. She plays first violin or she forgets the orchestra. Sexually excellent, but little else.

SCORPIO WOMAN WITH TAURUS MAN

Although these two are opposites, and things won't be easy, this partnership can succeed. For she admires his strength – and he loves her sensuality. He is a child of Venus and is romantic enough to cope with her watery emotions and bull-like enough to satisfy her sexual appetite. Mind you, he will sulk when she wants to take the reins and insists on making love her way. But his mood won't last past her transparent nightie. Both parties are capable of extreme loyalty, so with a certain amount of compromise this union can be made to work – but work is the operative word. An ideal business relationship.

SCORPIO WOMAN WITH GEMINI MAN

The Gemini man will initially be able to fool himself that he can keep up with the Scorpio woman, because he rarely looks deeper than the surface. She will admire his free spirit and lifestyle, but it will soon begin to make her possessive nature twitch. His superficiality and her sensitive depths bode ill for peach of mind. A love/hate relationship is likely to exist which may be quite exciting on occasions, but the Gemini may give up when he realizes that life is likely to be a constant battle with this female. The odds are that this union will be fun only for a while.

SCORPIO WOMAN WITH CANCER MAN

This is probably the most perfect match under the zodiac and it usually produces exceptional children. His is really the only sign that is absolutely right for her. They both love deeply, tenaciously too. She will hang on to him, even at emotional peril to herself, and he has the same single-minded devotion. Her Scorpio vitality will energize the gentle Cancerian, and his serene nature will help calm down her intensity. A love of the home and equal appetites in all give this relationship a great chance on any level.

SCORPIO WOMAN WITH LEO MAN

Not an advisable relationship if both partners are typical of their signs. In fact it's hard to imagine how they got together in the first place. He has to be the centre of attraction and she has a jealous nature which can't possibly permit this. Her temper is every bit as fierce as his; and his ego is likely to have an edge on hers. If he were the Scorpio and she the Leo, then they would both be sensible enough to pull out of the affair. But as things stand, it will probably be a fight to the death. Even in platonic friendship these two would have great difficulty getting along. An unwise relationship.

SCORPIO WOMAN WITH VIRGO MAN

This may be the first time the Virgo man has met anyone who can stand up to his critical tongue, and, what's more, can quickly silence it with her dazzling sarcasm. Neither party will wish to make their home a battlefield; therefore, provided they can keep the peace long enough, they'll discover that they can come to appreciate each other's qualities greatly. But she won't be able to resist the temptation to squash those wise-guy remarks. Emotionally they are poles apart. She's an ever-bubbling volcano waiting to explode, he constantly overrules his heart with his head. He may rightly point out that she is about to make a fool of herself, but she won't thank him for it. Ideally this relationship should stop at friendship.

161

SCORPIO WOMAN WITH LIBRA MAN

Believe it or not, this character can actually keep the Scorpion balance, provided she'll let him. But she will do the leading, and he'll need to do the peacemaking. His is a great need for affection, which will appeal to her strong passions, and his possessiveness may make her feel protected – well, for a while. So long as he doesn't mind being dominated every step of the way and in all spheres of life, then the relationship could work, but this is an unlikely match.

HOW WELL DO YOU KNOW YOUR SCORPIO WOMAN?

Answer honestly the questions below, scoring 3 for every Yes, 2 for Sometimes and 1 for No, then add up your total.

1. Does she know exactly what type of man she wants?
2. Does she suffer from jealousy?
3. Can she hold her liquor?
4. Do you think she is too critical?
5. Does she insist on her own way?
6. Is she a good judge of character?
7. Does she stick to the same friends?
8. Has she a sadistic streak?
9 Is she fiercely proud?
10. Is it hard for her to forget an injury?
11. Is she a demanding lover?
12. Is she ambitious for you?
13. Does she like a good mystery?
14. Does she have a sharp tongue?
15. Is she more lustful than loving?
16. Does she try to outshine other females in her circle?
17. Is she self-opinionated?
18. Is she impossible to shift once she has made up her mind about someone?
19. Do your friends feel uncomfortable in her presence?
20. Do you find yourself giving in to her when you feel perhaps you shouldn't?

(Answers)

1–30

This Scorpion female is a very positive woman, therefore on the surface quite easy to get to know. For you to be this far off-base, she is likely to be untypical to her sign. She is much more adaptable and easygoing than a true member of this sign would be. In an attempt to understand her, why not read under one of the Air signs, such as Libra or Gemini? These influences are sure to be strong on her chart.

31–50

You seem to have got yourself involved with one of the nicer Scorpions, and you understand her pretty well. You are either already married, about to be or are on course for a very lengthy and successful relationship. You are not a bit scared of your Scorpion woman, are you? You are clever enough to have discovered all those little ways you can please her and stimulate her devotion to you – clever boy.

51–60

Your Scorpio female may not be all bad, but she certainly has her fair share of the Scorpion faults. What's more, you appear to be fully aware of this. Maybe there's something masochistic in your make-up which appeals to the sadist in her. Or maybe you just haven't figured out a way of disposing of her yet – try reading the section entitled "How to End the Affair".

HOW WELL DO YOU KNOW YOUR SCORPIO MAN?

Answer honestly the questions below, scoring 3 for every Yes, 2 for Sometimes and 1 for No, then add up your total.

1. Is he possessive?
2. Is he envious of the success of others?
3. Does he tend to drown his sorrows in the bottle?
4. Is he opinionated?
5. Is he a male chauvinist pig?
6. Does he have a fiery temper?
7. Are you expected to wait on him?
8. Is he passionate?
9. Does he get upset if you refuse him sexually?
10. Is he ambitious?
11. Does he impose his views on other people?
12. Is he keen on self-improvement?
13. Is he physically powerful for his height?
14. Do you feel in danger of losing your own personality?
15. Does he stick to the same old friends?
16. Is he anti-divorce?
17. Is your appearance important to him?

18. Does he imagine slights from other people where none exist?
19. Is he against the medical profession?
20. Does he loathe women in trousers?

HOW WELL DO YOU KNOW YOUR SCORPIO MAN? (Answers)

1–30

Because the Scorpion is such a direct and honest person, it's inconceivable that you could have achieved this low score through lack of knowledge. Far more likely that this man of yours is not a true Scorpion, and I bet you are not a Water sign either. He is much too open-minded, adaptable and fair. I therefore suggest you read under the sign of Gemini or Libra. It's here you are likely to find your man.

31–50

You've managed to get yourself involved with a true-blue Scorpion all right, but fortunately he possesses more of the good attributes than the bad. You're clearly an honest, loyal and devoted lover or you wouldn't have got the chance to know him so well. You are either married or will be – I wonder if he's told you yet?

51–60

Despite all the warnings in every astrological book about the not-so-nice Scorpio, you have managed to get yourself lumbered with one. How can you know him so well and still be around? Obviously you enjoy being completely dominated, reorganized and bossed around. Don't think it's going to change; it won't. But as you appear to have accepted the situation, I wish you luck; you'll need it.

165

Sagittarius (the Archer)
Sign of the Lawyer or Philosopher

November 23 – December 21

The third Fire sign: Idealistic, jovial, intellectually inclined, outspoken
Ruler: Jupiter
Colour: Light blue
Careers: Interpreter, administrator, sportsman, scholar, civil servant, explorer
Famous Sagittarians: Beethoven, William Blake, Maria Callas, Dale Carnegie, Winston Churchill, Sammy Davis Jr., Walt Disney, Kirk Douglas, Jane Fonda, Paul Getty, Harpo Marx, John Osborne, Frank Sinatra, Dionne Warwicke

SAGITTARIUS MAN

The Sagittarian above all seeks space, having a keen sense of freedom, which he rarely completely gives up. He aspires to the highest of ambitions, both physically and mentally. He is optimistic, sincere, frank and impulsive. For he lives life like a ping-pong ball, passing from venture to venture, full of activity, bubbling with excitement, making friends and following tangents. Life is a circus and he relishes every minute of it. He has an inbuilt love of sports and natural pursuits like exploring or adventuring. He's idealistic, foresighted, jovial, with religious and moralizing tendencies.

166

He is capable of great brilliance and daring. Being very democratic, he has friends in every walk of life. He likes people to express themselves freely, he tends to speak his mind with great independence and can at times be too direct or blunt. He is usually an amusing conversationalist. He loves discussion and debate, being able to convert others to his viewpoint. At work he takes a direct approach and is usually very successful financially. However, he does not like routine and is bored by petty details.

For the most part, the Sagittarian is ruled by reason and logic, which he brings into play on everyone he meets. He is represented by the Centaur for good reason, for this half-man half-beast aims his arrows at some distant target most of us cannot see, in his need for an objective or a constant challenge. Anything that comes easy he figures is not worth having and that goes for the opposite sex too. He enjoys conquests for the sake of them and, when he loses, he doesn't mind at all; there's no malice in this type – just so long as you put up a good clean fight. And, talking of fighting – he does; for almost any cause he believes to be worthwhile, no matter if it is lost already. He will stand up with his arrows and his bow and fight.

Many gamblers are born under this sign, and few Sagittarians can walk past a one-armed bandit or a betting shop without wanting to try their luck.

He leads a hectic life, not necessarily because he craves a sophisticated social whirl like the Libran, but because he loves meeting people, exchanging ideas, finding out what makes them tick. This is a preoccupation of which he never tires. But one of his strongest characteristics is that aforementioned sense of personal freedom. Try stopping him taking off on his own and you'll see what I mean. He doesn't belong to anybody, and he doesn't expect other people to tie him down.

Mentally, he's a fair-minded person, and will never impose his ideas on anybody. He respects an individual's right to do or think exactly as he or she pleases – whether he agrees or not.

But even the good Sagittarian shows one of his weaker brother's faults, namely that of indiscretion. He is totally unaware that his many backhanded compliments can cause people untold frustration. Neither does he place too much store in deep emotional ties. He prefers to project the image of the carefree bachelor and he's also prone to exaggerating his conquests to friends.

However, because he is a lover of truth, the Sagittarian male finds it difficult to tell lies. This doesn't prevent him from trying on occasions, but he usually ends up in more trouble than he would have done had he told the truth.

Although the Sagittarian likes people to believe that he adores women, he is in fact a man's man – not necessarily a homosexual; he just regards the male as superior to the female. Everyone knows that women are ruled by their emotions and men by their logic – at least that's what he believes. The fact that there do happen to be emotional men and logical women around is something he finds hard to comprehend.

SAGITTARIUS WOMAN

This female shares many of her brother Sagittarian's characteristics. Her dynamic energy, too, bounces off walls, touching everyone it possibly can. Many describe her as superficial, because she is a collector of experiences. She is frisky, energetic and brings exaltation to any job she tackles. She can be aristocratic, kinky, serious-minded, frivolous – all in the space of an hour. She is invariably hopeless where money is concerned; if she isn't, it's because she has learned through sad experience. As with all members of this sign, her automatic instinct is to say thoughtless things, only realizing this when it is pointed out to her.

The typical Sagittarian woman is something of a tomboy. You won't find her hoping to compete with men on a physical basis, but she doesn't subscribe to all the old fashioned ideas about women. She is probably an avid feminist. She regards herself as equal to everybody, regardless of sex, and she acts accordingly.

On an emotional level, her sudden attractions often turn into lasting friendships, though such attractions to the opposite sex aren't always fortunate. However, her choices can be so impulsive that they don't work out, with broken engagements and marriages as the result. Sagittarians cannot tolerate any kind of restraint. They are not in the least bit domesticated and can be selfish and difficult to live with, even becoming critical or sarcastic when they are bored with their spouse.

As a rule, when facing a crisis in her personal life she has a happy knack of turning the situation into a joke, one which the hurt male for the most part can appreciate. She doesn't find it necessary to damage his pride just because a relationship is over. When she becomes a mother, children regard her more as a big sister than a maternal figure. The generation gap doesn't appear too wide with this woman. But she definitely wants more out of life than to be a baby machine and she generally avoids marriage until quite late. Like her brother she wants to experience almost everything life has to offer and the thought of a dull, domestic routine will make her cringe.

The Sagittarian female has a brilliant head upon her shoulders; many professional women such as doctors, lawyers and scientists are to be found under the sign of the Archer. Their probing minds attract them to research ways of helping other less fortunate beings.

Although the Sagittarian woman is often attractive, she is not the most graceful of creatures. In fact, she can be downright clumsy. You can bet that the female who knocked over the arrangement of display cans in the supermarket is a Sagittarian. Little mishaps seem to follow her around. Those who know her well no doubt constantly tease her about this. She has no intention of becoming the most elegant female around anyway, nor is she after the title of Miss Best Dressed Sun Sign of the Year. She is all for comfort in this particular direction, and it will be more by accident than by design that her clothes do anything for her physically.

Ms Sagittarius, like her male counterpart, is attracted to the outdoors; wide-open spaces make her feel freer than she probably is. And don't forget that personal freedom is highly valued and clung to tenaciously. The Sagittarian female doesn't always say the things that other people want to hear. Back-handed compliments sometimes smack in the face like a wet kipper. She doesn't mean to be rude, but more often than not her terms of endearment leave something to be desired. However, when she does put her words together in the correct order, she will enchant everyone with her sincerity. So much so that maybe someone will help her restack those supermarket cans.

THE HYDE SIDE

Weaker or more fault-laden Sagittarians are extremists; extravagant, tactless, boastful, inconsiderate, exaggerating, careless, restless, they strive to project the playboy/girl image. Their hot, quick temper will scorch everything in sight when it hits, but then will cool down instantly. Rather than holding grudges, they will avoid a person who has angered them for ever after.

These types invariably live in the present. Loyalty and faithful relationships are foreign to their nature. The end product of this is, of course, a total lack of consideration for those around. Reputation – including other people's – means little or nothing to them. Naturally, these tendencies on occasion cause many who cross their paths to suffer.

Their strong love of personal freedom may become distorted and they may become obnoxiously arrogant and rude. They run as soon as they meet anyone who can be a threat to their liberty. Nevertheless this type of Sagittarian is difficult to dislike, for their sense of humour makes them amusing to have around. Stronger personalities such as Leos will use them virtually as Court Jesters, though they may not realize straight away that those around them are laughing at them and not with them. But they love to be with people and if this is the only way, then they will grin and bear it.

It's unlikely that any Sagittarian can be conveniently slotted into either this category or the one before, probably being a mixture of both. But no matter what, they'll be fun to have around. If Sagittarians hurt someone else, they generally don't mean to; dropping bricks is just one of the hang-ups one must expect of this sign.

HOW TO CATCH AND KEEP YOUR SAGITTARIUS MAN

Not an easy task, for amongst other things, he is irresponsible, irrepressible and insincere. He is also lovable. This character loves a challenge and as a result he is often attracted to married women. Any female wishing to keep this type interested should never be seen to be too readily available. At the same time, a possessive and jealous woman is in for a lot of problems with the freedom loving Sagittarian. It may be a wise move for the aspiring female to reach some kind of agreement on how far each of them can go, outside of their relationship, for this is preferable to deluding herself into believing that this man will love one woman for life. He is repelled by clinging, demanding types; he will prefer a woman interested in her own activities and career, for in this way he will not feel oppressed by her dependency.

This is a dedicated sportsman and so where possible any interested female should try to share in his pursuit; if she does not, he will soon find someone else who will. The main thing to remember then, when determined to snare a Sagittarian, is that one must not let him know that he has been caught. He is attracted to the kind of female who appears independent and does not threaten his freedom in any way, shape or form. He'll be particularly impressed if she can become "one of the boys". She should not feel offended by this; it is the greatest compliment that the Sagittarius male can pay his woman.

HOW TO CATCH AND KEEP YOUR SAGITTARIAN WOMAN

This female is open, frank and optimistic, and most people regard her as a happy individual. Her projected image could make it seem a simple matter to ensnare the Sagittarian female, but not so. As soon as her overpowering sense of freedom is at risk in any way, she will disentangle herself from the offending relationship and look for something more easy-going. Possessive and jealous men should be warned that this is not the woman for them. She finds it extremely difficult to remain loyal to one person. It could, therefore, be advisable for both parties to reach a *modus vivendi* very early in their relationship and stick to it.

She is not attracted to smooth-talking men – those with silver tongues will be wasting their time. She is a pursuer of truth, and anything that rings false will annoy her intensely and her interest will disappear. In order to attract this woman, one needs to become more like her. The ideal image to project is one of light-heartedness, nonchalance, and the man concerned must make it quite clear that he has no wish to clip her wings. But it had better be the truth.

The Sagittarian lady loves people and if her mate should install her in a house miles away from anywhere one can be certain that somehow she will escape to find the company she desperately needs. Even when married with a stream of children, she will always have hundreds of interests outside of her home. This is an essential part of her personality which should be allowed to develop. One can only keep a Sagittarian lady by making her feel she does not have to remain against her wishes. She will probably be quite surprised when she finds out for herself that she does actually want to stay.

HIS IDEAL PARTNER

This male never consciously looks around for a mate. He may well somehow manage to find himself in an inextricable situation, because he cannot run fast enough (or because of his clumsiness he trips over and falls). He will be plucked and trussed before he knows what has hit him. Unfortunately for him, he is constantly challenged, sometimes taken over in his love life. Not surprising, then, that married women attract him. This can become a hard habit to break, not to mention a rather dramatic one. But when he does find true happiness and a mate, she is usually born under the sign of Aries or Leo. These women quickly learn how to understand and handle such a character. His personality fits in totally with their own.

When it comes to love, he will admit to being a cynic. He says he has been in love several times and will no doubt love again. It's unlikely that the Sagittarian is capable of deep or lasting love and those who come into contact with him should accept this or leave him be. Either they must respect his ideas on personal freedom or look for someone else to tie down.

This man's ideal mate probably doesn't exist, for if she did she would happily allow him to carry on his bachelor life practically undisturbed. She will have to resign herself to being left alone many evenings while he is out with the boys and occasionally the girls. There will, of course, be other evenings when they socialize together, though even then his mate will have to keep a sharp eye out while he flirts with every available female (and some of those that aren't).

But his chosen partner will get to know him well and come to realize that these other attentions are only needed to boost his ego. Here she can be clever, spreading flattery on a little thicker. Showing him that she cares will ensure that flirtations are kept to a minimum.

When he realizes he can do as he pleases, infidelity will lose its glamour, and the Archer may stay home a little more often than usual. But any woman who protests too loudly at his behaviour will have issued a challenge to him and the inevitable is likely to follow. Don't think just because he prefers to be honest he can't be as devious as a Geminian when forced to be. The fact that he's a bad liar only worsens the situation. In other words, a female with this man in tow has to take him as he is. He may change a little in mature life, but it will be a gradual process, and he will only change when he wants to. No female can keep this man locked up for her own pleasure.

Since the Sagittarian has many interests, his ideal mate will be willing to become involved in them, if she is not already. She may have met him at the local tennis, hockey, golf or rowing club. Any smitten female who refuses to go along with him shouldn't be surprised if he soon finds someone attractive who will. He's not short of telephone numbers or tennis partners.

HER IDEAL PARTNER

Although the Sagittarian woman gets along with most people, finding happiness with one man is never easy for her. When it does come to her, it's likely to be in the form of an Arietian or Leonine, who can appreciate her warmth, enthusiasm and her regard for personal freedom. They are also likely to go along with most of her cranky ideas and won't think her totally mad when she decides to take a risk or gamble, whereas such behaviour would horrify a Capricornian or Virgoan admirer.

Her ideal partner needs to be as similar to her as possible, someone who won't tie her too closely to the domestic scene and will always respect her individuality and independence, encouraging her to make something of her professional life or any pursuits she wishes to follow. If she loves her man enough she will slowly settle down with the passing years, but it isn't a change which can be forced upon her.

She does not want any man imposing his ideas or opinions

on her intellect; she is quite capable of making up her own mind, thank you very much. Don't ever order her to do anything. Ask her politely and she will oblige. A male who thinks he will impress her by being a club-swinging caveman is in for a shock. He had better change his leopardskin for a more up-to-the-minute outfit if he wants to capture her heart. Nevertheless there are occasions when her man needs to be firm with her, for she is not above testing him in this direction.

She likes to be reminded who is the man in the relationship, but only gently.

Her chosen partner will never listen to gossip about her from other people. It doesn't mean a thing. She is so truthful that all he has to do is ask and she will tell him where she's been and with whom; he'll get such a detailed report that he may wish he hadn't asked.

Realizing that he has a trusting, honest woman, her ideal mate also understands that where romance is concerned she is a bit of a sitting target, and whatever happens she shouldn't be shot down too many times.

SEXUALLY (MALE)

As you might expect, Mr Sagittarian's approach to sex, as with everything else, is candid. If he wants to go to bed with a particular female he says so, no beating about the bush. On the other hand, if he invites an admirer to see his etchings, that is exactly what she will be doing. Many women are taken aback by his approach and he will tease them unmercifully for being "old-fashioned", making whatever objections they put forward look ridiculous.

When not openly propositioning the opposite sex, he will try the corniest lines possible – not because he expects a woman to fall for them, but in an effort to laugh his partner into bed. All the old clichés are dusted down and trotted out. She will know exactly what he is after, and the beauty of it is that he knows that she knows. Strange as it may appear to some, this approach is often quite successful, if somewhat embarrassing.

He is not the most highly sexed creature on the carnal marketplace, but he usually has a fair number of notches on his bedpost. A Sagittarian man on the loose can make an incredible

174

number of conquests in one year. In many cases, it's just a bit of fun, while in others it is a desire to experiment that spurs him on. If he believes that he can learn something from a female, or teach her one or two new tricks, his interest is immediately aroused.

The unmarried Archer of approximately 30 will have tried most things at some point in his career. He doesn't believe in knocking anything until he has experienced it. But he will hide nothing from his woman. All she has to do is ask. His attitude is that you only live once, and therefore new loves in his life had better be warned that they are in for some interesting lessons. There's no point in taking him too seriously, simply enjoy.

SEXUALLY (FEMALE)

The Sagittarian lady has no problems about sex. She enjoys it and is not hampered by puritanical ideas or inhibitions. She is a free spirit. Simply because she gives in sexually does not mean that she feels that wedding bells are just around the corner; quite the reverse, she is capable of enjoying herself with one man and totally forgetting his name the next day.

Being an impulsive creature, she takes her pleasure where and when and with whom she chooses. More conventional types may find this a bit outlandish. Her attitude to the physical takes some getting used to, especially if the man involved is more familiar with the straight-forward female stereotype. But there's nothing in her rule-book which says she mustn't take the lead. It's equality for all, where she is concerned, and her man had better remember this.

This is a woman who likes to experiment sexually, and here she takes a leaf from her brother Sagittarian's book. Any male entering her boudoir had better be prepared for the unexpected, and all suggestions are welcome. She won't mind if he is less experienced than she is; she will be quite happy to make the running. She is an unselfish lover, always allowing her partner the freedom to do whatever turns him on. Her sense of justice presides in the bedroom, just as well as it does out of it.

Any unsuspecting man who expects things his own way in this arena is in for a lengthy debate. She is clever with words and he may well lose this particular contest.

Lastly, one of her most annoying habits is a tendency to discuss her past affairs in minutest detail. Sensitive members of the opposite sex are advised to take their ear-plugs along, while she is rambling on, or concentrate on finding various ways to keep her quiet.

HOW TO END THE AFFAIR

No problem at all. Because Sagittarians possess fair minds and tend to lack deep emotion, all one has to do to remove them is be honest. They won't even mind being told who their lucky successor is. In fact, they'll probably insist on knowing all the details. They have no objections to being pushed out of your emotional life in favour of someone else. And they will try to remain friends. Also they'll be interested to know how the successor is superior and in what way. Once this is understood, then it makes sense. If you are going one better, then they won't blame you at all for that.

If you can impress the Sagittarian with your new love's intellect then no attempt will be made to stand in your way. In fact, it's likely you'll get a kiss on the cheek or an affectionate pat on the back. But don't believe that you've seen the last of your ex, who will be around out of sheer curiosity just to discover how things are progressing and to make certain that you are being treated well. This is especially true if you were once very close.

In the highly unlikely event of a Sagittarian being difficult at your passing, there are a couple of dodges that can be tried. Let it be discovered that you are hanging around with those who might be considered to be beneath you, or general undesirables. Stay at home and refuse to join in outside interests. If you are a he attempting to dispose of a she, then throw in a few flirtations with other women for good measure, and issue one or two orders. It won't be long before she's telling you what to do, and in rather more basic language.

176

HOW TO ATTRACT THE SUN SIGNS

SAGITTARIUS WOMAN WITH SAGITTARIUS MAN

This combination doesn't usually work, oddly enough. But then what would you expect in a relationship between Moll Flanders and Casanova? Too many third, fourth, fifth and sixth parties interfering and keeping the two apart. True, they may begin by doing everything in tandem – sports, fun, games, social events, even visiting families. Then they may discover that they don't really feel free together. Somehow there's something forced. Because they have so much in common, they spend twenty-four hours a day together and though this may be willing captivity, it is captivity nevertheless. It is then that their tendency to stray takes over. One sense of freedom is something to contend with, but two?

SAGITTARIUS WOMAN WITH CAPRICORN MAN

Difficult to find two characters more opposed to each other. She is an optimist, he is a pessimist. She is a little crazy, something of a madcap – he is stone-cold sober and Mr Conservative. Furthermore, he is hardworking. He will spend all his time trying to keep her feet on the ground, while she is struggling to put his head in the stars. At first he will be fascinated by her wild and whimsical nature, but he won't be able to harness or live with it for very long. After a while, she will decide she cannot abide his predictability. If she reads economics and he reads philosophy or politics, then they may make the relationship last a little longer, but basically, if these two are typical of their signs, it's just not on.

SAGITTARIUS WOMAN WITH AQUARIUS MAN

This has all the makings of a perfect relationship. The Aquarian (air) is capable of providing a gentle breeze and helping the Sagittarian (fire) to grow and expand. Of course, air and fire aren't always compatible and there are bound to be occasions when the breeze becomes a gale and blows the fire completely

177

out. But in general this is a good union. She understands his moods, he gladly accepts her flights of fantasy. His detachment will allow her all the freedom she requires. They both love change and excitement: travel, new scenes, new sexual experimentaton. Providing they get themselves a good accountant – for both are hopeless with money – they should be able to enjoy each other's love.

SAGITTARIUS WOMAN WITH PISCES MAN

To the Sagittarius woman, the Piscean man is very heavy-going. There's no reason why they can't be friends, but as lovers they simply aren't on the same track. Initially things may go along swimmingly, for they will be intrigued by each other's strange and foreign characteristics, but it can't be long before she realizes that though "foreign" may be exotic, it's definitely not erotic or necessarily interesting. His sensitive dependency will prove to be a complete turn-off for her, whilst he will be desperately hurt by her refusal to make him the main pivot in her world. Even their interests are poles apart. The Piscean is essentially aesthetic and artistic, while she is more politically and philosophically inclined. He'll describe her as heartless, she'll describe him as wet. Hardly promising for any intimate relationship.

SAGITTARIUS WOMAN WITH ARIES MAN

When two fire signs such as these get together, there's promise of an explosive time. Both partners here are impulsive, energetic and full of fight. But both also know how to forgive and forget and don't take each other's failings too seriously. The Sagittarian woman will love his zest for living, share his enthusiasm for sport and match his ardour, generally bringing out the best in this man. Somehow, he always appears so much younger than she is, even if he isn't. Maybe it's his boyish sense of humour and wonder, which she could do worse than adopt for herself. If anyone can handle this egoist, it's got to be Miss Sagittarius.

SAGITTARIUS WOMAN WITH TAURUS MAN

She refuses to be hemmed in. He refuses to allow her freedom of movement and even thought. He feels the need to possess absolutely, while she needs to be unfettered. But he will be strongly attracted to her *joie de vivre*. She had better be warned that he is likely to get hurt and when the Bull is disturbed he can be quite a frightening sight. She is advised to read the chapter on ending the affair with a Taurus if she must get involved. Not a good relationship.

SAGITTARIUS WOMAN WITH GEMINI MAN

Although these two signs are at the opposite ends of the zodiac they have much in common. Their characteristics are similar, as well as their needs. Neither of them places too high a value on consistency and both adore freedom of mind and body. Neither will worry much if the other chooses to experiment outside the affair from time to time – it's in both of their natures. Both individuals tend to have many sides to their characters which need satisfying; put them together and confusion tends to reign. They may make it work, provided they can find enough time to spend with each other, though what's more likely to happen is that they'll slowly drift apart and probably won't even notice.

SAGITTARIUS WOMAN WITH CANCER MAN

He is likely to be attracted to her dazzling personality and would no doubt love to get near her; but if he does, he won't be able to cope with her for very long. He's tenacious, devoted and stay-at-home; she loves to flit and flirt, needing a base only as a place to go to get organized in order to go out again. Restaurants make her think of cooking, whereas they put him in mind of romance and love. He won't want to know about her past experiences, but she will insist on telling him and this perhaps could be the nail in the coffin of the relationship. As this is a fire-and-water union, you are likely to finish up with steam once again.

SAGITTARIUS WOMAN WITH LEO MAN

Although this is an excellent relationship, it will be anything but peace and quiet. The occasional explosions will detonate, as both parties love to dominate, and besides they enjoy the fighting plus the making-up. They share a love of luxury, excitement and being centre-stage. Providing each can learn to take turns in the limelight then they'll probably live happily ever after; but we are dealing with two egoists, and consideration for each other's feelings will have to be developed. Nevertheless it's a naturally compatible union.

SAGITTARIUS WOMAN WITH VIRGO MAN

He's meticulous and fastidious; she is a blithe spirit. He loves to pick – and she loathes nagging. He will be happy to make love to her, as long as she changes the sheets first and makes the bed after; but, let's face it, Miss Sagittarius just isn't the tidiest, neatest or most fastidious of females. It can only be a matter of days before he works this out for himself and tries to transform her; no way! However, if both parties decide to give this relationship a go, she must be prepared to cut down on her social life and re-organize her nest. Much then depends on how badly she wants this character.

SAGITTARIUS WOMAN WITH LIBRA MAN

This partnership will certainly be fun, at the beginning anyway. But what's going to happen when Mr Libra wants to take her home at midnight and Miss Sagittarius is just getting ready to paint the town red? He is an up-with-the-Sun person who is happiest in the early morning; she is a nightbird who prefers not to see daylight until at least noon. His sense of justice and fair play may make it work for a while, but he will be tormented by her whimsical ups and downs and soon both will realize this is an unwise emotional relationship. A good friendship.

SAGITTARIUS WOMAN WITH SCORPIO MAN

Another of those fire-and-water combinations; in this instance, they'll have a lovely time in bed, but I'm afraid there's not much in common elsewhere. He'll be determined to dominate her; she will be equally determined to elude him. He will try to make her more serious; she will want to make him laugh. They are the tortoise and the hare: he walks through life and she runs. All in all, it can be great if only a short-lived affair. But before long she will run up against his notorious jealousy, and this is just the girl to make it grow out of all proportion. The Scorpion man will want to ring her neck on occasions and may just do that. If she is wise she will get out of this relationship as quickly as possible.

HOW WELL DO YOU KNOW YOUR SAGITTARIUS WOMAN?

Answer honestly the questions below, scoring 3 for every Yes, 2 for Sometimes and 1 for No, then add up your total.

1. Is she the outdoor type?
2. Is she clumsy?
3. Is she tactless?
4. Is she talkative?
5. Does she hate formal occasions?
6. Does she think you are old-fashioned?
7. Is she hopeless with money?
8. Does she like to take risks?
9. Does she have a strong sense of freedom?
10. Is she untidy?
11. Does she dress for comfort rather than elegance?
12. Does she take the lead in sex?
13. Does she dislike cooking?
14. Does jealousy turn her off?
15. Can she easily become "one of the boys" when your friends come around?
16. Is she well versed in profanities?
17. Is she unshockable?
18. Do you wish she were a little more feminine?
19. Does she tell the truth even when it hurts?
20. Do you believe she should take life a little more seriously?

(Answers)

1–30:
If your lady is a typical Sagittarian you should have done a lot better than this. Either you are completely insensitive or there are other influences at work on her chart. The way you have answered seems to suggest a water influence, so try reading the chapters devoted to Pisces, Cancer or Scorpio, for there you may find the true character.

31–50
You've got yourself a mate, a friend, as well as a lover. What's

more, you know her well and accept her for exactly what she is –
a true-blue Sagittarian female. If you two are not yet married,
it's likely that you will be in the near future – but, if I were you,
I shouldn't let her read that!

51–60
You really are tied up with a Sagittarian who possesses more of
the faults associated with this sign. But all is not lost. For, this
woman being the type of character that she is, any time you
want to go will be all right with her. I hope you are not the
sensitive type, for this female is quite able to drive a bulldozer
over your feelings and opinions.

HOW WELL DO YOU KNOW YOUR SAGITTARIUS MAN?

*Answer honestly the questions below, scoring 3 for every Yes, 2 for
Sometimes and 1 for No, then add up your total.*

1. Is he hard to catch?
2. Is he interested in sports?
3. Does he loathe formal occasions?
4. Is he tactless?
5. Is he a "man's man"?
6. Would he be bored with a romantic dinner for two?
7. Is he hopeless with money?
8. Does he gamble?
9. Does he enjoy sexual experimentation?
10. Would he drop you if you got possessive?
11. Is he for ever changing his interest?
12. Does he find the female mind a complete puzzle?
13. Does he detest parties?
14. Does he go out drinking with the boys?
15. Does he forget special occasions?
16. Is he frightened of growing old?
17. Has he been attracted to married women?
18. Is he untidy?
19. Is he a sloppy dresser?
20. Is he stimulated by challenge?

(Answers)

1–30
This character you are involved with is much too practical, sensitive and considerate to be a true member of the Sagittarian fraternity; it's likely that other influences are at work on this chart, otherwise you couldn't possibly have answered so badly. If you read underneath some of the earth signs, you may find him there. The sections on Taurus and Capricorn may be quite enlightening to you.

31–50
You are lucky enough to have found yourself not only a lover, but a friend and confidant. Your relationship will never be completely ruled by sex alone. It takes more that that to keep you both happy. You seem to understand this man perfectly. Play your cards right and he might eventually walk you up the aisle.

51–60
How can you know your Sagittarian so well and still be around? After all, it's easy enough to get rid of him if you so desire. If you can accept his infidelity and shallowness, maybe you've reached some kind of arrangement between you. If so, I wish you the best of luck with this man.

Capricorn (the Goat)
Sign of the Economist and the Ambassador

December 22 – January 20

The third Earth sign: Patient, methodical, cautious, resourceful
Ruler: Saturn
Colour: Green
Careers: Scientist, manager, headmaster, engineer, civil servant, mathematician, farmer, politician, builder
Famous Capricornians: Muhammed Ali, Humphrey Bogart, Nat "King" Cole, Marlene Dietrich, Ava Gardner, Cary Grant, Howard Hughes, Joan of Arc, Martin Luther King, Mao Tse-tung, Richard Nixon, Aristotle Onassis, Edgar Allan Poe, Elvis Presley

---

CAPRICORN MAN

The Capricorn man is an iron-willed, strong-minded survivor. He is very power-conscious and can dominate everything and everybody who comes within his sphere. His intellect and pragmatism combine to make the most outrageous schemes work. But other people often find him hard work. He tends to look too deeply into even the simplest situations and over-intellectualizes them. Even the smallest problem requires endless mulling. There's no such thing as an impulsive goat. He is much too ambitious to leave anything to chance. He'll ponder

185

for days on whether to buy a £20 handbag for his woman, and then wait for months until it goes on sale. He is very quick to come up with new ideas, but unbelievably slow when it comes to putting them into practice.

Mr Capricorn always takes life seriously and tends to build a brick wall around his emotions. He is very willing to take on responsibility, though he may later complain about how many burdens have been thrust on his shoulders and point out how much more he has done than anybody else. But he is reliable, steady and faithful, sometimes to the point of extremes.

He knows where is is going and, just like the mountain goat, hardly ever puts a foot wrong. If he should slip, he picks himself up, looks to the heights and doggedly climbs again. And eventually he makes it to the top. Once there, he surveys his success and continues to strive to maintain it. The Goat never rests on his laurels. He knows there's always someone else trying to remove him from his lofty perch; but it will take a clever man to unseat him.

His physical powers are remarkable and he is one of the most hardworking characters in the zodiac. Honourable and self-disciplined, he commands the respect of mere mortals such as you and me. He is a relentless and honest worker. Don't think you will ever do a favour for him; he doesn't really need your help. If it is given, however obtuse, he will repay you in kind, for he hates to be obligated.

Financially he is extremely careful and thrifty – some may even say mean. He can usually exist on little and is able to make ends meet where others would fail miserably. Mind you, he can be extremely charitable, but he will never boast or publicize the fact. He likes to help in a quiet way and is a tower of strength when others are in distress.

In general, he is at his best when working with money and figures. Not surprisingly, therefore, many Capricorn men make excellent book-keepers and statisticians. If he makes a fortune, it will be solely through his own efforts. He can be trusted with other people's money and possessions and will be extremely hurt if this trust is not reciprocated.

Mr Capricorn hides any discomfort well. He may go through a really sticky patch, but no one will ever know. His world may be crumbling around his ears and he may be suffering great mental anguish, but he will not burden you with his problems.

He hates to make a fuss. Don't worry too much about him, he'll get over it.

Although capable of working long and arduously with an almost inexhaustible supply of energy, he has a tendency towards being moody and melancholic. Nervous troubles are likely to induce physical symptoms which are difficult to diagnose. Under strain, the Capricornian suffers from depression, and this can lead to over-indulgence in both food and drink, particularly the latter. But his amazing will-power, when it's given a new objective, will help him through.

If you are at the top of the mountain and see a Goat approaching, don't imagine that he is after your position or your glory; in fact, he probably has the deepest admiration for your getting there ahead of him. But look to the right a little – see that twin peak, on a level with yours? Well, it may be slightly higher, and it's labelled Capricorn. It won't be long before he is in occupation. Always remember, Goats don't keep up with the Joneses . . . they are the Joneses!

CAPRICORN WOMAN

The Capricorn woman is endowed with many of her zodiac brother's characteristics. She, too, is extremely ambitious and usually in a position of authority before the age of 30. But don't let that word "authority" fool you. For although she can be conservative in dress and manner, the female Goat can be ultra-feminine. Many men have been taken in by her icy exterior, only to discover, too late, what a warm, passionate little woman they have passed up. Just because she doesn't flirt with every Tom, Dick or Harry doesn't mean she should be overlooked.

Any man chasing this woman will know what I mean when I say that she tries to be just, in every aspect of life. If she feels, even once, that she has been used unfairly, she will drop into a chasm of moodiness so deep that even the longest rope of apology cannot effect a rescue.

Since she is invariably a career lady, you could be forgiven for wondering how she ever manages to get round to marriage and raising a family. But, strangely enough, she nearly always does.

She will invariably sacrifice her career for marriage. She just

187

loves to be the head of the household. Mistress of the Manor is better to her than Mistress of the Baron who owns the manor, and she will end up marrying the Baron. Remember, Capricornians are social climbers and only when they reach the top are they truly satisfied. The Capricorn woman has a steely determination to get the right man, and she will chase him until she catches him.

All Capricornians have goals, not the least of which is security. Not until she feels that her chosen mate can give her the best home and the most trouble-free existence will she kneel beside him at the altar. She may leave it until quite late in life, but she will eventually take the plunge.

Many are surprised to learn that the Capricornian has a fair share of artistic talent. She is an excellent orator and is always direct and to the point. Many famous writers, painters and composers are born under this sign.

However, Ms Capricorn should try to enliven her basically serious and unimaginative nature by joining in the gaiety and fun which she too often despises and regards as frivolous. Her conservatism is also expressed in the home surroundings. Not for her the flashy white plastic and chromium furniture of today. She favours traditional designs. She would prefer to live in an older house rather than a modern flat, just so long as it is dignified and well built. (That, by the way, is the way she likes her men). She abhors shoddy work around of any description; tradesmen who commit the unpardonable crime of not doing their work efficiently had better be prepared to wait for payment until things are put right. She doesn't like parting with her money at the best of times and a cupboard that keeps falling off the wall or a door that needs two people to open it will definitely not bring the green notes fluttering from her purse.

She likes to get a bargain and will not spend her money until convinced she is getting good value. She will run her home smoother than silk-lined roller bearings, on a budget that makes lesser mortals gasp with admiration. As a mother, she will be extremely ambitious for her children. In fact, she may tend to push them a little too hard, though in later years they will not regret this. Her ambition for them probably stems from the fact that as a child she was very mature for her age. It has been said that young Capricornians look like little old people and that older Capricornians must have found the elixir of youth. Nothing comes easy to this woman, especially early in life: her best years are after the age of 30. She is always ready to help those in need and goes about solving problems in a sensible and practical fashion, without expecting praise or reward for any good deeds.

The female Capricorn's greatest gift is the appearance of natural good breeding, whatever her parentage. She can be the most graceful creature on two legs without training of any description. She pushes her loved ones forward and helps them to reach their goals, which will always be realistic. She never nags her man, and as she grows older she grows more beautiful. Take a look at Marlene Dietrich and you'll see what I mean.

THE HYDE SIDE

These types are selfish, narrow-minded, too severe and exacting, cruel, unfeeling, critical, miserly, pessimistic, unnecessarily worrying and far too conventional.

They make excellent puppeteers – only they prefer to ma nipulate human marionettes, meddling in others' lives and having an uncontrollable urge to convert people. Their entire lives revolve around their ambitions, for this facet is all out of proportion. Such Capricornians are capable of making a mercenary marriage in an attempt to further themselves, and they base friendships upon usefulness.

Whether male or female, they are notorious scalers of the social ladder. It could be fatal for anyone to stand in their way or thwart their aspirations, whether personal or professional, for in the face of open opposition they become ruthless. The ciritical side of their nature will exaggerate the shortcomings and failures of other people. *Nobody* can measure up to their own set of standards. If others do not equal them, either morally or socially, the Goat pities them, doling out great handfuls of scorn and derision. A female of the species has great difficulty in making lasting friends, perhaps because she is moody, easily depressed or because her self-pity has driven her to drink.

But there is no such thing as a perfect saint or an absolute criminal born under the sign of Capricorn. It depends on circumstances and intellect as to which failures or attributes surface. Obviously there are certain people who bring out the better qualities and others are more negative.

HOW TO CATCH AND KEEP YOUR CAPRICORN MAN

Mr Capricorn is usually a pessimist. Even when the worst does not happen, he will sit back waiting for something else to go wrong. This is also an extremely ambitious man, persistent and determined. He progresses very slowly upwards in life and, because he does not take the easy way, spends much of his time involved with his work. Any female with her sights set on this character must allow for this. She cannot expect to have a monopoly on his attention and so this individual is rarely attracted to the kind of girl who is too demanding.

Capricorn is also the sign of the miser, and endless quarrels will result if his mate makes no effort to control her extravagance. But if a woman can make him laugh, then she is half-way to winning his heart. For he needs a light influence in his life somewhere, or he will become bogged down with responsibilities and worries. Therefore, when hotfooting it after a Capricornian, remember to show common sense in financial matters, but display a great sense of humour – if at all possible. Once this man realizes that life is suddenly taking a lift, due to the female present, he could be quite difficult to shake off.

HOW TO CATCH AND KEEP YOUR CAPRICORN WOMAN

This woman is a worrier: about money, about her job – in fact, she would not be herself unless she were worrying about something. She has a deep horror of debt and insecurity and will usually be drawn towards a man who puts her mind at ease in this direction. Because of her serious attitude to life, she could be attracted to someone who can introduce a little sunlight into her existence, maybe make her laugh occasionally, so designing males will need to develop a strong sense of humour.

The Capricorn woman is usually very involved with her career, and any domineering male who believes he can come along and alter this immediately is sure to be disillusioned.

190

Furthermore he should develop an interest in her work, for there will be times when she wishes to discuss her problems with him and will be grateful for a sympathetic ear. Shows of extravagance are deplored by this woman; she has a healthy respect for finances and her fear of insecurity compels her to lead a frugal existence. She will expect the same attitude from the man in her life.

Pessimism is also an integral part of her make-up, but on no account should a Capricorn-chaser treat this with scorn or be patronizing. Rather he must try gently to show her the more optimistic side of life. This can be done, for she is an intelligent creature.

HIS IDEAL PARTNER

The Goat takes his love-life, like his ambition, very seriously. Not for him the whirlwind romance that sweeps all before it, tossing his world upside down. You can forget the three-day romance and the ladder at the window; elopement is out. When he forges a bond, it won't be a rushed affair. His perfect mate should forget any ideas of wedlock, old shoes and rice until he has his career together. If he can't support her, he won't marry her. She doesn't necessarily have to be as beautiful as the spring – good looks take a back seat to good breeding; and she will have to measure up to his high standards. His ideal woman understands stocks and bonds, and will have to be an asset to him, creating a favourable impression on his business associates or work colleagues. And she needs to be able to wield a mean saucepan, if not have a degree in housekeeping.

When he decides she is worthy of him and his family, he will make no secret of the fact. The commitment will be made and the preacher informed. The Goat is an extremely loyal and faithful being and if he explains that the perfume she can smell is a new aftershave, that's exactly what it is. She'll never catch him with a shade of lipstick decorating his collar, no matter what the temptation.

His ideal mate is likely to be born under the signs of Taurus or Virgo, who share similar attitudes and the same practical outlook. Furthermore, she will never forget to be lavish with praise where he or his family are concerned. He will expect her to show them the same dog-like devotion as he does, even if she feels like snapping at the seat of their trousers. The family is an institution to the Capricorn. He will defend his loved ones against all comers, even down to his third cousin Bess, twice removed from Aunty Maud. As long as there are leaves on his family tree, no woodman will dare harm a single bough.

HER IDEAL PARTNER

Her ideal mate is likely to be born under the sign of Virgo or Taurus, the ones who are able to make her the happiest. A Taurean man, like her, possesses a morbid feat of debt and this mutual dread will prevent any financial difficulties undermining their relationship. Socially, they'll be blissfully happy together and may unwittingly sever all connections with the outside world. As for Mr Virgo, well, he will find that his inhibitions slip away in the company of this woman and he will be at his best with her. Many other interests are shared and companionship will burn warm and cosy within their home.

As previously mentioned, the Capricornian takes life far too seriously. She needs someone to make her laugh. I am not suggesting that suitors play the fool twenty-four hours a day, but her ideal mate should know exactly how to bring a smile to her lips every once in a while. However, he will never make jokes or tease at her expense: the man who does this may spend the rest of his life chuckling to himself, but she will be nowhere around.

Her chosen partner must learn to live with her moods. Her even-tempered exterior may be painted a golden shade of tranquillity, to gild the lily, but when she is upset she can brood for months. There's no use trying to cheer her out of her depression. You'd have as much chance of success as at trying to revive the dodo.

She needs a man who can compliment her. A little sincere flattery will go a long way (I say *sincere*, because she can tell waffle from the real thing), and just beneath that cool surface the embers of passion lie smouldering away, waiting to be fanned into life. But no man will get those flames leaping if his future is not sorted out. Show her a serious attitude to life and security and make sure that your cloud-cuckoo-land has destination signs that read "practical success", then pick her up gently but firmly and walk positively into paradise. And you'll be able to warm your heart on her for a very long time.

SEXUALLY (MALE)

The Capricorn man is acutely conscious of the difference between the sexes, and in the company of females he simply cannot be himself. He may wring his hands, shuffle his feet, flirt so obviously that he is an embarrassment. One thing he finds it difficult to do is be himself.

However, don't get the idea that he doesn't like women: nothing could be further from the truth. In his youth particularly he probably broke more hearts than Clark Gable and Rudolf Valentino rolled into one. But this slowly begins to change in later years. He will still cast a glance at the stills outside a topless club, but should a girl make a blatant pass and offer some straightforward proposition, he will find it impossible to feel at ease in her company. Ideally he needs a light-hearted influence.

Sex is frequently taken too seriously by the Capricorn. It will be on his curriculum, probably slotted in somewhere not too inconvenient to his everyday activities. He needs to be taught that it can be funny, even hilarious. If a woman can laugh him into bed, this is probably the best way. Relaxing him is half the battle. Once this is done, he is quite capable of handling the sexual combat that follows. Anything that will break down his tension is permissible: massage, warm bath or shower, aromatic herbs – all these may help, but his lady will also have to know how to unwind him. Few Capricorn men set aside much time for sexual experimentation, due to the pressure of work. Any new ideas will have to be introduced slowly and they'll need to build up their joint repertoire gradually.

If the Capricorn man's love-making is criticized too many times, and his mate insists that he is too preoccupied with ambition and should be more into the physical side of things, he will immediately drop into a deep depression. And one thing no one wants is a depressed Goat. It's almost impossible to arouse one anyway. Yes, he must be treated carefully when it comes to sex. And the watchword should, at all times, be: smile.

SEXUALLY (FEMALE)

Capricorn woman is the original "nobody wants me" type. When a man advances, she looks over her shoulder just to make certain that it is *her* he wants. Her pessimistic nature will make her doubt that anyone could be strongly attracted to her, nor will she take it for granted that a second date will follow the first. A man who boosts her ego and makes her life full will find himself on the right side of her bedroom door in a short while.

It's highly unlikely that she will ever directly approach a member of the opposite sex herself. She is far too inhibited and has difficulty expressing her feelings; no matter how attracted she is to a man she will always let him make the first move. Not that she will expect him to notice her existence at all: she will just sit hoping.

Sexually, as in all else, she is straightforward and conservative. Many men see this as a challenge, but when they fail to break down the cool façade they will leave empty-handed. Patience is the key. Don't get the idea that she can do without her sex. She needs to fulfil herself on this side just like the rest of us; it's just that she rarely admits it. It needs to be pointed out to her, though not too obviously. Anything that can induce a state of complete relaxation should be utilized to get her in the right mood. Soft lights, sweet music, a bottle of wine and good food may be hackneyed, but they still work wonders for this lady. But don't take her to Joe's café or the Wimpy Bar; make it somewhere expensive. Remember, we are talking about a snob. Mind you, her suitor should never overstep the mark with wine. One glass too many and he will have lost her to a depression. But if she is allowed to pour out all her worries and inner fears she will probably dissolve into a mass of self-pitying tears, at which point she is emotionally at her most vulnerable. Supply that shoulder to cry on which she so desperately needs, and before you know what has happened, the amorous side of her nature will have been aroused. It is now that she needs tender love, the emphasis on love. Any attempts at ravishing will only be repelled. It's important that her first sexual experience in a relationship should be gentle; after that she will be back for more.

She needs a man who likes a woman who can make him feel like a man. Then she will be a tower of strength in any crisis and will not leave when the going gets really rough.

HOW TO END THE AFFAIR

Spend his money and insult his parents. Develop excessively expensive tastes and unforgivably sloppy ways. Show no interest whatsoever in his career. And if that doesn't cool his ardour, try poking fun at him. Although he enjoys a joke, he isn't too keen on being the subject of them. Plastic spiders in his soup and imitation ink-blots – or better still, real ones – on important papers will be guaranteed to turn him off in record time. Keep this up for at least a week, and good-bye time will be just around the corner. Don't expect him to be friendly afterwards; Capricorns go off the opposite sex rather quickly and usually for good. When disillusionment sets in, he will be gone. There'll be no angry scenes, for he will ignore them. There's no point in raising your voice; he won't be listening. In fact he won't hear you, because he will already be half a mile away.

The same procedure should be followed if it is a female Capricorn who is cramping your style. She too is an extremely ambitious person. She has a clear-cut mental picture of the type of man she needs, and he had better shape up – unless he wants to be rid of her. Therefore, all any man has to do to lose her is to fall short of her expectations.

When her mother is expected for a short stay, kick up a stink. Tell her the old bat isn't welcome in your home and you never liked her anyway. And if you can throw a word or two of abuse at a kid brother or any other relative, this will help too.

At this stage, she is sure to threaten to go back to Mother or her flatmate. Show her you don't care if she swings from the rafters, and the last rays of the relationship will be delivered as she slams the door in your face.

ATTRACTING THE SUN SIGNS
CAPRICORN WOMAN WITH CAPRICORN MAN

This relationship may be somewhat ponderous, but there is no question as to whether it can survive. Neither party will be able to find much fault with the other, for their faults are identical. They share each other's ambitions, materialism, an ability to love ardently and respect for the family. However, they must be prepared for this to be more of a steady partnership than a dazzling love affair. Since this particular sign isn't one to expect nor really want wild, passionate affairs, this may be OK by them. Let's hope, though, they have some amusing friends; somebody has to raise a smile on occasions, and it's certainly not going to be either Mr or Miss Capricorn.

CAPRICORN WOMAN WITH AQUARIUS MAN

Intellectually, these two possess tremendous insight and incisiveness, which characteristics are sure to bring them together. Apart from this, though, it's a rather heavy-going union. Aquarian man (air) misinterprets her practical, feet-firmly-planted-on-the-ground stance, while she won't be slow to describe him as flighty and detached. When she states that she needs him *here*, he'll escape by instinct – which, in the final count, will be the best thing that could happen to them both. Two such diverse personalities find it extremely hard to compromise or rub along in any way.

CAPRICORN WOMAN WITH PISCES MAN

A relationship with possibilities, this is a case of opposites attracting. Dependent Pisces man loves the Capricornian dominance. The sensible Capricorn lady thinks the Piscean intuition is immensely useful. On a sexual level they are extremely compatible. His sympathy and understanding tend to bring out the best in her. However, if both are true to their signs, then she must be happy to lead in this relationship. Remember that this doesn't necessarily mean that he is a weakling (after all he can play the big boss at work); he simply likes a strong woman. If both can accept their inevitable roles, then this partnership may succeed.

CAPRICORN WOMAN WITH ARIES MAN

Aries (the Ram) and Capricorn (the Goat) are sure to lock horns on the slightest pretext. It's true that her practical nature will admire his ability to get things done, but both need to rule. His fiery, quick temper will make her resentful and she will spend many hours trying to find a way to retaliate – as well as to keep a part of her life for herself, while sharing some of it with him. Financially he is impulsive and extravagant, she is conservative and even mean. There's a sort of conflict, then; all in all, a relationship destined to fail.

CAPRICORN WOMAN WITH TAURUS MAN

Initially to the warm Taurean she may seem cold and distant, but if he hangs around long enough and really gets through to her, he will penetrate her superficial façade. Once he has turned on the charm, he will elicit her underlying tenderness. Both belong to an earth sign and are beautifully suited to sharing any kind of relationship. One thing she will have to bear in mind is that he must be allowed the upper hand every day with a W in it. This is one of those relationships where both parties can bring out the better sides of each other.

CAPRICORN WOMAN WITH GEMINI MAN

If both partners are typical of their sign, then the best thing they can do is to part company. Patience is a Capricornian byword; Geminians don't have any in their book at all. She is methodical and practical, he thinks systems are only good for IBM machines. There's no doubt this could be an interesting intellectual friendship, but for a mad passionate affair, both are advised to look elsewhere. And as for marriage – forget it.

CAPRICORN WOMAN WITH CANCER MAN

Not an impossible combination, but one that is basically an attraction of zodiac opposites. She has the ability and intellect to make him feel safe and protected; his sympathy and understanding are food and drink to her suspicious ego; yet, in truth, the two signs would be much better matched if the sexes were reversed. For it won't take the Capricorn woman long to work

197

out that she can dominate this man and, whether she likes it or not, this wouldn't be good for her – not all the time.

CAPRICORN WOMAN WITH LEO MAN

The exuberant Lion feels first and tends to think later. The conscientious Capricornian thinks first and continues to think, even while she is feeling. He is outgoing and his outlandish antics will drive this doubting lady practically up one side of the wall and down the other side. When she has worked this all out for herself, she will need to be careful how she ends their episode, because although Leo man never holds a grudge, she may at a later date decide she would like him for a friend.

CAPRICORN WOMAN WITH VIRGO MAN

Capricorn is the only sign which is one hundred per cent capable of satisfying the Virgo's manic perfectionism. Her exactitude and precision manage to keep his nagging to a minimum and they will both live contentedly in a sparkling clean world with everything in its place. The only problem likely to spoil their otherwise golden relationship is the fact that both will expect to make all of the decisions. However, compromise should be easy for those two, as feelings are likely to run deep enough to achieve some kind of balance.

CAPRICORN WOMAN WITH LIBRA MAN

Like all women, she can hardly fail to be attracted to Mr Libra. On a temporary basis he may race her motor, but her tendency to ride with the brakes on is hard for him to bear. He won't understand her need to be surrounded by luxurious possessions – velvet drapes in the living-room, the best crystal and linen in the dining-room – while she is unlikely to understand his need for constant social activity. His wish constantly to get out and about will be viewed with suspicion by her, for she will believe he wants to escape from her – and eventually he is sure to.

CAPRICORN WOMAN WITH SCORPIO MAN

Unless both partners enjoy deadly combat, this match is most inadvisable. Mr Scorpio's sharp verbal sting and her stubborn temper will have a way of wearing each of them out. Although these two are worthy opponents, who wants to spend all their life making war, not love? It is debatable that they could even get on as friends, for they would still drive each other crazy.

CAPRICORN WOMAN WITH SAGITTARIUS MAN

Her steadfast, pragmatic nature will set the Sagittarian man's teeth grinding, because he is diametrically opposite to what she is and believes in. She may be at first attracted by his free-wheeling, but when it comes to anything more than a casual date every other month, they'll both be climbing walls. If she is smart, she will doubtless keep this relationship on a purely platonic basis.

HOW WELL DO YOU KNOW YOUR CAPRICORN WOMAN?

Answer honestly the questions below, scoring 3 for every Yes, 2 for Sometimes and 1 for No, then add up your total.

1. Does she always look on the gloomy side of things?
2. Does she professionally expect you to succeed?
3. Is she a snob?
4. Does she secrete money away in strange places?
5. Does she loathe parties?
6. Does she possess a sense of occasion?
7. Is she responsible?
8. Would she be upset if she were improperly dressed for some social function?
9. Is she persistent?
10. Is she conservative?
11. Does she have a sense of history or tradition?
12. Does she choose her friends because they can be useful to her?
13. Is she a hypochondriac?
14. Is she anti-speculation of any description?
15. Is she in charge of the money in your household?
16. Is she reserved?
17. Is she inhibited?
18. Does she find it difficult to relax?
19. Does her sexual appetite depend on success or failure outside of the home?
20. Does she drink when she is unhappy?

(Answers)

1–30
Either you have just met the lady, in which case you are totally on the wrong tack, or she is not typical of her sign; for she is far too scatty and extrovert to be a true Goat. It's more likely that she has some affinity with one of the more irresponsible signs, such as Gemini, Sagittarius or Pisces. And if you read these chapters, they will help you to go a long way to understanding her – somebody needs to help you.

200

31–50

You've obviously got yourself a true-blue Capricorn lady in tow and one who possesses one of the nicer aspects of the sign; furthermore, you understand her pretty well. If you have only just met, then you may be on the verge of something big. It's more likely that you've been involved with her for some time, though.

51–60

Somehow you've got yourself involved with a Capricorn female who is in possession of more of the faults than virtues associated with this sign. And somehow you have managed to survive. It's likely that you are rather weak and deficient in some way and need this sober, strong influence in your life. One thing's for sure: there's not going to be an awful lot of fun around. Better make sure you really want to take on this rather heavy-going girl.

HOW WELL DO YOU KNOW YOUR CAPRICORN MAN?

Answer honestly the questions below, scoring 3 for every Yes, 2 for Sometimes and 1 for No, then add up your total.

1. Is his career the principal thing in his life?
2. Is it important to him to do better than his friends or aquaintances?
3. Is it difficult to prise money out of him?
4. Is he extremely strait-laced?
5. Does he demand absolute loyalty?
6. Does he abhor all kinds of sexual deviation?
7. Is he uncomfortable in the presence of women?
8. Has he a sense of history or tradition?
9. Would he be surprised if you took the lead sexually?
10. Does he find it difficult to switch off from work in the evenings?
11. Does he drink too much?
12. Does he adore special occasions?
13. Does he love a bargain?
14. Does he hold the purse-strings?
15. Does he lack a sense of humour?

16. Do you sometimes find him unapproachable?
17. If given too much change, would he take it back to the shop?
18. Do you sometimes think he is a little too superior?
19. Is he or would he be ambitious for his children?
20. Is he embarrassed if you kiss him in public?

(Answers)

1–30

It could be that you have just begun your relationship with your Capricornian man and haven't really got to know him yet; if so you are on the wrong track. However, it's more likely he is not true to his birth sign. There could be another influence – something more versatile and crazy, such as Gemini or Sagittarius. If you look at these chapters, you may find help in understanding him. Don't reject the Capricorn chapter completely; the characteristics are there, even if well hidden.

31–50

You know your Capricorn man extremely well; there's no doubt he's grateful for this. You seem to be able to accept some of his faults, and he is probably going to be in your life for some considerable time to come. You're a lucky girl. You have a protector, lover and father all in one.

51–60

I'm afraid you seem to be lumbered with a Capricorn male born on the rather wet side of this sign. Life is going to be rather short on laughs and fun. This is OK if you are a serious type yourself, but you are in danger of being swamped by this sober character.

Aquarius (the Water Bearer)
Sign of the Humanitarian and Truth-Seeker
January 21 – February 19

The third Air sign: Broadminded, imaginative, reformative, inventive, intuitive, unpredictable
Ruler: Uranus
Colour: Electric blue
Careers: Scientist, photographer, broadcaster, publisher, aviator, electronics engineer
Famous Aquarians: Lord Byron, Charles Darwin, Charles Dickens, Galileo, Mia Farrow, W.C. Fields, Zsa Zsa Gabor, Abraham Lincoln, Yoko Ono, Ronald Reagan, Vanessa Redgrave

---

AQUARIUS MAN

The Aquarian male has strong ideals and humanitarian feelings. He is original and is a progressive thinker. He puts intense energy into any cause, but can be dogmatic. He is scientifically inclined, unpredictable, friendly and invariably attracted to the unusual. At times he is so abstract and philosophical that even his closest friends find this emotional detachment maddening. He must be constantly on his guard against being unreceptive to new ideas. He thrives on brainpower – possibly learning French to impress the waiter, the trombone to amuse company. Any job that ties him down makes him feel trapped. He lives exclusively in the future.

Helping friends and fighting causes, whether lost or otherwise, appears to be the Aquarian's lot in life. He'll wave his banner with the best of them, and then hurry along to bail a friend out of prison or rescue a stranded acquaintance. Never delude yourself that because he is your friend, or even lover, you will ever get really close to him. The Water Bearer is known for his detachment and independence and this is of enormous importance to him. He is capable of making great sacrifices for it, almost to the point of rejecting personal relationships.

Being used to being different from everyone else, he will always have a streak of originality and his application of it covers a wide range of subjects – new outlets for his artistic talents and even scientific ability will be exploited in this way. This can lead to pseudo-artiness or wildly unconventional pursuits.

Although he is much in favour of reform and change, and the advancement of those around him, he is equally stubborn in outlook and fixed in his opinions. He is never easily persuaded that he is wrong. Some find this mixture of kindliness and obstinate insistence on the rightness of his own opinions very disconcerting; the Aquarian's aloof glamour is fascinating and dynamic, but not warm or endearing.

There are times when he doesn't care for the opinions of others and will often simply not bother to form any view of their behaviour. Not that he lacks imagination; his thinking is often ahead of his time, clean-cut, clinical in style. He is also broad-minded, though often what others take as broad-mindedness can be a display of indifference.

Never tell a bald lie to an Aquarian; he will be able to see through the fabrication. He has an uncanny knack of sifting truth from falsehood. Not only does he know when you are lying, he probably knows it before you open your mouth. However, where he is good at spotting a falsehood, he is extremely bad at perpetrating one, and usually won't even try. He knows he is a bad liar so he tries to fool you in a more subtle manner. That way he can never be accused of going against that which he preaches.

The Aquarian is a digger. He will dig into other people's personalities, their family history, their bank account – anything they consider too personal to make public; and he won't stop doing it until he knows them through and through. But just try turning private detective with him. He'll throw his hands up in horror. How dare you pry into his private affairs! It would be easier to find out the workings of MI5. He doesn't like revealing his true feelings; no matter how much he has found out about other people's, his will remain secret. And when he says, "I love you," the person concerned had better make certain that he's talking to them, for he loves just about everybody.

AQUARIUS WOMAN

The female of the species shares many of the qualities of her male counterpart. She is often a dedicated career girl with little or no maternal instinct, and she rarely rushes into marriage. But she does try to reorganize her life with every man she meets.

The more sensitive members of the human race will feel that she tends to analyse their emotions too much. Although she's very attractive, other people are often disillusioned or disappointed by her cool façade. She can discern everybody's virtues, and will not be that interested in their bank balance. Mind you, others won't be too pleased when she brings out their vices and sticks them under their nose alongside their failings.

She tends to look at life from the outside and is rarely able to place trust in others until they have been scrutinized and probed. Friendship for her is founded on understanding and respect, but when she gives her affections, they are well worth having. She tries to be sincere, but can also be lonely, since it is difficult for her to find anyone to measure up to her ideals.

The Aquarian woman rarely belongs to anyone in particular. There is an elusive quality about her affections that is always just out of reach. Don't imagine that chaining her to the kitchen sink and keeping her housebound will reveal all. This couldn't be further from the truth. It will not take her long to break the shackles and flit off to someone less restrictive. However, when she finds a man who understands that her freedom is paramount and accepts a relationship along these lines, then her love will be limitless.

There's an impulsive side to her too, and others may find her grasshopper mind rather disconcerting. She can switch directions in mid-sentence. Discussion about the world situation may easily lead to a discussion about interior decorating, which may lead into a discussion about her childhood and then back to the world situation. Of course there's no relevance. Her head can change direction quicker than the traffic lights change colour. And with the same predictability.

THE HYDE SIDE

These characters are perverse, eccentric, fanatical, unconventional, touchy, rebellious, rudely tactless and lack integrity and principles. They are also far too detached and erratic.

The Aquarian's splendid originality, the ability to be a step ahead of time, in these types reveals itself as crankiness and, in some cases, absent-mindedness. They'll do anything simply for the sake of being different. That wonderful broad mind? It's distorted to the point of inefficiency. Practical considerations are lost in confusion. Opportunities that arise are lost by indecision. Time is wasted over trifles. Lack of tactics and consideration lead them blundering into difficulty, and the power of concentration is almost non-existent. Self-opinionated behaviour is also out of all proportion. They absolutely refuse to believe that *anybody* is as intelligent as they are. Other's feelings and opinions will be brushed aside, given labels like "mindless", "ineffectual". No doubt these Aquarians do have good ideas, but their unfortunate manner will put others on the defensive as soon as they walk into the room.

The female of the species wishes deep down she had been born a male, feeling that there are too many disadvantages to being a woman. For this reason, she will never resort to using sex in order to advance herself: you won't find many Aquarian women on the casting couch. She objects strongly to not being treated as an equal and can become over-bearing and undiplomatic. Both sexes tend always to tell the blunt truth and this on occasions can be impossible for others to live with. Their remarks, unlike the Sagittarian's unintentional *faux pas*, are meant to hurt. And they do. The more sensitive amongst us find them extremely difficult to forget.

But few of us are perfect. We all have our positives and negatives, and Aquarians are no exception. If involved with one, you will discover that fur-lined emotions are a pre-requisite.

HOW TO CATCH AND KEEP YOUR AQUARIUS MAN

Any scheming female who has set her cap at an Aquarian must be prepared to take on half the world as well, for he is greatly concerned with the progress of mankind; if she can bring herself to share this interest, he will be extremely grateful.

However, he rarely allows himself to become personally involved. He does as much as he can for his fellow human, but in a detached kind of way. He rarely becomes emotional and this in most cases makes his help invaluable, for he doesn't let personal feelings cloud his judgement and usually knows what should be done in a logical way. Because of these involvements, his woman is going to have to adapt to the fact that he is frequently away when she needs him. Nagging, however, will prove quite useless. The only thing she can do is make it obvious that she too has a problem which needs solving. Then he may turn his attention to her. This man does not go for frilly flounces on the female form. He respects a woman's independence and that she has a personality of her own. So any woman who wants a man who does nothing but whisper sweet nothings and constantly shower her with devotion should cast her eyes elsewhere.

This man's partner needs to project an intelligent and humanitarian image, but it must be sincere or she'll never keep him.

HOW TO CATCH AND KEEP YOUR AQUARIUS WOMAN

Any man who attempts to limit this woman to what he imagines to be a female role in life is in for a disappointment. She concerns herself with mankind, worries about world starvation or the exploration of natural resources, and is usually caught up in some cause or another. He must either enjoy this or dump her. For she cannot change.

You must also expect plenty of interruptions in your few moments alone with her, for there may be many evenings when the phone rings and she rushes out in answer to some party's desperate plea for help. If her man attempts to restrain her in any way, she will only decide that he is selfish and will probably dismiss him from her mind.

It is also possible that the designing male is under a false illusion that he is doing the chasing. The Aquarian woman, if she wants a man, has no hesitation in telling him so. She is fully liberated and does not subscribe to the old idea of passive woman. If the man in her life believes her to be rather detached or bordering on frigidity, he should think again. It's simply that this woman does not go in for lavish displays of affection. It's not part of her nature, but that does not mean that she cannot feel quite deeply. If he begins to get the distinct impression that he is being neglected, there's no point in nagging or bullying her. The only thing to do is to make it evident that he too is in desperate need of care and attention.

HIS IDEAL PARTNER

In his emotional relationships, the Aquarian male likes to retain a certain amount of independence. Any female who can't appreciate this is definitely on to a loser. Nevertheless, this tendency obviously doesn't make serious relationships easy. It is perhaps true that Aquarians feel most at ease when they are alone and can feel free in all respects. Mind you, if he has investigated his woman thoroughly – which he certainly will have done before committing himself – and has decided she is his ideal, then their partnership will be extremely stable. He can be loyal and faithful, though his dispassionate nature can be a source of conflict.

It's likely that his ideal mate will be born under the signs of Gemini or Libra, for they find this puzzling character relatively easy to fathom, where others are totally mystified. He prefers a woman who already has her own career going full steam ahead. This way he does not feel she is totally dependent on him, and she will also remain interesting to him.

He'd rather come home to an empty house than be greeted on the doorstep by a dowdy, uncommunicative drab. He needs a girl with whom he can exchange ideas and views.

His ideal female is unlikely to be particularly highly sexed, or hyper-sensitive – not that he's sexless, but the physical side of life does come rather low on his list of priorities. It's there when he wants it, and if he doesn't – well, he completely forgets about it.

His perfect woman needs abundant patience, for he does not take to marriage easily. She must be prepared for a long engagement – say about ten years to be on the safe side. Who knows, she might be pleasantly surprised when he proposes after five or six years, although he might consider this to be a bit rushed. And she mustn't expect him to descend upon her with armfuls of lovely flowers and poetic words; she may receive the odd dog-rose, thrust under her nose, and he may even write a love letter at some point, but the message will be the same as if the flowers were an expensive bunch of red roses or the poems written by Robert Browning. She must never try pushing him into marriage. Playing hard to get may arouse his interest, but any female who attempts to prompt jealousy by telling him that she is thinking of marrying someone else is in for a disappointment. He will just use this for an excuse to duck out of the affair.

When he finally marries his ideal partner, she will have more than just a husband. She'll have a crusader, reformer, idealist, truth-seeker and an eccentric, all rolled into one. But faint-hearts should stay away.

HER IDEAL PARTNER

She needs a man who won't only expect her to be a lover but also a friend. One is inadequate without the other. Her ideal man is free from pettiness, having no desire to keep her in his pocket. Those with the best chance are born under Libra or Gemini, for they are capable of making her happy.

Should she eventually get around to marrying and having a family – something she will not do until she has checked out her mate thoroughly – she will want her offspring to be as independent as she is. Many Aquarian women can be found among supporters of advanced educational techniques. She may force her ideas on to young shoulders and discuss controversial topics with her children. And she will always need to know what is going on in the minds of her loved ones. Her ideal mate won't mind if she probes deeply into his most private thoughts. It's unlikely he will have a secret left by the time she is through with him. But he must never try the same tactics with her.

The Aquarian woman has undoubted charm but does tend to be something of a bossy-boots. Therefore, the opposite sex may either adore her or loathe everything she stands for. Her perfect man will respect her need for a busy life outside the home, someone who will not be amused by her constant cause-fighting; furthermore he must be open-minded and emotional and not too highly sexed. (Does that rule out everybody? Possibly.) She in turn will respect a man who has ambitions of his own. He must never lose sight of his ultimate goal, for, in her eyes, compromise is tantamount to failure.

Obviously, then, she is not an easy girl to please; nor is she the epitome of passionate delight and togetherness. But once she has chosen her mate, and he turns out to be the ideal one, wedded bliss is just around the corner. It may always be just out of reach, but it is there – somewhere.

SEXUALLY (MALE)

The Aquarian is the truth-seeker, and although he won't like it, I think it's permissible to hit him with the truth right now. Sex, and all that sex entails, is not high on his list of essentials. Certainly it is there and has to be recognized, even indulged in occasionally, but he counts it a small part of any relationship. He is not a creature of extremes, believing that moderation is to be adhered to in all things physical. For this reason he is unlikely to be attracted to women with keen sexual appetites. Well, not for more than the occasional one-nighter! The female who likes sex for breakfast, lunch, dinner and supper had better find somewhere else to dine; she isn't going to be satisfied with a few crumbs dropping from this particular table.

When he meets an interesting woman, he is more likely to attempt to get into her head rather than into her bed. He will, of course, appraise her physical appearance, but only to ascertain whether or not she is his type. Having passed this test, she will be expected to spend the rest of the evening talking about world politics, mutual careers, prison reform, violence on television – or other such erotic subjects. Only when he catches sight of her stifled yawns will he realize he must be doing something wrong. It is at this point that he will gather that discussions on international conflicts or the death penalty are not necessarily the best aphrodisiacs on the market. He may then attempt to make a quick adjustment, rushing the overtures and inspiring no response whatsoever.

This man believes in equality, and if he finds himself in the happy position of being propositioned by the female, he will see nothing wrong or peculiar about it. To him it's perfectly natural. He is the liberated woman's delight.

Because he is preoccupied with externals, he tends not to give the sexual side of life a great deal of thought, unless he is with a girl who can really light his fire. Aquarian sexuality largely depends on experience. If at some time in the not too distant past he has been fond enough of a female to allow her to introduce him to the many physical aspects of life, she may have whetted his appetite. In this case, he will thirst for experience, and here Aquarians can have very dry throats. But it must be remembered that when he indulges it will be done in a rather clinical fashion. It is the experiment that fascinates him, rather than the actual sensation.

If he has been unfortunate enough to go through life without a purely sexual affair, his interest will be practically nil. Any girl with designs on this particular character will need to introduce him to the better things of physical love. Shock tactics can work miracles. Not surprisingly, a sense of humour is important when becoming involved with this individual, who responds with vigour to anything he finds amusing.

SEXUALLY (FEMALE)

Members of the opposite sex who have a smooth line in small-talk and love to pile on the flattery are definitely playing the wrong game with this lady. It will get him absolutely nowhere. In fact, she is quite likely to turn around and laugh in his face. It's always better by far to use an open and direct approach with this truth-seeker. Just so long as sex isn't taken for granted.

The Aquarian woman is not hampered by old-fashioned ideals and if she sees someone she likes, she will go right ahead

211

and tell him. The way through to her is via her intellect. Conversation should centre on politics, religion or careers – perhaps not the most erotic of topics, but ones guaranteed to stimulate her interest and her mind, and it won't be long before he can change the subject to more personal matters. One or two compliments are permissible. She will know her best feature and it will pay him to discover it and play on this. She is not one to fool around in a long-term relationship; if her man says he is going to phone at quarter past eight, then he had better do it on the button, unless he wants to listen to the unobtainable signal. The moment she senses he is not being totally straightforward, she will be off.

She won't really mind if he may have half a dozen other girl-friends, so long as he is where he says he is going to be. She dislikes deception of all description.

Sexual curiosity gets through to her. She is not spurred on by any tremendous appetite. She can discuss, quite clinically, the quirks and practices of others. If they happen to strike a bell along the line, she will suggest they try it out. Regrettably, she believes one can become sexually adept without practice or thought. The man who tries to tell her she is wrong will finish up with a full-scale war on his hands. With other sun signs, this could lead to an interesting kiss-and-make-up session, but not with the Aquarian woman. Her glacial side will come to the fore and he will end up sharing his bed with Sally the Snowwoman.

Neither does she go in for the kinkier side of life and she won't be aroused by the sight of hobnailed boots or handcuffs. But she is able on occasions to come up with a variation on a theme. Imagination, intellectual stimuli and sexual creativity are there in the offing, providing the poor man can get her off the starting-blocks. But do leave your running spikes at home.

HOW TO END THE AFFAIR

This is a relatively easy task, for the Aquarian never sticks around where he isn't wanted. He will always, therefore, appreciate honesty. However, if you suspect that he is deeply in love with you, then a little tact is called for (although it's unlikely that he would think the same, were the position reversed).

Try applying claustrophobic tactics. Restrict him, demand to know where he is going, with whom and what time he will be returning. A couple of weeks of this behaviour and you wouldn't be able to keep him around you even if you wanted to. But if this doesn't have the desired effect, try taking a conservative attitude towards all things. Don't allow him to be the good Samaritan at 3 o'clock in the morning, or if it is impossible to hold him back, don't let him bring home his rescued friends. Cut him off from all his acquaintances. Keep him to yourself.

The same policy can be adopted by males attempting to rid themselves of a female Aquarian. Make a stand by telling her that you believe that a woman's place is in the home and that her role, from now on, will be as mother and housekeeper. See how her face drops a few inches? That sweeping glance she gave towards the door? It won't be long before she is sitting you down, saying, "Darling, there's something I'd like to discuss with you . . ." She may not even get around to it, since she does tend to change her mind quite often. Once she has sensed that you are losing interest, her bags will probably be packed long before you get around to throwing her out.

It's not hard to dislodge an Aquarian – they never stick around where they know they aren't wanted.

ATTRACTING THE SUN SIGNS

AQUARIUS WOMAN WITH AQUARIUS MAN

Who can understand the crazy Aquarian lady's needs to go flying kites, roller-skating in the park, running barefoot, splashing in puddles, better than another Aquarian? She is sure to meet him somewhere unusual – at a demonstration, on an archaeological dig or in a Moroccan bazaar. Sexual attraction is strong between this couple and when it comes to love-making she can be as inventive as he is. All very nice, one might think, but don't forget the other side of the Aquarian nature, the self-opinionated side, which often fails to consider the opinions of other people. Two personalities inclined this way could make life pretty rough, and in a long relationship it wouldn't take much to kill off the romance. When confronted with the realities of what is left, one or maybe even both of them could depart in record time. An excellent relationship on a short basis.

AQUARIUS WOMAN WITH PISCES MAN

The kind Piscean man will be attractive to her because he can tolerate her tendency to go off in several directions at once. He has probably studied her astrological chart and might even tell her what to expect from life each day. He is invariably glad to make her a hot drink, warm her slippers when she comes in from the cold, and in fact warm her up physically any time. But will she be as considerate? Most unlikely. While the Piscean man can go on giving and giving and giving, even he must eventually reach the limit of his patience. Mind you, it's likely that she will be extremely sad when their relationship does end, as she won't have realized just how many of those endless little things he had done for her. A rather one-sided affair.

AQUARIUS WOMAN WITH ARIES MAN

Dynamic, unstable and with a hint of explosion is the best way to describe the Aquarian/Aries combination. She must expect a certain amount of friction and some emotional beating. The Aquarian woman likes to take risks occasionally and may therefore investigate at least one Aries man in her life. However, her intuitive common sense will doubtless keep her from making it permanent. Initially she may find his hyper-sensitive ego somewhat amusing, but whoever laughs at the Aries man does so at their peril. When she realizes he is deadly serious, and that he genuinely does put himself first in life, disenchantment is sure to set in double-quick. In order to attract him, she would have to suppress her own personality. If she is content to play second fiddle to his needs and desires, and is able to pander to his vanity, then all will be well. But all this is extremely unlikely. Friendship maybe, but a successful love affair? Never.

AQUARIUS WOMAN WITH TAURUS MAN

In order to attract this man, a certain amount of deception is necessary, which is alien to her personality; for she would need to pretend to be more practical, down-to-earth and convention-

214

al than she really is. Otherwise she will drive the rather rigid Taurean crazy with her Aquarian restlessness. True, they both love comfort and luxury, but they won't agree about exactly what it entails. Worst of all, perhaps, he'll want to know all the details of every affair she has ever had. She considers this to be her own business and certainly won't want to share her secrets, with anyone. An unlikely combination.

AQUARIUS WOMAN WITH GEMINI MAN

This is a perfect partnership. The many-faceted Aquarian woman is highly compatible with the Geminian's dual nature. They will love surprising each other, and neither will be baffled or offended by the other's changeability. She may need to take care not to allow him to feel shut out when she goes off in a corner to contemplate her navel, but the ability to consider each other's feelings should solve any problems in this particular union. True, she won't be mad about the way he flirts with anything that remotely resembles the opposite sex, but she basically will understand his need for intellectual stimulation, therefore an excellent relationship is on the cards.

AQUARIUS WOMAN WITH CANCER MAN

Her constant need for external stimuli, her chasing of causes, plus her busy social whirling, are likely to put Mr Cancer into something of a state of shock and send him ranting and raving to the nearest psychiatrist. Between her eccentricities and his moodiness, they could both spend much time on the analyst's couch, especially if they decide to make this togetherness last for ever. In general two personalities so opposed should stay as far apart as possible.

AQUARIUS WOMAN WITH LEO MAN

This is an interesting combination, made up as it is of zodiac opposites. She can provide the surprises Mr Leo so loves; and he's strong enough to withstand the whimsies of her

215

offhanded, detached intellect. Each will get a kick out of complementing, observing and in some instances sharing the other's talents. But the Aquarian woman will never be happy to pander to his enormous ego. If anything, she finds it rather amusing. However, if they don't decide actually to get married, maybe they could consider going into business together. They could certainly make a go of it in that direction.

AQUARIUS WOMAN WITH VIRGO MAN

If opposing personalities could be made not only to attract but be compatible, then these two would make a fine couple. He needs order where she thrives on disorder; he loves to criticize, she won't tolerate rebuke. She knows his soft spot and cannot help but appear to be constantly homing in on it. She would be better off bargain-hunting than hanging around this character for any length of time. An unlikely union.

AQUARIUS WOMAN WITH LIBRA MAN

Her intrinsic abilities and his gift for generally getting along will make this a near-perfect partnership. At first he may be tempted to interfere with her liking for occasional solitude, but once she has explained this need, he is perfectly able to understand. Venus (Libra) and Uranus (Aquarius) are capable of fulfilling each other's wishes with ease. An ideal relationship of any description is forecast.

AQUARIUS WOMAN WITH SCORPIO MAN

She is likely to have the possessive and jealous Scorpion in a padded cell within a month. Her reserve in love-making is no match for his passion; her social flitting will make him prepare to sting and her external philanthropic interests will seem intolerable to one who believes that charity definitely begins at home. Furthermore, both can be immovably stubborn and self-opinionated with the wrong mate – and they are definitely wrong for each other.

216

AQUARIUS WOMAN WITH SAGITTARIUS MAN

On a short-term basis these two blithe spirits can prove extremely well suited, for both love freedom, excitement, frivolity and constant change. He will be delighted to discover that she knows what he wants before he does. He will reciprocate by showing her all the wonderful sex he has longed for but perhaps didn't know where to find. After a while, however, differing interests could mean that a large part of their time will be spent apart, and although they won't want it to happen, it may only be a matter of time before they slowly, but surely, drift apart. An excellent friendship or affair.

AQUARIUS WOMAN WITH CAPRICORN MAN

Although these two share complementary intellects, this alone is not enough to keep the Aquarian woman from breaking out of the Capricornian prison. He will constantly strive to reorganize her and tie her down, while she will overwhelm him with her free-spirited thinking. She will be horrified at the strength of his possessiveness, and will quickly realize that he is not going to be easy to elude, once he has decided that she is the girl for him. One can only hope his common sense will make him realize that this match could never work permanently.

HOW WELL DO YOU KNOW YOUR AQUARIUS WOMAN?

Answer honestly the questions below, scoring 3 for every Yes, 2 for Sometimes and 1 for No, then add up your total.

1. Is she for equality for all?
2. Is sex low on her list of priorities?
3. Would she be off if she detected any signs of jealousy or possessiveness?
4. Is she a bad liar?
5. Is she forever chasing lost causes?
6. Do you find her cool detachment difficult to understand?
7. Does she detest housework?
8. Is she sexually conventional?
9. Would she be appalled if you didn't keep your promises?
10. Is she an unconventional dresser?
11. Do other people regard her as eccentric?
12. Is she unpredictable?
13. Does she put the outside world before you?
14. Is she lacking in tact?
15. Does she loathe emotional outbursts?
16. Is she unsentimental?
17. Would she wonder what you were after if you bought her a dozen red roses?
18. Does she get restless at romantic dinners for two?
19. Is she attracted to lame dogs?
20. Does she often think you'll never never understand her?

(Answers)

1–30
If your lady regards herself as a true Aquarian, and you've known her for any length of time, you must be completely confused. From your score it's quite apparent you don't really know her at all. However, there's another explanation: there may be other influences at work on her chart, for she seems to be more romantic, feminine and domesticated than the average Aquarian. Perhaps if you read the chapters devoted to Pisces, Scorpio and Cancer you may find her true character.

31–50

You have in tow, my friend, a true Aquarian. You seem to be doing an admirable job when it comes to understanding her. You are probably a freewheeling type yourself, in which case you are perfectly suited. If you are not already married, that happy state can't be too far off.

51–60

I'm afraid you have found yourself an Aquarian female with more of the faults associated with this sign than the virtues. If you are married to her, then life can't be exactly a bowl of roses. If you're not, it's unlikely she will ever succumb to this final commitment. No Aquarian likes to be known and probed as deeply as you have been able to do.

HOW WELL DO YOU KNOW YOUR AQUARIUS MAN?

Answer honestly the questions below, scoring 3 for every Yes, 2 for Sometimes and 1 for No, then add up your total.

1. Does he expect to share his interests with you?
2. Is he interested in politics?
3. Does he loathe routine?
4. Would he offer assistance if he saw someone lying on a pavement?
5. Does he frequently fail to notice when you are upset?
6. Does he prefer to sit up all night talking, rather than making love?
7. Would he be upset if he caught you telling a lie?
8. Would he use evasive action if he sensed you were spoiling for a fight?
9. Do you wish he were more imaginative in bed?
10. Is he unmaterialistic?
11. Is there a private side to him you don't understand?
12. Does he regard his work as a vocation rather than simply a job?
13. Is he something of an eccentric dresser?
14. Does he have no sense of occasion?
15. Does he have a wide circle of friends all from different backgrounds?

16. Does he lack tact?
17. Does he fail to consider your sexual needs?
18. Would he tell you if he thought you looked a mess?
19. Do other people find him somewhat odd?
20. Is he opinionated?

(Answers)

1–30

In a word, no, you don't – not if he is a true Aquarian. If he is, you are totally on the wrong track. Perhaps you should make a more concerted effort to get to know him. However, another possibility may be that there are other influences at work on his chart, possibly Pisces, Scorpio or Cancer. A quick read through these chapters may prove quite enlightening.

31–50

You've found yourself a true Aquarian man of the nicer type and seem to know and understand him very well. You are a perceptive but independent type yourself and you'll make him an excellent mate. Maybe you already are.

51–60

Clearly, your Aquarian is not one of the nicer types, I'm afraid. Your life must be full of confusion and chaos. However, you seem for the moment able to adapt to all of this; whether you could for life is another matter.

Pisces (the Fish)
Sign of the Musician or Artist
February 20 – March 20

The third Water sign: Considerate, sensitive, intuitive, imaginative, suggestible, impressionable
Ruler: Neptune
Colour: Sea green
Careers: Artist, writer, actor, poet, sailor, social worker
Famous Pisceans: Harry Belafonte, Chopin, Albert Einstein, Jean Harlow, George Harrison, Michelangelo, Rudolf Nureyev, Sidney Poitier, Prince Andrew, Lynn Redgrave, Renoir, Elizabeth Taylor

PISCES MAN

Because the male Piscean is idealistic, he doesn't appear as practical as he often is. When he has to choose between common sense and utopianism, he uses down-to-earth methods. He usually manages to have the material things necessary to comform. If, however, there is a big difference between his ideals and the real conditions of his life, he tends to be restless and discontent, and to compensate can become obsessed by insignificant detail. He is very sympathetic to others, but usually modest and unassuming, often lacking confidence in himself. He has an extremely agreeable love

221

nature and is very domesticated. He is so pleasant that frequently he is the pet in the family.

He is totally unconcerned with superficial appearances, but more with the inner being, the essence of spirit, rather than concrete physical fact. To him there's little difference between reality and fantasy. He writes and speaks fluently. He is a mystic and may write about religion with divine inspiration. Other people often think him weak, but then you would be mistaken if you described him as strong. The Fish is such a modest creature that when things go well for him it may not occur to him that he had anything to do with it. Whenever life looks black, he waits fatalistically for somethign to turn up. If it does, all will be well; but if it doesn't then a well aimed kick up the rear may help the situation quite dramatically.

This character feels all emotion keenly, so experiences extreme happiness as well as unhappiness. Since he is very much influenced by prevailing conditions and those around him, these can either make or break him. He is also the type who from time to time is best left alone. It is not that he desires to be anti-social, it is simply that on occasion he needs a period in which to recuperate from the world and sort himself out. Other people may try to force him to face life head-on, but their efforts will be totally wasted and only serve to push him deeper into his own secret world, where he can dream, plan and think alone.

Not surprisingly, the Fish is drawn to liquid; he likes to be in it, on it and to consume it. It's rarely enough for him to have a quick sip of sherry at a christening party, once he's got the taste, he will imbibe until he drops beneath the baby's cot. Of course, not every Piscean is alcoholic, but I wouldn't mind betting that the Salvation Army have tried to save more Pisceans from the demon drink than any other sun sign.

The Fish was designed to see the world as a great big bowl of cherries. He does, of course, recognize the pips when he sees them, but he would rather dine on the flesh of the fruit floating through his liquid world where everything is beautiful. When he does receive a body-blow from life, it takes the wind out of him. He tends to hide beneath the cloud until the storm passes; making a practical decision which will once more bring him into the sunlight of reality seems beyond him.

The Fish doesn't like restriction. Admittedly he is somewhat indifferent if it doesn't take away his ability to dream a little, and he's not the violent type. Others may rant and rave at him, only to find him looking at them in a rather patronizing fashion. He always bears in mind that sticks and stones can break his bones, but words can never harm him. He may even be attempting to stifle a yawn while others are becoming blue in the face with rage.

But don't get the idea that he cannot be roused to anger. He wouldn't be human if he was always able to turn the other cheek. His retaliation won't be physical but rather verbally caustic. He can take most people by surprise with a few well chosen words. Then, as quickly as his venom has been spilled, he will revert to his smile with a look that makes you wonder if you imagined it. But invariably the line of least resistance is thought to be the best remedy.

The Piscean man may think that he can live for ever, and there's no point in other people attempting to disillusion him. He'll believe he will go on to be 210 anyway. What's the point of shattering his dreams? Better that other people climb aboard his gentle cloud and float along with him until he reaches the star that only he can see. Of course they may never get there, but what a superb journey they will have.

PISCES WOMAN

This is a sympathetic and poetic person. Her sixth sense understands, soothes and transmutes other people's troubles. She has a strongly protective streak and often a weakness for the lame dog. Sometimes this involves finding jobs for friends, homes for lost kittens and new girlfriends for old lovers. She possesses little self-confidence, and the fear of overlooking vital matters causes her to overwork, check and recheck every project, date and business contract six times before she commits herself.

She can be extremely eccentric. She may fast for days, then eat her way through the refrigerator. Her pessimism and prudence can lead her to buy a bus ticket to the airport, then hail a cab at the last minute because she is afraid she will miss the flight, even though she is two hours ahead of time.

She has a tremendous fund of affection and love; she is

devoted to those who are close to her, sometimes overly concerned about their welfare. In fact she is so self-sacrificing, does things so unselfishly and with so little fuss that other people may not fully appreciate what she does for them apparently so effortlessly. And though she is not the kind who expects any kind of reward, ingratitude can hurt her deeply.

The Piscean female is one hundred per cent woman and as such she is extremely attracted to the opposite sex. She has great compassion, and her friends will include a few waifs and strays of all ages. And they are not always human: there's always free milk for the neighbourhood cat outside this lady's back door and her garden will be chock-full of breadcrumbs and titbits for the birds during the winter. Her man will never be able to complain of neglect. She has enough love to go around a thousand-fold. If his boss has barked at him a little too loudly or a taxi driver been insulting, she will soon soothe his hurt feelings with a cool hand and a whispered word. Many of these delightful women will be found nursing the sick and infirm or offering comfort in their very own kitchen.

Unfortunately, like her male counterpart, she cannot stand too much harsh reality. That horrible, noisy, dusty world on the other side of her front door will send her finely tuned notes into complete and utter discord. If she is sensible she will escape through the arts, develop a flair for acting, mime or poetry, or may even take to dancing, whether of the disco variety, ballet or free, exotic dancing in the style of Isadora Duncan.

It's easy to use watery metaphors when speaking of the Piscean, for her characteristics are often those of the sea with its hidden depths, sudden storms and shifting currents.

Her emotions are so strong that she, as well as others, can be in constant turmoil because of them. The more she can impose creative shape upon her feelings, the greater her chance of coming to terms with them pyschologically.

Children adore her. It won't upset her at all to discover her son or daughter with hand stuck in the peanut-butter jar or mouth crammed full of cream biscuits. She will most probably laugh at the spectacle, even when it happens time and time again. She finds it hard to discipline and needs help in this direction. Should she ever resort to her first whacking, perhaps because her man suggested it was the thing to do, there will be tears in her eyes. It doesn't come naturally to her to give the children the rough side of her tongue and her offspring may be somewhat spoilt. She will do her best to instil in them an artistic love of beauty, but she must recognize her failings in practical matters.

When she works, on no account should she consider a career where discipline or noise play too great a part. She needs beauty, peace and tranquillity. It's unusual to find a Piscean woman in a job where figures are paramount; all numbers confuse her gentle mind.

The female Fish doesn't find it easy to conform; she cannot cope with discipline or routine and will not run her life in anything like an orderly fashion. Her natural kindness, sympathy, charm and general softness will impress her man and inspire her friends. They will probably think so much of her that they won't even notice the chaos that abounds in her home. Her sentimentality can sometimes annoy a more practical person but her dream-weaving impracticality is bound to win over even the most staid and critical types. And when she sits beside you and turns those beautifully expressive eyes on you, who could possibly fail to be won over?

THE HYDE SIDE

When Pisceans are weak, they are very, very weak: impractical, over-emotional, too soft, careless, indecisive, touchy, secretive, incomprehensible, confused in handling their affairs, gullible, extravagant, temperamental and completely dependent on other people. The fine, vivid imagination which is a source of positive direction to the stronger Fish is abused in the negative types, taking the form of delusion, and they are inclined to over-indulgence in drugs or alcohol. There's a tremendous difference between the good and the bad Piscean, the one being able to rise to the top of every field, the other sinking to the depths of degradation and despair.

The Hyde side of Pisces promotes the types who tend to be lazy and attached to the home mainly because it is the most comfortable place to be. They have to fight hard for stability and to resist the impulse of the moment. They fight hardest when their pride is threatened. Friends expect them to talk behind their backs, enemies are deceived by their surreptitious plotting and they can never be pinned down. They also tend to imagine snubs and don't forgive easily.

The astrological symbol of Pisces is two fishes with their tails tied together, which aptly illustrates these characters' attitude to life. First, they are pulled one way and then the other. Naturally enough they get nowhere at all.

Hypochondria is often found in those born under the sign of the Fish, who are prone to strange attractions and ideas which they make no attempt to control. The desire for their own secret world is inflated out of all proportion in these instances.

Financially speaking, those with a strong negative influence could be regarded as completely hopeless, an accountant's nightmare – totally unable to budget, always in debt and sparing little or no thought for the discharge of their creditors. If this sounds a little Victorian and gives the impression that these types are wastrel – you are right first time. But to be fair, it isn't really all their own fault. Their troubles can stem from emotional upsets. Couple this with any form of financial strain and you get a serious drain on their health. The problem is that they will never learn to conserve what energy they do have, and so they become victim to their own fatigue. Medical cabinets are crammed full of all sorts of pills and potions which they imagine can give them good health.

But let's be realistic. Most of us are a fair mixture of good and bad, therefore a Piscean who is one hundred per cent worthless is a rarity. But it does no harm to be prepared.

HOW TO CATCH AND KEEP YOUR PISCES MAN

This is probably the most sensitive sign in the zodiac. Mr Pisces is usually also Mr Romantic. He will run from any aggressive or possessive female. He needs to feel free to grow and develop in his own particular way. He is quite happy to give his love and he cannot be forced to express it constantly; if this should be expected, then he will withdraw into his own secret world where he will be impossible to contact.

The Piscean is usually an artistic soul; even if he works in an office or factory he will generally indulge his aesthetic instincts in a hobby such as music or painting. He will expect his woman to show as much interest in this as he does. The sensitivity

226

lurking beneath the surface of this individual makes him greatly concerned with all vulnerable beings and he will weaken to anyone likewise inclined. The Piscean is not fitted to take responsibility or pressure in any guise. This means that his mate must be prepared to take over the practical side of life without reproach or resentment, for nagging and bullying will achieve nothing. This man is impressed by the woman who is gentle, kind, feminine and just as sensitive as he is.

HOW TO CATCH AND KEEP YOUR PISCES WOMAN

No one could accuse the Piscean woman of being anything but feminine. She is the softest type of female in the zodiac: romantic, highly sensitive and emotional and usually aware of it. She will be attracted to a big, strong, protective man, one whom she feels she can rely on totally and who will appreciate her need for constant reassurance and romance, without thinking she is the least bit stupid. She is a lover of children and animals and her home will be bulging with the most unlikely pets; she finds it impossible to walk by any bedraggled suffering part of humanity. There's no point in attempting to change her, one must just accept this as part of her personality.

She has a rather secretive side, and there are times when she needs to be on her own in order to sort herself out. The man in her life must stifle any impulses to be hurt or annoyed when she refuses to let him in. She will re-emerge when she has put everything in its proper perspective and knows exactly how to act next. Bullying will only result in her withdrawing further, and communication will become almost impossible.

Although the Piscean female is attracted to the very masculine male, macho types are wasting their time, for her man must also have a well defined streak of sensitivity and sentimentality.

HIS IDEAL PARTNER

This man needs a very special type of woman with certain specifications, and very often she is to be found under the signs of Scorpio or Cancer. These are both equally emotional, sensitive and sympathetic as Pisces, and they do not find him nearly so complex as other girls are sure to. With the wrong girl, the Piscean man can end up a complete neurotic or a gibbering alcoholic, for he is very easy to undermine. He needs someone like himself, gentle, kind. But his ideal mate needn't bother to get too maternal about him, since he also needs someone with a sense of the romantic, without which he is unable to face up to the harsher realities of life. Pisceans like to be told that, no matter what storms are on the horizon, one day the rain will stop and sunshine will prevail.

Above all, his ideal woman must eventually want to settle down and have children, for he makes an excellent father. They love the way he readily joins in their games, for like them he has dreams and fantasies of his own. If the children want him to play cowboys and Indians with them, he'll slip into the spirit of it with great relish. His ideal mate won't get uptight when her full-grown Piscean male dresses as a gorilla, charging through the kitchen chased by a whole posse of little big-game hunters!

Most of his appetites are well developed and that includes sexual, so the undersexed female should stay away. If kept in short supply where physical love is concerned, a Piscean withdraws into his own little world. No one can enter, he'll want to be alone. Neither should she be surprised to find a goodbye note from him when he does eventually emerge. His ideal woman will be able to build his ego physically, but, most of all, must love him quite desperately. Any hard-hearted Hannahs had better stay away from him. He must be allowed to keep his dreams intact, for someone who shatters the thin crystal of a Piscean dream bubble is never forgiven.

Money can also cause trouble in Piscean relationships. He is not exactly noted for his six-figure bank account, unless it's on the red side – and that doesn't worry him, for red is such a nice colour. His perfect woman will take command of the purse strings long before he learns how to untie the knot. That won't of course give her *carte blanche* for extravagance, for if he sees her throwing money around he's likely to follow suit. She will have to look after his money, then, for it's hard to come by. The Piscean doesn't earn that easily.

HER IDEAL PARTNER

Because of the gentleness of her nature, it is extremely important that the Piscean woman become involved with the right
man, and her chances of happiness are increased with those
born under the signs of Scorpio and Cancer. These types can
handle her complex nature without too much trouble, and their
characteristics complement and enhance hers.

Her ideal man's imagination is on a par with her own. He will
enjoy being spoilt and flattered and believe in keeping romance
alive just as she does. She does have a jealous streak which can
surface on occasion, but when taken by such a mood she is
rarely given to ugly scenes. In fact she can appear so appealing
at such times that the man concerned will end up feeling guilty
as hell and hating himself for causing her a moment's suffering.

Emotionally she is definitely demanding, a leaner. A mate
who is insensitive to this will destroy her completely. Love is
very closely tied up with sex, and she needs to feel that she is
the only girl in her man's life. Any man who is so uncertain of
himself that he finds it necessary to improve his ego by having
a little bit on the side will not be welcome here.

She has no desire to dominate her man or to wear his
trousers. She may don his jacket on a couple of occasions,
should he sink into a lazy phase, but only to give him a nudge
in the right direction. She needs someone to protect her from
the harsh world and will be absolutely convinced that he is able
to do so; and if he is the right partner for her, he will. His
shoulders must be big enough for her to cry on and, when
necessary, to blot out any day-to-day nastiness that might come
her way. In return she will certainly make him feel all male.

A man who can help her overcome her natural timidity and
self-doubt will be the one to win her heart and soul. Then she
will sacrifice all for him. If times get hard along the way, she is
prepared to give and give, just as much as she may receive. And
she will always stand by her man when life takes a turn for the
worst.

SEXUALLY (MALE)

Being naturally charming and having a certain appeal all of his very own, the Piscean man is hard to resist. Most girls find it extremely difficult to say no to him. Turn him down and those hurt Piscean eyes make a woman feel extremely guilty. For he gives the impression that she has denied him what he believes to be the most precious thing in the world. She may be so filled with remorse that she eventually changes her mind.

For the most part, this man's approach to sex is a romantic one – that is, unless life has led him to become old before his time, in which case he may be rather cynical and disillusioned. Generally speaking, though, he is the type to send his woman armfuls of daffodils, still wet from the morning dew, or a velvety orchid on a warm summer evening. He will pamper her and treat her like a lady and the least she can do is be appreciative. His wooing must never be greeted with derision or taken for granted, otherwise he will be off. Fortunately for him, there are enough romantic women in this world to bring out the best in him.

His imagination, where sex is concerned, serves him well. He can do anything she wishes. Given the right sexual partner, there's no stopping him. His aim is not only to please himself but to satisfy her desires and he will go to any lengths to achieve this.

Because he isn't the strongest of characters, there are times when he is drawn to the dominating kind of woman; it is then possible for him to become some kind of sexual slave to her desire, but it won't last, of course. He will never force his desires upon the girl he loves; she must be willing. He would rather satisfy them in his head than offend her.

SEXUALLY (FEMALE)

It is difficult for any male to resist the female Piscean. She is naturally charming and always seems in need of protection. But she is a dreamer, and the only way she can be appealed to is through romance. She is very hard to forget once you have shared her company. Any man who approaches her with a direct manner will mortify her and send her scurrying for her hidey-hole. But the smoothy with the fancy words cannot overdo it. She will melt under the moon in June and go in for all the other lyrical clichés. She will sit wide-eyed and innocent as all the old lines are trotted out, sending her up on to her own romantic cloud of fantasy.

When she is flying high in her golden puffball, she is sexually ready to go, but things have to be taken easily. Gentle and tender is the only way. Animal lust should be left in the farmyard where it belongs, in her opinion. Cavemen types get absolutely nowhere with her. Also it should be borne in mind that this lady will never ever approach a man; no matter how much she wants him to make love to her, she will never proposition him. She doesn't have to, however; she is expert in all the feminine wiles and is clever at drawing attention to herself without being obvious.

Apart from the need for romance, imagination is another prerequisite, for hers is inexhaustible. She will have a million ways of pleasing her man and then some more which will come to her while they are tangled up in the sheets. It is important that her lover attempt to join in with her fantasies and, where he can, make them reality. She is not unreasonable in her demands and will not expect you to do anything that is unattractive to you.

HOW TO END THE AFFAIR

Don't for one minute think this is going to be easy. The Piscean, if he believes himself deeply in love, places his woman on a pedestal a mile high and it could be hard for her to step down that far. She can do no wrong – ever. He will stubbornly disbelieve anything bad about her.

This situation requires a great deal of tact and diplomacy. Whatever you do, don't turn around and say "It's over and I'm off." Have you ever seen a Piscean with a broken heart? A fallen angel couldn't look more desolate. It may be several weeks before you are able to shake this gentleman loose, even if you intend to leave him with his sanity. The first step is to mention that you are beginning to have doubts and are no longer certain that you are compatible with each other as you first thought. Now you have to prove it to him, and this can be quite hard. The Piscean character is split in so many different directions that only you will know what he considers to be his ideal. It is up to you to disillusion him. But here are one or two other suggestions.

Since this is the most impractical of men, you could try becoming the most practical of girls. There is a chance this could endear you to him even further, but if he has gone as far as asking you to marry him, you should sit down with pencil and paper and tick off the relevant items that a wedding entails. Tell him of the cost, bore him to tears with figures: the cost of your trousseau, the bridesmaids' dresses, the hire of the reception room, etc. Then get on to the expense after the happy day. Work out how much you are going to need for housekeeping, electricity, gas bills, laundry, etc. – and that's before any children come along. There's nothing like a balance-sheet to destroy his romantic mood and send him screaming to the hills. Whenever you see the romance welling up in his eyes, switch the conversation to money or any mundane subject. Two or three weeks of this and he will begin to agree that you are indeed totally incompatible.

The same procedure should be used when attempting to dispose of the female Piscean. She is an extremely feminine woman and totally at a loss when it comes to practical considerations. If she thinks you are going to bully her about expenditure, saving for the future, etc., she will become quickly disillusioned.

Whatever you do, don't keep your Piscean hanging on any longer than necessary. Don't suggest a temporary parting; that will keep the flame of hope burning a little too brightly, and as the Piscean's life is built on dreams this is the cruellest thing you could do. Always let him or her down very gently. Don't drop a Fish with a hard bump; they bruise easily.

ATTRACTING THE SUN SIGNS
PISCES WOMAN WITH PISCES MAN

This affectionate and loving relationship can be nearly perfect, providing one of the partners can manage to be realistic. Both are turned on by beauty, peace and homelife. Fidelity is essential too. Watch out, though, for the mutual tendency to melancholia. These two have no trouble attracting each other, sharing sensitivity and a need for romance. But it should be remembered that both are extremely intuitive; so apart from knowing how to make each other happy, they also know how to make each other miserable. The sexual chemistry between them will be supercharged and inescapable. They will both be determined to keep the romance alive, and an active imagination will aid the situation. A pretty memorable relationship, but one or other would have to be very untypical of this sign to make a go of it permanently.

PISCES WOMAN WITH ARIES MAN

She's all woman and he's all man, and therein lies the attraction. However, her romantic soul yearns for flowers and soft music to set the scene for amorous encounters. Direct, macho Mr Aries will happily make love in the back seat of the car or in the kitchen cupboard, if that's the nearest available spot. Unless she happens to get a kick out of always being the one who loves the most, she is in for a very rough ride on the emotional level. If he can resist always putting himself first, then things may work out, although it's doubtful.

PISCES WOMAN WITH TAURUS MAN

The Bull adores to be pampered so he will be in his element with this woman, who loves to look after and fuss over her man. Although he too can be romantic, he is also a very practical person and mutual romantic frames of mind may never coincide. However, it is a relationship that can result in total bliss. She is loyal and needs a happy home; he is eager to provide it and will stomp all over anybody who tampers with his possessions. His will is ruled by the planet of love, namely Venus, and he will love faithfully and lustfully. She will quickly discover that she needs his strength and his gentleness. Providing he can learn when and when not to be overly practical, things may work out well. He will need to accept her world of fantasy and not try to change her.

PISCES WOMAN WITH GEMINI MAN

In a word, disaster. The Gemini man needs to indulge in mental gymnastics with the opposite sex and this will be extremely hurtful to the Piscean woman. He will also rebel against the fact that she likes to spend a certain amount of time playing house. That's not for him. Sometimes he likes cocoa by the fireside, but he wants to choose the moment for himself. She may be left at home reading love poems while he is out gallivanting with his secretary. He may indeed love her with some side of his character, but the many sides are likely to consider her a bit of a drag. Furthermore, objectives, needs and intrinsic ideals are totally dissimilar. All in all, it doesn't smack of success, does it?

PISCES WOMAN WITH CANCER MAN

An excellent relationship, and a blissful one. Both parties are sensitive, sentimental and home-loving. He effortlessly understands her, and vice versa. He will adore the way she runs after him, trying to see to his every comfort, and if it is romance she wants, romance he can give her – oodles of it. They'll cuddle up together by the warm fire in their own home with a full larder, both finding utter fulfilment. Her deep-rooted urge to be needed will keep their affections within the relationship and that's the way they both like it. There will, of course, be moments of gloom, but a jam sandwich, a warm bed and a big hug will cure practically everything.

PISCES WOMAN WITH LEO MAN

Although Leo the Lion has a warm, soft, generous heart, it isn't always apparent. His arrogance and pomposity could make life for this sensitive lady uncomfortable by making her nervy. Mind you, at least she'll be able to provide all the ego-boost he needs. But she may begin to feel somewhat inadequate when he brings his important business friends home. Financial gambles will scare the hell out of her, and such tension is sure to reflect on their sex life. But she will at least cheer his brilliant coups at the office, although secretly hoping he will be so grateful in return that he'll pamper her tender ego just a little. Unfortunately he considers her adoration his due, rather than a generous gift. This match may be more than her already nervous nature can possibly handle.

PISCES WOMAN WITH VIRGO MAN

The Virgo man, as we all know, is practical, cool, detached, unemotional and not particularly highly sexed. From this description one wonders what on earth he's doing even thinking of becoming involved with a sensitive Fish. Her self-willed sentimentality will go to any lengths to tickle his fancy, only to find there's no way to satisfy a nit-picking perfectionist. This realization is blood-curdling to her and they'll find that emotionally they are just not going to make it. Her water and his earth combined are unlikely to do anything except make one great big pile of mud.

PISCES WOMAN WITH LIBRA MAN

For a short-term affair this partnership is excellent, for the Libran loves to play at love and Miss Fish will lap it up. She will seem fragile, unworldly and ultra-feminine to him. Unfortunately once these superficial attractions are set aside, there isn't much here to sustain the relationship. Her idea of togetherness simply does not comply with his social butterflying and constant flirting. One of this couple's biggest problems is that neither of them will really want to work hard at their relationship. Like water from the bath, it's likely to slowly gurgle away down into emptiness.

PISCES WOMAN WITH SCORPIO MAN

Mr Scorpio has all the strength, passion and sensitivity that this lady requires. He also has an excellent imagination and plenty of love to give to the right woman and she could be Miss Pisces. He's bound to find her muddle-headed at times and somewhat over-sentimental, but these characteristics, far from making

235

him angry, may in fact eventually endear him to her. This relationship consists of a constant expression of deepest emotion and passion. Sensation after sensation will be experienced. All feelings will be tasted and savoured. An excellent match of watery affection. But she'll need to face up to the fact that he is at least twenty times stronger than her. But she always said she wanted a strong man.

PISCES WOMAN WITH SAGITTARIUS MAN

Initially they may be dazzled by each other. His happy-go-lucky character will appeal to her, especially when she sees him making a fool of himself at someone's birthday party. She'll laugh at his funny red nose and join in the musical chairs with him; but when things get a little more serious, she will quickly discover he is a fairly superficial character. This partnership is a steamy combination of fire and water, hot stuff at first but quick to cool off. He is bound to conclude that she is over-sensitive, even when he is absolutely crazy about her. She will find his compulsion for adventure and thrill-seeking frivolous as well as frightening. A good passionate affair, but little else.

PISCES WOMAN WITH CAPRICORN MAN

Not one to shy away from a shoulder to cry on, Miss Pisces may initially be attracted to this man's strength and dependability. She will feel that here is someone who can shelter her from that ugly, nasty world outside. And up to a point she is right. He will be delighted when she waits up for his return from some big business dinner. Her romantic sexuality will be flattered by his conscious need to please, especially in bed. While he is keeping her secure and protected, she will be keeping him warm and loved, possibly permanently.

PISCES WOMAN WITH AQUARIUS MAN

The Pisces woman will wish she could be as cool and detached about life as this character is. What she will not appreciate is the impersonal way in which he tackles sensitive situations. He likes to go fishing alone, so that he can commune with nature. She will want to tag along just to be near him, even if she can't bear to look at bait without vomiting. These two have many sensibilities in common, but before making this a permanent relationship they had better play house first to be sure. What's likely to happen is that once feelings of neglect set in, she'll wallow in self-pity. When he does finally arrive home, he will be verbally attacked. She will accuse him of being thoughtless, for that is the way she sees it, even though he doesn't deliberately go out of his way to ignore her. It just happens – it's like that with most Aquarians.

HOW WELL DO YOU KNOW YOUR PISCES WOMAN?

Answer honestly the questions below, scoring 3 for every Yes, 2 for Sometimes and 1 for No, then add up your total.

1. When you look in her eyes can you tell what she's thinking?
2. Is she a romantic?
3. Is she anti "women's lib"?
4. Is she secretive?
5. Is she against pure lust?
6. Is she jealous?
7. Does she prefer to wear skirts?
8. Is she indecisive?
9. Is she emotional?
10. Is she easily hurt?
11. Is she childlike?
12. Is she baffled by financial affairs?
13. Do you always need to initiate things sexually?
14. After she has had a little weep, does she like to make love?
15. When watching an old weepie on television does she have a little cry?
16. Is she an animal-lover?
17. Does she prefer you to make the decisions?
18. Would she be deeply hurt if you forgot a special occasion?
19. Has she been known to drown her sorrows in the bottle?
20. Is she extremely moody?

(Answers)

1–30

You obviously haven't known your Piscean woman long, for you appear to know little about her. However, there may be another reason for your score and that is that your Piscean lady has another strong influence on her chart. She is far too practical and liberated to be all Piscean, and it's likely there's an earth influence. Try reading the chapters devoted to Taurus, Virgo and Capricorn, and you may be able not only to understand her a little better but to find the real lady.

31–50

You are a lucky man; you appear to have got yourself involved with a true Piscean in possession of more of the positive qualities associated with this sign than the negative. If you are wise, you will hang on to her. She is about as close to an ideal woman as you'll find. Not only that but you seem fully to understand and appreciate her, and you should find great happiness together.

51–60

I think you must have cheated! It's extremely difficult to get to know a Piscean woman as thoroughly as you appear to know her. They always keep something back. But if you do know her this well, I shouldn't think she's exactly wild about the fact, for familiarity often leads to complacency and in that there's not much romance – an essential for this lady.

HOW WELL DO YOU KNOW YOUR PISCES MAN?

Answer honestly the questions below, scoring 3 for every Yes, 2 for Sometimes and 1 for No, then add up your total.

1. Does he like to get away on his own?
2. Does he tend to drink too much when he's unhappy?
3. Does he avoid decisions whenever possible?
4. Is he a romantic?
5. Is he a hypochondriac?
6. Is he an animal-lover?
7. Does he like you to take the lead in sex?
8. Is he artistic?
9. Does he have a happy way of making you feel all woman?
10. Is he sentimental?
11. Is he unambitious?
12. Can you hurt him easily?
13. Does music affect his mood?
14. Is he hard to get to know?
15. Is he highly sexed?
16. Would he find sex without love distasteful?
17. Does he love children?
18. Does he enjoy drinking with the boys?
19. Is he frequently given to self-pity?

(Answers)

1–30

You can't have been with this character for very long: you seem to have made little progress towards understanding him. Either this or he just isn't a true Piscean, in which case it's likely that there's a considerable amount of earth on his chart. If you read the chapters of Virgo, Taurus and Capricorn, you may find him secretly lurking there. If you happen to be born under one of these signs yourself, it will help you make the most of your relationship.

31–50

Without any doubt, you have a true Piscean man in tow and you seem to understand him extremely well. Go easily with him, it is within your power to influence his life to such an extent you can help him be a success or a failure, both professionally and personally. It's likely you've been together for some time, or you certainly will be in the future.

51–60

Because the Piscean is so secretive, nobody, not even his mother, ever really gets to know him that well. Therefore, it's extremely unlikely that you've been one hundred per cent honest with yourself when answering this quiz. And if you have, then your Piscean won't be particularly delighted. If you really can read him as well as this, then he will feel he has lost part of himself, and no doubt that you are too familiar with him and are taking him for granted.

THE MARRIED WOLF
AND ASTROLOGY

The married wolf is not only one of the oldest problems a woman has to face but also one of the most heartbreaking. Some already-spoken-for gent will state, "My wife doesn't understand me," another: "What the hell, baby! Let's live for the moment." But the worst type of all is the one who completely forgets his spouse altogether. There are various ways or reorganizing and coping with the above if astrology is used as a guide. It's to be hoped you are being honest and logical with yourself, in which case the following could be invaluable.

THE ARIES MARRIED MAN

To be fair to Mr Aries, he may not have intended to complicate your life – or his own, for that matter – but as well as being ardent and passionate, he is a creature of impulse. He probably took one look and fell for you like a ton of cement tossed from a ten-storey building. However, be warned; his passion dies just as quickly, if not quicker! Will he tell you he's married? It's unlikely. He lives in his head and prefers to keep his thoughts to himself. He won't exactly lie, but watch out for those half-truths and the swift change of subject. Reorganizing the married Aries is relatively easy. He's a tidy dresser, but remember, no husband can afford to spend as much on clothes as his bachelor counterpart. Look out for the tell-tale signs: the clean but slightly frayed collar or cuff, the well pressed but shiny suit. If you are still in doubt on the sixth date, try and recall how many different outfits he has worn. One or two? You can bet your bottom dollar he is married, and possibly with children who need new shoes, and a wife expecting a new winter coat. If, despite all this, you decide that you want him, then the only course of action is to refuse him your company until he is divorced. If he's really serious (which I doubt), his divorce will go down in the *Guinness Book of Records* as the quickest on file. This man does nothing at a slow pace. If he backs away, then good riddance!

THE TAURUS MARRIED MAN

There are two types of Taurean married wolves. The first is one hundred per cent Bull with a gross sexual appetite which he wishes to satisfy whenever and with whomever he can. The second is the character who has been married for some time and is plodding along, ignoring his romantic instincts and telling himself he is being sensible. If you stumble across the latter, you'll be wooed in a way that would do credit to Casanova. Should his guilt allow you to see him more than twice, you can be sure that he is smitten. But unless you are prepared to be a home-breaker, you'd better move on – but fast. For when this type talks of divorce, he means it, even if he does move more slowly than his Arietian brother. The sexual Bull is fairly easy to recognize. He expects a quick conquest with no complications. Deny him this and your problem will disappear in a cloud of dust. Should this Taurean gent swear that he is not married, then insist on a Sunday lunch date. This is the time when he will be expected to be at home – furthermore, a time when he will be reluctant to give up his roast beef and three veg. But ideally you shouldn't fall for this character at all. He will stampede into your bedroom or your emotions and he is very difficult to budge.

THE GEMINI MARRIED MAN

Oh, the innocence! Beware the dreaded married Gemini wolf. He operates so smoothly, it is pretty to watch – provided you are on the outside, that is. All Geminians have multiple personalities, although you will only ever see one. Elegant, good-looking, romantic and devoted – liar! He thinks he is clever and usually he is: too darn clever. Any girl needs her wits about her when confronted by this character, no matter how experienced she may be. He loves to flirt and romance, but as soon as you reciprocate, he's off. For this is an egoist and once he has satisfied himself that you have fallen beneath his spell, he loses interest. Sometimes sex doesn't even come into it, not if it is too easy anyway. Of course, he may admit to being married, but if he does, his wife will be an adulterous alcoholic who beats the kid (according to him). How you will sympathize! But he is more likely to flatly deny that he is already hitched, and you will probably believe him. Therefore why not offer to cook him a meal at his place? And ring him constantly in the evening. If that doesn't scare him, maybe, just for once, he is telling the truth. Little things can also give him away. Yes, he's a snappy dresser but he isn't too good at repair work. Check his buttons and watch out for tiny, neatly sewn tears. If he is immaculate and all is in place – then he's married. Get out your skateboard and take off.

THE CANCER MARRIED MAN

Once you have discovered that this character is married, he is one of those rare men who will offer just as much as you do. He may not be madly in love with his wife, but she is familiar and secure, and his kids mean the world to him. Therefore, this type does not deliberately set out to recapture his bachelorhood. If he is involved with you, it is accidental. This doesn't provide you with a green light to break up his home; it's not that easy. In the first place, he will not deny his married state, provided he is asked in a straightforward fashion. But he will do credit to Laurence Olivier when it comes to confessing. He loves drama, it is natural to him. After this he will assure you that he loves both you and his wife; and will, if you permit it, spend the next two years openly playing you off against each other. Not because he is heartless, he simply cannot bring himself to hurt anyone. Even if you should finally drag him away from his wife and up the aisle, he will spend the next five years seeing her every time you do something wrong. Yes, he's a real pain in the neck! And if someone else has staked claim first, you'd be wise to turn your sights elsewhere – unless you are a Cancerian yourself, in which case there'll be enough tears shed over the next few years to flood the River Thames. Is it worth it? A quick answer to that is: definitely not.

THE LEO MARRIED MAN

The Lion is the king of the jungle, and don't you forget it! And as such he likes to surround himself with subjects and courtiers.

The more flattery you throw in his direction, the more devoted he will become. His poor wife has probably run out of superlatives or may have finally realized that he is, after all, just a man. Her mistake. Hence his attraction to you, so you'd better watch out. He is certain to have several lady loves and you'll have to be an expert with honeyed words to win through. However, this man dislikes lies and will not hide his status. Neither will he promise to marry you, unless you are elegant, intelligent, utterly feminine, a cordon-bleu cook and an art expert, so don't kid yourself. You are there to impress him and others. If you want to get rid of him, just make him feel inferior to you intellectually, sexually or professionally, and he will be off with a somewhat tarnished crown. Which brings us to the fact that royalty must have its crown jewels and, unless he is stinking rich, there will be only a few adorning his person if he is married, whereas a fancy-free Lion will be dripping in gold or will own status symbols.

THE VIRGO MARRIED MAN

Mr Virgo has the reputation of being cold, pure and practical – in other words, a bit of a bore. Not so. When he is in love he can be just as exciting as any of the other eleven signs. But in most cases, he is ruled by an intellect which tells him that extra-curricular fun is nothing more than a pain in the backside! And he's probably right. The only Virgo wolf you are likely to run across is the one who has already made up his mind that his marriage is at an end. Therefore, there will be no deception. He is quick to recognize his feelings for you and, if they are genuine, he won't lose any time extricating himself from his dead marriage. Any female who has told herself that it might be fun to fool around with this chap could suddenly find herself in a very difficult situation, even embarrassingly so. For she is liable to be named in the divorce. Be warned, ladies: if you don't want your married Virgoan, don't muck him about.

THE LIBRA MARRIED MAN

It is widely believed that you can spot a married man a mile away by his resigned expression. Forget that, at least where this man is concerned. He has been in love with women ever since he opened his eyes and saw Mummy, and he will flirt with them until he is an old-age pensioner. Mr Libra is attractive, a lover of beauty, interested in fashion, and charm positively oozes from his every pore. He also possesses the happy knack of being able to say the right thing at the right time. If he admits to having a wife, which is unlikely, he is a classic example of the "she doesn't understand me" type. But then would you smile benevolently while your man courted every beauty within a fifty-mile radius? If he refuses to confess his married state then take a second look at his appearance. Even if he is immaculate, isn't he just a touch 1970s? He hasn't had time to keep up to date since he met "the little woman". Assuming you have realized your mistake, what do you do? Nag him: he walks away from arguments. Let your appearance go: he was only attracted to your looks in the first place. And lastly, open your own doors and light your own cigarettes: he will wonder why he ever thought you so deliciously feminine. If you are hooked, then you have my sympathy. You can only hope that he is quickly charmed away by a more glamorous lady – and, believe me, you won't have to wait too long.

THE SCORPIO MARRIED MAN

Passionate Mr Scorpio has the reputation of being the sexiest thing in the zodiac. This may be true, but another strong quality of his is loyalty. He tends to channel his sexual energy in one direction at a time and if you become involved with this character, you could be biting off more than you can chew. It could well be that he is looking to end his marriage and is searching for another life partner. There are, of course, exceptions, and when it comes to Scorpio these are usually the types who have been told repeatedly by astrologers that they are over-sexed and have something to live up to. In this particular instance you have a man whose sole interest is getting you into the bedroom. How do you unmask him? By arousing yet another of his characteristics; namely, jealousy. If he scowls every time you look at another man, his intentions are serious. If you kiss the next man you meet and he doesn't bat an eyelid, then you will know exactly what he is after and the rest will be up to you. He won't lie about being married, and if you wish to discover if he still cares for his wife, intimate very gently that perhaps she too is being unfaithful, and then watch for the explosion. If he razes the restaurant to the ground, you can pick up your coat and leave him to pay the bill. For a violent Scorpion is not a pretty sight.

THE SAGITTARIUS MARRIED MAN

The single Sagittarian man is a keen sportsman, a lover of justice, untidy, clumsy and regards you simply as a challenge – characteristics that are somewhat incompatible with the married state. Scrutinize your supposedly single Archer: does he straighten the carpet after he has tripped upon it? Use ashtrays, beer mats and napkins – yes? Then, my friend, someone has been training this fine specimen for some time. He may try to tell you he is unmarried, but this is a transparent lie. Look him straight in the eyes and observe guilt at its most classic. If he suspects that you may be almost as intelligent as he, but not quite (as he feels no female could possibly be), then he belongs to the "let's live for the moment" brigade, in which case it is over for you. How to dispose of the cad? Make demands upon his time; he is an independent soul and loathes to be tied, hence his incompatibility with the married state in the first place. Make him feel as if he has been with you for twenty long years and he will be off. Probably to the nearest cricket pavilion or rugby club, for sport is such a nice safe hobby.

THE CAPRICORN MARRIED MAN

Extra-curricular activities in the married state and your average Capricornian don't mix – well, not for long anyway. Not because the Goat is so virtuous or even faithful, it is merely a matter of economics. Our friend likes money and he wants to hang on to it. And two women can be expensive. He will see nothing wrong in an overnight flirtation with a pretty girl met while on a business trip, but when the trip comes to an end, so will the relationship. This is, of course, general, and there are

246

bound to be exceptions, which may stem from his ambition. For, next to money, the Goat loves position in life and success, and if he believes that you can help him or improve his chances, then he will hang around. Or, if he is already successful, but his current wife couldn't keep up with him, then he may be looking to trade her in for a later and more sophisticated model. Not very nice, you may say, with reason; but at least he is being honest. Our friend is rarely swayed by emotions or sheer romance. If he claims these are his motives then be suspicious. Try to discover what he stands to gain from an association with you. However, we are dealing with a very determined character and if he has made up his mind that you are going to be wife number two, you could have difficulty in escaping. The only way to shake him off is to let him down socially. There are millions of ways this can be done: the wrong use of cutlery in an expensive restaurant, the blank expression when the menu is presented to you in French, the fact that you can't come out tonight because you promised to babysit for your sister who has gone to play bingo. Use your imagination, and your Capricornian will melt away like the morning dew.

THE AQUARIUS MARRIED MAN

And now for something completely different – the Aquarius married man. In actual fact there isn't much to choose between the married variety and the single in this particular instance. Both are eccentric, vague and honest. If you look directly into their clear blue eyes and ask: "Are you married?" you'll get a simple yes or no. Whichever it is, this will be the truth. You can depend upon it. This type is always caught out when he attempts to tell lies, he just isn't good at it. Mind you, he may have to stop and think for a moment, for he is so vague that he might have forgotten the little woman he marched down the aisle with six months ago. Just as in two weeks' time he is equally capable of forgetting you existed at all. Therefore, there is no need to get into a lather over this character. Furthermore, he is unlikely to be with you because he fell in love with you at first sight; he probably thought you had a nice face or that you might be fun. The Aquarian always looks for charm, rather than a lover or a wife. Show temper on your part and it will send him into the arms of the next friendly lady, or perhaps home to his wife who hasn't seen him for a couple of days. This is a difficult character to gauge. He will refuse to discuss his married life with you, neither will he make plans for the future. In fact, he could find it tough-going talking about anything, unless you have some common interest. But watch out: you could get used to him popping in and out of your life, and something deeper could develop. If it happens on his side and you want out, a show of emotion or hysterics should do the trick nicely. On the whole, the Aquarian married man is a waste of time.

THE PISCES MARRIED MAN

This character is literally a different kettle of fish from the one above. If you get involved with a Piscean married man, life will be anything but boring. Happiness and heartache all the way. Only you can decide whether it's worth it all. In the first place, the Fish is modest and it is probable that you will be the one doing the landing; and because he is great at deception, and that includes deceiving himself, he will not admit to being married until you are too deeply involved to be able to help it. If you have been with him for some time and are determined to find out the truth, you may have to don your Sherlock Holmes deerstalker and get out your pipe. A work colleague or a friend might be tricked into giving you his address, and you can then make it as difficult as you can for Mr Pisces, so that in the end he has to tell you. Suggest weekends away, meet him from work – anything to force him into making a decision. Before you plunge in head-first and swim around in the Fish's crazy pool, make certain you really think he is worth the trouble – for trouble you can expect, and oodles of it. If you are wise, you'll cast your line elsewhere.

HER FIRST LOVE – ARIES

There's only one word to describe the Arietian female's attitude
to first love – enthusiastic. She is passionate and impetuous,
therefore although the relationship will be hearts and flowers
all the way, it will also be fiery and quickly forgotten. This
woman's head remains stubbornly in the present; she rarely
wastes time in longing for the past or planning the future.
Neither is her man likely to be the type that Mother would
approve of. She is far too impulsive to consider anything but
the initial chemical reaction. At least she is honest. No coquet-
tish games for her – it's a spur-of-the-moment thing and, after a
couple of weeks, she may begin to wonder what it was that
fascinated her in the first place. She will then proceed to forget
him with the speed of light.

HER FIRST LOVE – TAURUS

The Taurean woman is no side of beef to be tossed this way or
that by any man, as she quickly makes plain. She likes to be
wooed. This doesn't mean that she waits for or expects marriage, but she does need to feel that the relationship is strongly
emotional as well as physical. So she waits and waits. However,
when the time is right, her sensuality is fully woken. She writes
– and expects to receive – love letters, the contents of which
would do credit to Elizabeth Barrett Browning. The affair is
certain to be of a longer duration than those of her friends.
Furthermore, it is something she will never forget. Decades may
pass, but mention her first love and she will dissolve into a
mass of sentimentality.

HER FIRST LOVE – GEMINI

When it comes to flirting and handling the opposite sex, the
Gemini girl is a very early starter. She has been doing it ever
since she uttered her first word, and that was probably before
the rest of us. But when she grows up, she generally enjoys the
chase rather than commitment. Although she will never admit
it, she is emotionally insecure. Therefore, her rule is: safety in

numbers. She is an intellectual and will enter into endless discussions on the subject of love before she appears to be swept off her feet. This may be a rather cold-blooded operation, resulting in her reaching the conclusion that it's about time she found out what all the fuss is about. So she experiments and, not surprisingly, is often disappointed. Queen of the flirts she may be, but love is instinctive and not a subject for dissection. Luckily for her, the opposite sex frequently finds her fascinating, therefore her knight in shining armour is sure to be strong on patience. Once she feels secure enough, she may allow herself to be taught how to participate in this much talked about and popular pastime. In retrospect she will look back with a certain amount of emotional fondness – provided she has time, with the queues of suitors standing outside her door.

HER FIRST LOVE – CANCER

This girl is a complex bundle of femininity. She is emotional and romantic and will wait for that special someone. She is also a sentimentalist and will remember her first love with fond affection, even when she is a grey-haired grandmother. His letters and photos will be locked away somewhere, probably tied up with the inevitable piece of blue ribbon. However, the first experience isn't always a happy one for the Crab. Some Cancerians are rather slow and worry about being hurt – and unless she is careful, some glib-tongued smoothy may break through and conquer before she has had time to catch her breath, and this will often lead to a broken heart. It is important that she discerns the difference between love and infatuation, pity and friendship. She needs to recognize her various emotions and, until she can, she should stay at home in front of the television.

HER FIRST LOVE – LEO

The Leonine girl has no hesitation or hang-ups when it comes to something she wants. And although her love life is generally postponed until she has found someone who makes her feel like Bo Derek, she possesses a healthy, sensitive ego and her special man will have to be unbelievably complimentary and faithful to her and her alone. When satisfied in this direction, she will usually leap in paws first. Nevertheless, she should bear in mind that the same ego can make her extremely vulnerable to convincing liars. Fortunately, if he is broke, there is no way this can happen, for she expects to be wined, dined and cossetted at regular intervals. These days, no male throws away money that easily! Provided she can distinguish sincere flattery from flannel, exercise a little common sense, then her first love can be exactly as she wishes. But once this romance is over, she will not be slow to make a move towards the next one.

HER FIRST LOVE – VIRGO

The Virgoan girl is supposed to be the virgin of the zodiac – untrue. What she is, in fact, is critical and intellectual and not given to flights of fancy. Neither is she easily touched by emotion. She may fool around with love quite cold-bloodedly in order to get an idea of what makes it so popular. She will not really enjoy senseless flirting, unless she becomes emotionally involved. When this occurs for the first time, the relationship will be a lengthy one, for she demands mental compatibility as well as emotional. Once she has launched herself, so to speak, she is a quick learner and a white-hot lover. If things should eventually go wrong, she becomes very distressed, taking a considerable time to recover. She may not have as many admirers as her friends, but she is mature and realizes it takes more than a simple physical attraction to get the most out of a relationship. And this doesn't mean marriage: that is something she avoids for as long as possible.

HER FIRST LOVE – LIBRA

The Libran girl adores the opposite sex and probably can't remember a time when she didn't have a string of suitors at her door. Nevertheless, she is not prone to making an early commitment. She is far too busy playing at being in love. The objects of her affection do not realize, of course, that she is playing. "Why are there so many attractive men around?" she often wonders.

She never was any good at making decisions. Her first Romeo will have to be a cut above the average in some way – glamorous job or rich parents. She isn't mercenary but she can usually have her pick, therefore why shouldn't she choose what she considers to be the best of the crop? To her, the first love is something special, never to be forgotten. She overlooks the fact that she will have fallen again within a week of the relationship ending. Many girls envy this type and admire her style. Love is never basic, it is a work of art.

HER FIRST LOVE – SCORPIO

A female Scorpio is reputed to be the "sex bomb of the zodiac". Her sensuality can be likened to a volcano – it bubbles until one day it erupts. This girl is exclusive and highly critical. It is immaterial to her how long she remains unattached, just so long as that first love really means something. She may smoulder several times before she actually allows her feelings to ignite. She has amazing self-control and sees through insincerity immediately. Eventually the day comes when she is unleashed, and at this time she is a willing, one-hundred-per-cent female. Her first love can be expected to last for some time, and furthermore, it often leads to marriage.

HER FIRST LOVE – SAGITTARIUS

The Sagittarian constantly reads or is told of other people's emotional hang-ups and problems. She cannot understand this – it's all really quite straightforward to her – not unlike eating and drinking, come to think of it. Furthermore, she is quite happy to make the advances if she thinks it is necessary. Mind you, she wasn't born with too much confidence – in her early teens she suffered from notorious clumsiness and a lack of tact, which was always accentuated by the presence of someone she really cared for. The word "care" is aptly used. She doesn't expect to be swept off her feet or to hold hands in the moonlight. She just wants someone to care. And as she is probably the tomboy of the family, the boys in the neighbour-hood take to her at an early age, so that her love life really begins in a chummy and friendly way rather than in the heat of the moment. If she had been riding on Cloud Nine she would have fallen off anyway. In retrospect she will, no doubt, remember that it was her first love who taught her to climb trees and play a mean game of marbles. His name? That's something that escapes her.

HER FIRST LOVE – CAPRICORN

The young Goat is a slow developer. She is still out camping with the Girl Guides at 17 when all her friends are dating. Of course, she is aware of the opposite sex and knows that at some point she is going to have to do something about them. She is in no hurry to fall in love. When the time arrives, that spotty, gangly Goat turns into an elegant female who probably looks five years older than she is. She then proceeds to spend a couple of years dating and having fun, steering clear of anything intense until that special someone eventually arrives. She was a slow starter, but she now learns in record time. Furthermore, you can bet that her first lover will be socially or financially her superior, for the Goat is a snob and fiercely ambitious. She puts a certain price on her affections. She carefully assimilates as much knowledge as she can from her first lover, both emotionally and socially – and when a better proposition comes along, she is off. She is rarely governed by her emotions, so take a second look at that calm, poised exterior and don't bother her with your love problems; there are more important things in life.

HER FIRST LOVE – AQUARIUS

The Aquarian girl is another late starter, maybe because she is too busy worrying about the world to give much thought to individuals. No doubt her first lover will be someone with whom she shares a conviction or a cause, or who, like her, is committed politically. The relationship itself doesn't have to be passionate. When it comes to love, she thinks rather like the Sagittarian – it is pleasant; end of story. Because of this her lover may think that her heart is never quite winning, that in the midst of pretty speeches she is thinking of those in prison in South Africa or somewhere else. What is more, he is probably right. Some find this elusive quality challenging and attractive, others are bored and cannot be bothered. One thing is certain, however: they cannot be indifferent to this lady. Ask her to name her first lover, and initially she will argue about what exactly you mean by "first lover". Secondly, you will notice that fey look of hers which means that her thoughts are elsewhere; and that's the end of the conversation.

HER FIRST LOVE – PISCES

Pisces lady is romance personified. She cannot function properly without a man to love and indeed her helplessness attracts them to her in droves. Letters and tokens are carefully stored away and brought out whenever depressed. Emotionally, she finds it difficult to separate infatuation from love and her first affair will not only have to have rainbows and moonlight but violins as well. No doubt her hero will be as romantic as she is – if not, he won't get very far, I'm afraid. While this can be one of the most magical moments of her life, at the same time she should try hard to use some common sense. It is only too easy for her to be lumbered with a thoroughly unsuitable husband. Old-fashioned, her friends may call her, but I doubt whether the Fish would have it any other way. When she is old and wrinkled, she will at least have plenty to remember.